BAR **GOTO**

KAMONEGI

JON & VINNY'S
ITALIAN

BÉPUBLIQUE

CALL YOUR
MOTHER
=A JEW-ISH DELI=

ZOE'S
FOOD
PARTY

Mi
TOCAYA

KISMET

PIZZA NAPOLETANA

TOKI

THAI DINER

Golden
Diner

PONDICHERI

AL FORNO

kasama

Compère Lapin

CÚRATE

a.o.c.

OZ

MONTEVERDE

eem

JALEO
BY JOSÉ ANDRÉS

BRIDGETOWN

zahav

HIGHLANDS
BAR & GRILL

COFFEE
BETTER HALF
COCKTAILS

down north

frenchette

Dame

DIMES

SWIFT & SONS
STEAKHOUSE

SPOON AND STABLE

INDO

Mc LOONS
ESTD 2012
LOBSTER SHACK

compass
rose

La Taqueria

Petit Trois

EnB

Xi'an Famous Foods

HONEYPIE
milw, wi

HIPPO,

CHILI
Camp Washington
since 1940

EATER

100 ESSENTIAL RESTAURANT RECIPES

From the Authority
on Where to Eat
and Why It Matters

EATER

100 ESSENTIAL RESTAURANT RECIPES

Hillary Dixler Canavan
Photography by Laura Murray

ABRAMS, NEW YORK

CONTENTS

LETTER from EATER'S EDITOR in CHIEF

AT EATER, WE'RE OBSESSED WITH RESTAURANTS.

We've been chronicling the world of food and dining since 2005, when we started as a New York City blog covering openings and closings; big-name chefs and up-and-comers; and menu items making a splash in a hard-to-impress city. Since then, we've grown in so many ways: expanding to more than twenty cities across the world, adding travel coverage and home cooking tips, producing documentary-style videos on what it's like to work in restaurants and our very own TV shows. Now, we're in print with our very first cookbook.

Even before I started working at Eater, I considered it my job to figure out the best places to eat around the country. Whenever I was visiting a new city, I made lists on lists of where I wanted to eat, including both classic and new spots, doing my best to understand what makes a city's food scene sing. And dining out in New York City, where I live, never got old—I was constantly in search of the magic that comes together in a vibrant space, with just-right hospitality and flavors you can still recall long after the meal is over.

This cookbook is a testament to our long-standing love for restaurants—the people who run them, the way we're taken care of, and the surprise and delight that comes with discovering a place you can't wait to share with all your friends. We asked our team of nearly eighty writers, editors, producers, and artists to nominate the restaurants and recipes we had to include from their cities and travels, looking for a mix of old and new, fancy and casual, and, of course, the spots we recommend over and over again. The recipes the restaurants so generously shared with us are results of years of work, refined by line cooks and prep teams, designed to serve entire dining rooms, and so the chefs spent even more time helping us understand what's feasible for the home cook, offering sensible adaptations and substitutions for those of us who don't have a walk-in cooler.

Another way to think about this book is a one-of-a-kind travel guide to America's essential restaurants. Make these recipes, and then go experience the real thing—walk through the restaurant doors, soak in the soundtrack, admire the decor, peruse the menu, and enjoy a meal exactly as the chef intended. Or flip the order and go first, then recreate a seminal dish after an unforgettable meal. However you do it, this cookbook is a celebration of restaurants, both in reverence for what they do, day in and day out, and a cementing of their place in the culinary pantheon.

STEPHANIE WU
Editor in chief, Eater

HOW TO USE THIS BOOK

Eater's favorite restaurants are old and new, they're brick-and-mortar, and they're trucks, upscale tasting menus, and holes-in-the-wall— bakeries, cafes, street stands, and bars. The restaurants we obsess over span a dizzying array of cuisines and styles, but what the best have in common is the way they surprise and impress. Nothing beats a restaurant firing on all cylinders, at the top of its game, the creativity and excellence of its team on full display.

That level of expertise is not easy to achieve at home. So, when we gathered recipes, we also asked the pros for shopping lists and gear recommendations, for tips, tricks, and how-tos to help anyone who loves going out to eat capture some of that restaurant magic at home—without your own prep team or extensive pot collection. If you're not sure where to start, the guides and the shopping lists are a great place.

As for the recipes, here's how to set yourself up for success.

READ THE WHOLE RECIPE before you start shopping, let alone cooking. Restaurant recipes are typically executed by more than one person. The cook who preps the broth one day isn't necessarily the cook who preps the meat the next, or the cook who plates it when a diner orders the dish. At home, you can use that to your advantage: Many of the components can be made in advance, making the actual serving (and eating) of the dish easier and faster. Reading the recipe in full will help you understand how to plan.

Invest in **THE HIGHEST-QUALITY INGREDIENTS** you can. The best restaurants are sticklers for fresh produce, top-of-the-line proteins, and exceptional finishing oils and spices; your final product will taste more like it does in a restaurant when you're using the good stuff.

When it comes to salt, unless otherwise specified (which it most often is in baking), recipes rely on **DIAMOND CRYSTAL KOSHER SALT**, the go-to in most restaurant kitchens. In most recipes, you'll see instructions to taste and adjust seasoning, or to salt to taste. You might wonder whose taste? What taste? This is a chance to build your palate and learn what you like. Go slow: You can always add more, but you can't take salt out once it's been added. Speaking of seasoning, pepper means freshly ground, always.

If you buy one tool to better use this book, make it a **KITCHEN SCALE**. Weighing your ingredients is the most precise way to cook, and it's how restaurants do it. Once you spend the $10 or so, and get the hang of it, it's actually easier and leaves less to clean up.

It's okay to cut corners! We've adapted these recipes to make them more home-friendly, subbing in store-bought products when they work and highlighting ways to vary or change the recipes for ease without sacrificing flavor. Feel free to **INTERPRET THE IDEAS**, flavors, and techniques and try something that feels true to your skill level or preferences.

Last, please add each and every one of these restaurants to your itineraries if and when you find yourself traveling. There's nothing we at Eater love more than connecting you with the best restaurants out there. So go, read, cook, and *eat*.

BRUNCH

1

IN DEFENSE OF BRUNCH

The best restaurant brunches are intensely social affairs. Customers packed into crowded dining rooms or on sunny patios catch up with friends, and regulars take their place at their usual Saturday table. The conversation is part of why you're there. There's gossip, of course, but also eavesdropping. And then there's the strategizing, a true joy if you're eating with fellow obsessives. Who's going savory and who sweet? Pancakes for the table? Bacon? Both?

Part of the fun of brunch is the way it absolutely destroys the arbitrary boxes that we force our food choices into when we declare something like a sunny-side-up egg a "breakfast food" and fried chicken a "lunch or dinner" food. At brunch, things are more porous—there is simply no reason not to include whatever favorite dish from the repertoire in the mix.

If you've gone to brunch, you've already done something fun with your day. You could spend the rest of it running errands, doing chores, or just staring at the wall for that matter—all of it will be more palatable because you had delicious fun before noon.

Which is why the joy of doing a proper brunch at home cannot be overstated. Make yourself something fancy, throw an elaborate mid-morning party for your neighbors, gather your loved ones, and pull out your punch bowl (any bowl can be a punch bowl). It's your party, and anything goes.

TAYLOR HAM, EGG, AND CHEESE

SUMMIT DINER
Summit, New Jersey

Welcome to New Jersey, where a great breakfast is available at any time of day or night at one of its fine diners. The Summit Diner is widely considered the state's oldest in operation, occupying a 1930s train car on one of the town's main streets. Its untouched old-school interior and textbook diner fare are the stuff of local legend and happy childhood memories. Like a good Jersey diner proprietor ought to, owner Jim Greberis offers a Taylor ham and cheese sandwich. Taylor ham, a spiced, cured pork roll created by Trenton-based Taylor Provisions in 1856, is rarely seen outside of the state, so you can use another ham or Canadian bacon instead. Regulars at the Summit Diner often add home fries to their sandwich—ask for "the slider"—and if you want to do the same at home, just fry sliced, boiled potatoes in a bit of oil and bacon fat. If you do find Taylor ham, watch the salt in your eggs; the pork roll is plenty salty on its own.

Serves **4**

Soybean or other neutral oil

4 eggs

8 slices Taylor ham or Canadian bacon, cut ¼ inch (6 mm) thick

4 kaiser rolls, halved

8 slices American cheese

Freshly ground black pepper

Ketchup

Heat a griddle or large heavy pan with a splash of neutral oil over medium-high heat. Add the eggs and fry to your liking. Set the eggs aside.

In the same griddle or pan, cook the ham until heated through and slightly browned, about 30 seconds each side. Set aside, leaving the heat under the pan on.

Toast the cut sides of the kaiser rolls, both tops and bottoms, then place them on a clean work surface cut side up. Place a slice of American cheese on each. Place 2 slices of the cooked Taylor ham on each of the bottom pieces, then layer with the fried eggs and the roll tops.

Put the sandwiches back on the griddle or in the pan, still set to medium-high heat, and cover them to melt the cheese (you can use a grill dome, bowl, lid, or foil to do so). Alternatively, you may transfer the sandwiches to a hot oven (about 350°F/175°C) for 2 to 3 minutes. Serve the sandwiches with black pepper and ketchup.

CHINATOWN EGG AND CHEESE SANDO

GOLDEN DINER
New York City

◇◇◇

New Yorkers love arguing about what makes a good breakfast sandwich. Roll or bagel? Bacon or sausage? Hash browns on the side or in the sandwich? On that last front, there's been a growing consensus: If you're not putting hash browns inside your egg sandwich, you are missing out. At Golden Diner, chef Sam Yoo's ode to the bodega breakfast includes a thick potato hash cake, its browned crust a thrilling contrast to impossibly soft cheesy eggs, all on a sesame scallion milk bun that would be at home at any one of Chinatown's nearby bakeries. The buns are a project—but so worth it, as they can be enjoyed for breakfast, snack, or as a dinner roll alternative, and you can make them ahead—so we've gone ahead and subbed in frozen hash browns, which crisp up perfectly. Of course, the cheesy eggs are plenty delicious on their own.

Makes about **12** buns & **4** sandwiches

◇◇

For the dough starter:

5½ cups (680 g) all-purpose flour

1 tablespoon plus 1 teaspoon (16 g) instant dry yeast

2 tablespoons (40 g) honey

2¾ cups (160 g) chopped scallions, green parts only

For the dough:

5⅓ cups (640 g) all-purpose flour, plus more for dusting

⅔ cup (80 g) nonfat milk powder

1 tablespoon plus 1 teaspoon (14 g) instant yeast

1½ tablespoons (24 g) fine sea salt

1¼ cups (256 g) butter, at room temperature

1 egg, whisked until very smooth with 1 tablespoon water, for the egg wash

Sesame seeds, for garnish

For the sandwiches:

8 frozen hash brown patties

12 eggs

¼ cup (½ stick/57 g) butter

Salt

8 slices American cheese

Bacon, sausage, or avocado (optional)

To make the starter, combine 3⅓ cups (795 ml) water with the flour, dry yeast, honey, and scallions in a large bowl. Whisk until smooth and scrape down the sides. Set aside and let the starter activate for about 5 minutes.

For the dough, whisk to combine the flour, milk powder, and instant yeast. Sprinkle this on top of the dough starter and cover with plastic wrap. Let the starter mixture ferment at room temperature for 2 to 4 hours.

Add the salt and butter to the starter mixture and mix with a wooden spoon or spatula until all the flour is moistened. Knead the dough in the bowl until it comes together and then scrape onto a lightly floured surface. Knead the dough on the counter for about 5 minutes, adding as little flour as possible, just to keep the dough from sticking too much. The dough will be sticky at this point.

Cover the dough with an inverted bowl and allow it to rest for 20 minutes at room temperature.

Knead the dough for another 5 minutes, or until smooth and elastic.

Cover the dough with plastic wrap and let rise in a warm (not too hot) place for 1½ to 2 hours, until it doubles in size. Punch down the dough and use a bench scraper to portion about twelve 120 g dough pieces. Shape each piece into a ball and place on a baking sheet lined with greased parchment paper. Lightly cover with plastic wrap and rest the dough until each bun doubles in size, about 1 hour.

Continued

As the dough rises, preheat the oven to 350°F (175°C).

Brush the buns with egg wash, sprinkle with the sesame seeds, and bake for 25 to 30 minutes, until the buns are golden brown.

Let the buns cool for 20 minutes. If making a day ahead, store in an airtight container or wrap, or keep wrapped in the fridge and use a toaster oven to warm them the next day. Fully baked buns also freeze well: Once fully cooled, wrap any buns you don't plan on serving in plastic wrap and freeze for up to 1 month. To serve from frozen, defrost and heat them in a toaster oven.

To make the sandwiches, bake or air-fry the frozen hash brown patties according to the package directions.

Heat a large skillet over medium heat. Halve and then toast 4 of the sesame scallion buns in the skillet. Set aside.

Crack 6 of the eggs into a large bowl and whisk to combine. Melt 2 tablespoons of the butter in the same skillet over low heat. To soft scramble the eggs, add the whisked eggs to the pan, season with salt, and stir with a rubber spatula or wooden spoon continuously. Just when the eggs start to set, top with 4 slices of American cheese, then continue stirring so the cheese melts into the eggs. Once incorporated, divide the eggs into 2 portions and place on the bottom halves of 2 of the buns. Repeat for the remaining 6 eggs and 2 buns. For each sandwich, add 1 or 2 cooked hash brown patties on top of the eggs and then place the top bun to finish. Serve the sandwiches with bacon, sausage, or avocado on the side, if you like.

Ranch Water Is a Perfect Brunch Drink

When Molly Austad, the wine director at the hit Houston restaurant Bludorn, hosts brunch at home, she relies on a Texas classic: ranch water. It's easy, refreshing, and make-ahead friendly, leaving her plenty of time to focus on food instead of serving drinks. Here's how she does it:

RANCH WATER

The night before, mix two parts blanco tequila (Austad likes LALO tequila best) and one part fresh lime juice and store it in the fridge overnight. In the morning, serve the tequila-lime mixture in shot glasses alongside bottles of Topo Chico mineral water. Instruct guests to take a big sip of Topo Chico and then pour their shot directly into the bottle.

How to Make Eggs Like a Busy Line Cook

As told to by PETIT PESO chef RIA DOLLY BARBOSA, who's run brunch services at beloved LA restaurants like Canelé, Sqirl, and Paramount Coffee Project.

To cook better eggs at home, you need practice. That's where restaurant cooks have the leg up on home cooks: We're doing it every day at huge volume. You have no choice but to improve. Or get fired. If you really want to master a technique, you need repetition: When you practice, you'll ruin a bunch of eggs. That's okay: It's how you will learn and get better.

Eggs are super easy to mess up but also super rewarding when you get them right. And they're surprisingly personal. Everyone has a different preference.

SOUS-VIDE

At restaurant brunches, you'll see a lot of poached eggs—that's easy to do at scale with sous-viding. You can sous-vide at home, and that will keep things more consistent. For home immersion circulators like the Anova, 167°F (75°C) is the sweet spot: Bring your water up to temperature, add whole eggs, cold from the fridge, and cook for 14 minutes. Then run them under cold water from the tap until they're cool enough to handle. Crack and use right away!

POACHED

If you don't have a home sous-vide setup, don't let poaching intimidate you. The secret is extremely fresh eggs. Fresh eggs have firmer, tighter whites, which means you don't need to use the infamous vortex technique to keep the whites together. Just add a very fresh cracked egg into a shallow pot of simmering water, leave until the white sets, and remove carefully with a slotted spoon.

BOILED

Boiling eggs is easier still. Add eggs to a pot of boiling water (there should be enough water to cover the eggs). Experiment with cooking the eggs anywhere from 5 to 9 minutes to find your personal preference when it comes to where your yolk lands on the runny to jammy to firm spectrum. Even for a hard-boiled egg, you don't want to overcook it, or it will head into gray yolk territory.

FRIED

When it comes to frying eggs, try adding just a bit of oil to a pan, enough to do a shallow fry. Then, using a spoon, baste the egg with the oil so you set your whites but leave the yolk uncooked. Flipping the egg and quickly letting the yolk set will get you eggs over easy or medium.

SCRAMBLED

Combine your eggs and a splash of milk with a fork. The way I was taught to scramble eggs for brunch services might feel counterintuitive, but it's the key to not overdoing it: Keep your heat low. Melt the butter over low heat, add your eggs, and stir often with a rubber spatula or wooden spoon until the curds set. You can go two ways from there: For a creamy scramble, stir often from start to finish and stop before the eggs firm up. If you want larger pieces and dryer curds, let it set a bit between stirs so the eggs firm up a bit more. To season, sprinkle on a pinch of Maldon salt just before you take the pan off the heat, and gently stir to incorporate.

OMELET

For a three-egg omelet, use a fork to combine 1 tablespoon milk with the eggs. From there, melt butter over low or medium-low heat. Add your eggs and start stirring counterclockwise around the diameter of the pan. Then do some smaller swirls until they're soft and set. When the eggs are in a nonstick, they'll start to pull away from the sides of the pan; that's when to take it off the heat. Pulling away means it's ready to roll. Add any fillings, then tilt the pan upward and coax the egg to fold over itself and roll it off onto your plate.

ORANGE BLOSSOM BRIOCHE

THE PURPLE HOUSE
North Yarmouth, Maine

About a half hour's drive past Portland, the quiet town of North Yarmouth, Maine, is home to some of the country's finest baking. The aptly named Purple House is where chef Krista Kern Desjarlais showcases her wood-fired baking skills, serving up coveted Montreal-style bagels, Roman-style pizza al taglio, and an ever-changing array of pastries, like these orange blossom brioches. These gorgeously golden buns can absolutely be enjoyed on their own, or with butter and jam. At the Purple House, Kern Desjarlais has been known to sandwich creamy ricotta mousse inside. She also recommends toasting and dotting them with some olive oil, chocolate, and sea salt. But don't stop there. The Purple House and Desjarlais's other restaurant, the summer-only spot Bresca & the Honeybee, serve up killer homemade ice cream, so consider making a Sicilian-style brioche con gelato; a scoop of pistachio or vanilla gelato would be excellent sandwiched inside this soft, fragrant brioche.

Makes **9** brioches

For the orange blossom syrup:
2½ cups (500 g) granulated sugar

1½ teaspoons to 1 tablespoon orange blossom water

For the brioche:
1⅔ cups (200 g) all-purpose flour

2⅓ cups (300 g) "00" flour

1 teaspoon (5 g) fine sea salt

½ cup (100 g) granulated sugar

2 teaspoons (5 g) instant dry yeast

2 large eggs

⅓ cup (75 g) butter, melted and cooled

Zest of 1 lemon

Zest of 1 orange

1 cup (240 ml) whole milk

2 eggs, whisked with a fork till smooth, for the egg wash

¼ cup (50 g) coarse sugar, for sprinkling

To make the syrup, in a medium pot, bring 1¼ cups (300 ml) water with the sugar to a boil over medium heat until it thickens, 10 to 15 minutes. Remove from the heat and let cool to room temperature. Stir in the orange blossom water, then store in an airtight container in the refrigerator for up to 2 weeks.

To make the brioche, in the bowl of a stand mixer fitted with the dough hook, combine the all-purpose flour, "00" flour, salt, granulated sugar, and yeast. In a separate bowl, whisk together the eggs, melted butter, lemon and orange zest, and milk. On low speed, mix the wet ingredients in with the dry ingredients for about 10 minutes, until a smooth dough forms.

Transfer the dough to a clean bowl, cover the bowl with plastic wrap, and leave in a warm place to proof for 1 hour, or until it rises by about 50 percent. Then move the covered bowl to the refrigerator and chill overnight. Expect the dough to rise a bit more in the fridge.

Remove the dough from the refrigerator and weigh out 9 portions at 75 g and another 9 portions at 15 g. Shape the dough into balls—the larger one is your bun, the smaller one is the *tuppo*, or hat, the topknot found on Sicilian brioches. Form a deep indent in the bun with your finger and slip the tuppo as far into the hole as possible, so it will stay attached while proofing. Transfer to a parchment paper–lined baking pan with ample space between each, as they will expand in size. Lightly cover the buns with plastic wrap and proof at warm room temperature for 1 to 2 hours, until puffy. To test if the buns have proofed enough, gently poke the side of one with your fingertip. It should not spring back. If the indent springs back, continue to proof. When done proofing, gently brush with the egg wash all over the top and sides and sprinkle all over with coarse sugar.

When the buns are almost done proofing, preheat the oven to 375°F (190°C). Bake the buns for 20 minutes, or until golden brown. Remove the brioches from the oven and brush with orange blossom syrup while hot.

BROCCOLI TOAST

In the stylish neighborhood of Los Feliz, Kismet is a destination: The regulars are local, but visitors from near and far stop by to enjoy natural wines, an airy dining room, and dishes that make the most of California's bounty without being preachy about it. While Kismet may seem "effortlessly cool," we know that requires a heck of a lot of skill and planning. Take the broccoli toast, from the restaurant's beloved brunch menu. Chefs Sara Kramer and Sarah Hymanson created a main-event dish out of this humble vegetable—it arrives speared through with a steak knife, showered in seeds, and well-dressed with mint leaves and citrus. The broccoli salad alone would shine at any time of day; but with a cool spread of labneh on top of a buttery slice of sesame toast sourced from beloved LA bakery Bub and Grandma's? It's California brunch perfection.

Serves **4** to **6**

Salt

Florets from 2 average-size heads of broccoli (7 cups/630 g), cut into bite-size pieces

2 cups (250 g) toasted pumpkin seeds, pulsed to pebble consistency in small food processor, or ground with mortar and pestle

1 teaspoon salt, or more to taste

1 tablespoon plus 1 teaspoon (10 g) Aleppo pepper

1 to 2 cloves garlic, grated

½ cup (120 ml) olive oil

¼ cup (½ stick/57 g) butter, softened

4 to 6 (1 inch/2.5 cm thick) slices sesame sourdough bread

2 cups (448 g) labneh

1 cup (225 g) assorted citrus fruits, segmented and thinly sliced

Fresh mint leaves

Bring a medium pot of salted water to boil over high heat. Prepare an ice bath. Add the broccoli florets and cook for about 2 minutes, until bright green and slightly tender. Drain. Transfer to the ice bath to cool and then drain.

In a large bowl, combine the pumpkin seeds, 1 teaspoon salt, the Aleppo pepper, and garlic. Add the blanched broccoli and olive oil and toss to coat the florets. Taste and adjust the seasoning.

Heat a cast-iron pan or griddle over medium-high heat. Butter both sides of the bread slices. Working in batches if necessary, toast in the pan until golden on both sides. Slather one side of the toasts with labneh, top with the broccoli mixture, and garnish with the citrus and mint.

Uppma and Eggs with
Cilantro Chutney,
Spanish Fried Chicken
and Cornmeal Waffles,
Blueberry Pancakes

UPPMA AND EGGS
with Cilantro Chutney

For more than ten years, Houston diners have flocked to Pondicheri for a taste of chef and co-owner Anita Jaisinghani's self-described "nontraditional authentic" Indian cuisine. During the popular daytime service, that looks like a comforting bowl of uppma topped with fried eggs and a pool of bright green cilantro chutney. Uppma, a breakfast porridge popular in India's southern states, can be made from semolina, polenta, or corn or rice grits—Jaisinghani leans into the Texas spirit with local stone-ground grits. At home, you should experiment to find what you enjoy working with best (or what you happen to have in your pantry). She also recommends using uppma as a vehicle for breathing new life into leftover vegetables, so don't be shy about mixing it up and adding whatever you have on hand. Feel free to use store-bought chutney if you don't want to make your own. To really achieve a Pondicheri-style brunch at home, serve your uppma and eggs with warm masala chai.

26

For the uppma:

½ cup (90 g) semolina or grits

3 tablespoons sesame oil (coconut or peanut oil would also work)

1 teaspoon dried green lentils

1 teaspoon black mustard seeds

10 to 12 curry leaves

2 cups (250 g) diced vegetables (such as corn, bell peppers, and cauliflower)

2 to 3 whole dried red chiles (optional)

1 serrano chile, minced (optional)

½ teaspoon ground turmeric

1½ teaspoons salt

1 tablespoon grated unpeeled fresh ginger

* * * * *

Neutral oil such as vegetable or canola, for frying the eggs

4 eggs

Juice of ½ lemon

Sesame seeds

Handful of your favorite herbs

Olive oil (optional)

Cilantro Chutney (recipe follows)

Preheat the oven to 350°F (175°C).

Spread the semolina or grits on a baking sheet and roast in the oven for 10 to 12 minutes, until golden brown.

Remove and set aside.

In a stockpot, heat the sesame oil over medium-high heat until it's just shy of smoking. Add the lentils and mustard seeds and cook until they pop and sizzle, then immediately add the curry leaves, diced vegetables, and red chiles and serrano chile, if using.

Increase the heat to high and cook, stirring frequently, for 5 to 7 minutes, until the vegetables wilt and have a slight char. Add the turmeric, salt, ginger, and 2 cups (480 ml) water and bring the mixture to a boil. Add the semolina or grits in a steady stream, stirring constantly to prevent lumps.

Lower the heat to low and cook for 3 to 4 minutes, until almost all the liquid has been absorbed. Turn off the heat, cover the pot, and let the uppma rest for 10 to 15 minutes.

In a large skillet, heat some neutral oil over medium-high heat and fry the eggs according to your liking. Serve the eggs as a side to the uppma.

Garnish the uppma with lemon juice, a sprinkling of sesame seeds, fresh herbs, and a drizzle of olive oil, if desired, before serving. Serve with the cilantro chutney.

Cilantro Chutney
Makes 2 cups (480 ml)

1 bunch cilantro

¼ unpeeled Granny Smith apple, cored and sliced

½ serrano chile, seeds left in, plus more if you want it spicier

½ cup (75 g) unsalted dry-roasted peanuts

1 cup (240 ml) plain whole-milk yogurt

Juice of 1 lemon

Salt

Trim the cilantro, removing the bottom 4 inches (10 cm) of the stems. Wash under cold running water. Shake off excess moisture and transfer to a colander to drain.

Put the sliced apple, chile, peanuts, yogurt, and lemon juice in a blender. Start blending on low speed, increasing the speed to high, and blend until completely smooth.

Add the cilantro in small batches and continue to blend until smooth. Taste and season with salt. If you would prefer more heat, add more serrano chile and blend. Transfer to an airtight container, where it will keep in the refrigerator for up to 2 days.

SPANISH FRIED CHICKEN AND CORNMEAL WAFFLES

A.O.C.
West Hollywood, California

There's something deeply romantic about A.O.C. The walls are covered in ivy, the dining room has old-world dark woods and a fireplace, and the dreamy patio is strewn with twinkly lights. Even the most stubbornly casual Angelenos will throw on something a little special for a visit. Suzanne Goin's elegant, easy, Mediterranean-leaning menu has something for everyone, with classics like bacon-wrapped dates and Moroccan chopped chicken salad. And while brunching under the sprawling Brachychiton tree branches outside certainly feels fancy, it's also *fun*. Like fried chicken and serrano ham on top of waffles fun. Goin imbues her fried chicken with the flavors of Spain: It's marinated in an array of spices, including coriander and Aleppo pepper, the dredge is seasoned with paprika, and it's all topped with butter infused with chile, cumin, and a heck of a lot of garlic. If you're not ready to tackle the full monty at home, the waffle recipe is great on its own for breakfast with a pat of good butter and drizzle of maple syrup, and the fried chicken is a showstopper worthy of your next dinner party.

For the chicken:
½ teaspoon ground cumin

¼ teaspoon ground coriander

½ teaspoon Aleppo pepper

2 cloves garlic, smashed

1 tablespoon plus ½ teaspoon smoked paprika

Salt and freshly ground black pepper

1½ pounds (680 g) boneless, skinless chicken thighs, cut into strips

1½ cups (360 ml) buttermilk

1 cup (120 g) all-purpose flour

1 teaspoon cayenne pepper

2 quarts (2 L) vegetable oil, for frying

For the cornmeal waffles:
1 cup (120 g) cornmeal

½ cup (65 g) cornstarch

½ cup (65 g) all-purpose flour

1 teaspoon salt

1 teaspoon baking powder

¼ teaspoon baking soda

¾ cup (180 ml) buttermilk

½ cup (120 ml) milk

⅓ cup (80 ml) vegetable oil

2 large eggs, separated

1 tablespoon sugar

½ teaspoon vanilla extract

To serve:
1 cup (227 g) Chile-Cumin butter (recipe follows)

8 to 10 ounces (225 to 284 g) jamón serrano, thinly sliced

Maple syrup

Combine the cumin and coriander in a small pan over medium heat. Swirl the pan and toast until fragrant. Immediately remove from heat and transfer the toasted spices to a small bowl. To make the chicken, combine the cumin, coriander, Aleppo pepper, garlic, ½ teaspoon of the smoked paprika, ½ teaspoon salt, and ¼ teaspoon black pepper and rub it into the chicken. Place on a tray and marinate in the refrigerator for at least 4 hours or up to overnight. Pour the buttermilk over the chicken and let it sit in the refrigerator for another 30 minutes.

Meanwhile, combine the flour, cayenne, and remaining 1 tablespoon paprika. In a heavy wide-bottomed pan, heat the vegetable oil over medium heat to 350°F (175°C) according to a deep-frying thermometer.

Drain the chicken and dredge it in the spiced flour. Shake the excess flour from the chicken strips and gently drop them into the hot oil. Cook the chicken until golden brown, about 3 minutes, then, using a slotted spoon, remove from the oil and set on a tray lined with paper towels to absorb excess oil.

To make the waffles, in a medium bowl, whisk the cornmeal, cornstarch, flour, salt, baking powder, and baking soda. In another bowl, whisk the buttermilk, milk, vegetable oil, and egg yolks. Add the wet ingredients to the dry ingredients and gently mix until just combined. Do not overwork the batter.

In a stand mixer fitted with the whisk attachment, whisk the egg whites to almost soft peaks. Add the sugar and continue mixing until the peaks are firm and glossy. Beat in the vanilla.

Gently fold the egg whites into the batter until just incorporated. Cook in a waffle maker as per the manufacturer's instructions until crisp.

To serve, melt the chile-cumin butter in a small saucepan over low heat. Place a hot, crispy waffle on a plate. Assemble a couple pieces of fried chicken on top, then drape some sliced jamón serrano over the chicken. Nestle a couple more fried chicken pieces on top, then loosely weave more jamón serrano around and over the chicken until you have a pretty stack sitting on top of your waffle. Drizzle maple syrup and melted chile-cumin butter over the whole stack. Repeat with the remaining waffles, chicken, and toppings.

Chile-Cumin Butter
Makes 12 ounces (340 g)

2 ancho chiles

5 arbol chiles

1 cup (2 sticks/225 g) butter, softened

½ tablespoon whole cumin seeds, toasted and coarsely ground

3 cloves garlic, smashed

Salt and freshly ground black pepper

* * * * *

Soak the chiles in a bowl with hot water for 30 minutes. Remove from the water, remove the seeds, and finely chop the chiles by hand or in a food processor. In a stand mixer fitted with the whisk attachment, or in a mixing bowl and whisking by hand, whip the butter until airy. Fold in the chiles, cumin seeds, and garlic and season with salt and pepper. Transfer to an airtight container and store in the refrigerator for up to 1 week.

BLUEBERRY PANCAKES

Diners can thank baker and co-owner Melissa Weller for making it so delicious to see and be seen at Sadelle's. The brunch menu offers modern interpretations of New York daytime staples like bagels and Waldorf salad; think less ladies who lunch and more trendsetters who brunch. And on table after marble table, Instagram post after Instagram post, there is at least one plate of these sugar-dusted blueberry pancakes. Weller is known for being a master technician as well as a creative powerhouse, so consider her pancake recipe the ultimate blueprint for perfecting your own. But do it Weller's way first: The SoHo fashion crowd knows these are a classic as-is—and classic is always in style.

Makes **8 large pancakes**

1⅔ cups (200 g) all-purpose flour

½ cup (60 g) whole-wheat flour

1½ tablespoons (23 g) baking powder

3 tablespoons (38 g) sugar

1 teaspoon (6 g) salt

1¾ cups (420 ml) milk

4 large eggs (200 g)

¾ cup (1½ sticks/168 g) butter, melted and cooled slightly

1 tablespoon (14 g) butter, for cooking the pancakes, plus more for serving

1½ cups (260 g) fresh blueberries

Maple syrup

In a medium bowl, whisk together the all-purpose flour, whole-wheat flour, baking powder, sugar, and salt. Set aside.

In a larger bowl, whisk together the milk and eggs. Add the dry ingredients to the liquid ingredients, whisking well to get rid of any lumps. Gradually whisk in the melted butter in increments. Let the batter rest for about 10 minutes at room temperature or place in the refrigerator to rest overnight.

Heat a large skillet over medium-high heat. Melt a little butter into the skillet and then ladle about ½ cup (120 ml) batter into the skillet.

Scatter some blueberries over the pancake and cook until the edges are cooked and the pancake sets up a bit. Flip the pancake over and cook for 1 to 2 minutes more. Repeat for the rest of the pancakes. To keep the pancakes warm while working in batches, place finished pancakes on a plate in a very low oven (250°F/120°C).

Serve the pancakes warm with butter and maple syrup.

SHAKSHUKA
with Baguette

RÉPUBLIQUE
Los Angeles, California

In a chapel-like building built by Charlie Chaplin and once home to the legendary LA restaurant Campanile, a line of people stretches toward the sidewalk in the morning sun. They're waiting for their turn to choose from master baker Margarita Manzke's impeccably stocked pastry case and grab their morning coffee. Her husband, Walter Manzke, runs point on the restaurant side, offering a French-leaning menu to couples on dates and other revelers. Pioneers of "all-day dining"—a restaurant that purposefully blurs the lines between breakfast and lunch without closing in between—the Manzkes have created a mainstay in République. It's considered a must-do for visiting food writers and chefs. The move is to go in the late morning: Take a seat in the cathedral-ceilinged dining room, keep an eye out for A-listers, and order a pastry or two and the shakshuka. The oven-baked tomatoes, nestling two perfectly cooked eggs, arrive bubbling in a small cast-iron skillet with spears of flawless baguette ready for the dipping. The restaurant makes its shakshuka with sous-vide eggs to allow them to prep ahead; at home, you'll be doing it in a more typical way (in your oven). And while making Margarita Manzke's famed baguette is an advanced bake, this shakshuka is far more forgiving and you could serve it with baguette from your favorite local baker.

Serves 4 to 6

For the yogurt-pimentón sauce:
⅓ cup (80 ml) plain whole-milk yogurt

2 teaspoons pimentón (Spanish smoked paprika)

2 teaspoons finely chopped shallots

1 tablespoon finely chopped fresh mint

Salt and freshly ground black pepper to taste

For the shakshuka:
2 tablespoons olive oil

1 tablespoon minced garlic

½ medium white onion, diced

1 (28-ounce/794 g) can crushed tomatoes

1¾ cups (455 g) chopped roasted piquillo peppers (canned; look for them online or in Spanish grocery shops)

2 tablespoons harissa

1 tablespoon ground cumin

½ tablespoon ground black pepper

1 tablespoon ground coriander

Salt

4 to 6 large eggs

Fresh mint, fresh cilantro, and/or za'atar, for garnish (optional)

1 baguette (recipe follows)

To make the yogurt-pimentón sauce, in a small bowl, combine all of the ingredients. Taste and add more salt and pepper as needed. Store in an airtight container in the fridge while you make your shakshuka, but don't make this too far ahead of time (don't leave it overnight).

To make the shakshuka, heat the olive oil in a large skillet over medium heat, add the garlic and onion, and cook until caramelized; they should be soft and brown. Add the tomatoes and piquillo peppers, reduce the heat to low, and simmer for about 30 minutes, until the sauce comes together. Stir in the harissa, cumin, black pepper, and coriander. Season with salt.

While the sauce is cooking, preheat the oven to 375°F (190°C).

Transfer the shakshuka to an ovenproof serving dish and make pockets for the eggs with the back of a large spoon. Gently crack one egg into one hole at a time, watching out for the shells. Place the baking dish in the oven and bake for 10 to 12 minutes, until the eggs are fully cooked.

To serve, drizzle the shakshuka with yogurt-pimentón sauce and garnish with mint and cilantro, if using. Finish with a sprinkle of za'atar seasoning, if using, and serve with a quarter of a baguette per person.

Baguette

Makes 3 baguettes, about the length of a sheet pan

For the sponge:
¾ cup (104 g) Central Milling Artisan Baker's Craft Plus organic bread flour (see Note)

Pinch (0.25 g) instant dry yeast

For the dough:
3 cups plus 1 tablespoon (415 g) Central Milling Artisan Baker's Craft Plus organic bread flour (see Note), plus more for dusting

⅓ teaspoon (1 g) instant dry yeast

1¾ teaspoons (10 g) fine sea salt

* * * * *

To make the sponge, in the bowl of a stand mixer fitted with a dough hook, mix the flour and yeast with ¼ cup (60 ml) water on low speed for 4 minutes. Put the sponge in an airtight container and ferment in the refrigerator for 24 hours.

The next day, to make the dough, mix 1 cup plus 3 tablespoons (285 ml) water with the fermented sponge, the flour, yeast, and salt in a stand mixer. Place in a container and ferment in the refrigerator for 12 to 14 hours.

To shape the baguettes, after the fermentation, dust flour over your workspace and divide the dough into 3 equal pieces. Gently pat to deflate slightly and to create rough rectangular shapes. Each portion should be slightly smaller than your baguette pan or sheet pan.

Work one portion at a time. For each portion: With your rectangle in front of you (longer sides at top and bottom), fold the top over, longer side toward the bottom, almost folding the entire thing in half. Flatten and seal along the seam with your palm or the heel of your hand. Then turn the dough 180 degrees, so the unfolded long side is now on top. Fold the long, top edge over, flattening and sealing the seam just shy of the bottom edge. Repeat the process, making and sealing 2 more folds.

Using your palms, starting at the center, gently roll the dough back and forth to elongate to 12 to 15 inches (30 to 38 cm). (Again, you do not want the logs to be longer than your baguette pan or sheet pan.)

To proof, if using a couche (a cloth specifically designed for this task), transfer the logs seam side down onto the cloth, creating wrinkles in between each piece for separation. Or transfer the logs seam side down onto a lightly greased or parchment-lined sheet pan, or, if using, a lightly greased baguette pan. Cover with lightly greased plastic wrap and let proof at room temperature for 30 minutes to 1 hour, until the baguettes double in size.

Preheat the oven to 450°F (230°C). Line a baking sheet with parchment paper.

Fill a skillet or shallow baking pan with ice or fill a spray bottle with water to create steam in the oven. When the oven is fully heated, transfer the baguettes seam side down onto the prepared pan, or, if baking in the baguette pan, move right to scoring. Score the baguettes by making 3 diagonal long cuts along the top of each baguette.

Place the baguettes in the oven and put the skillet or shallow baking pan in the oven on the bottom rack, if using, or spray the sides and bottom of the oven with water from the spray bottle. Bake for 10 minutes and then remove the pan that held the ice, if using (if not using, leave the baguettes undisturbed). Bake the baguettes for another 10 to 15 minutes, until they are a deep golden brown.

Take the baguettes out of the oven and cool on a wire rack. Freeze baguettes you don't intend to eat within a day or two for up to 3 months.

→ NOTE: République uses Central Milling Artisan Baker's Craft Plus organic bread flour, which is a white flour derived from hard red winter and hard red spring wheats and malted barley flour. You can order it online (the orders are bulk, so go in on it with a fellow baking friend or plan to use the flour for other projects like sourdough, pastry, and pizza), and there are also some distributors nationwide. You can try subbing in another artisan bread flour, but note that each brand will have variance. King Arthur European-style artisan bread flour has a similar protein structure.

MUSHROOM ADOBO

◇◇◇

Commanding long lines since the day it opened, Kasama is part bakery, part Filipino gastropub. Baker and co-owner Genie Kwon is in charge of pastries, filling the case with jamón-topped éclair-shaped Danishes, croissants stuffed with coconut cream and passion fruit jam, and ube-laced Basque cheesecakes. Her husband, Tim Flores, handles the savory side, serving up a daytime menu drawing from his Filipino heritage, whether subbing in shaved pork and longganisa for roast beef and sausage in a riff on an Italian beef combo or staying truer to the classics with crunchy lumpia and earthy chicken adobo. Mushroom adobo is a brilliant approach to the classic Filipino technique that leans all the way into its umami goodness (for a totally meat-free version, just sub in vegetable stock). With garlic-fried rice and a fried egg, it's also a low-key megahit.

Serves **4**

For the garlic-fried rice:
3 tablespoons vegetable oil

12 cloves garlic, minced

4 cups (788 g) cooked and cooled white rice

Salt and freshly ground black pepper

For the mushrooms:
1 pound (455 g) mushrooms of your choice (oyster, maitake, beech, and shiitake will all work well individually or mixed), torn or roughly chopped

6 cloves garlic, minced

¼ cup (60 ml) distilled white vinegar or rice wine vinegar

¼ cup (60 ml) soy sauce

1 cup (240 ml) unsalted or low-sodium chicken stock

3 tablespoons dark brown sugar, plus more as needed

2 tablespoons butter

Salt

For serving:
4 eggs

1 tablespoon vegetable oil

Sliced scallions (optional)

To make the garlic-fried rice, in a large wok or skillet, heat the vegetable oil over medium-high heat. Lower the heat to medium and add the minced garlic. Cook for 2 to 3 minutes, until the garlic turns a light golden color. Carefully strain the garlic from the pan, leaving the garlic-infused oil behind. Drain the fried garlic on paper towels until cooled.

Add the cooked rice to the garlic oil in the wok, stirring to coat all the grains with oil. Spread the rice out in the wok, covering as much surface area of the hot pan as possible. Let the rice cook, undisturbed, for 3 to 5 minutes. Stir the rice well, then spread it out again and cook, undisturbed, for 3 to 5 minutes more. Continue this process until the rice is cooked to your liking. Season the rice with salt and pepper and set aside.

To make the mushrooms, heat a large sauté pan over medium-high heat without any oil. Once the pan is warm, add a handful of mushrooms and sear to get some color. Work in batches and be careful not to overcrowd the pan, as the mushrooms will release liquid, and you want them to stay crisp.

When the mushrooms are browned, add the garlic and continue to cook until the garlic is golden brown. Add the vinegar, scraping up any browned bits stuck to the pan to incorporate them, and continue cooking until the liquid is reduced by half. Add the soy sauce, chicken stock, and brown sugar to the pan and reduce the sauce by half. Stir in the butter to emulsify the sauce. Season with more brown sugar and salt as needed.

In a large skillet over medium-high heat, fry the eggs in a little oil.

Serve the mushroom adobo on top of the garlic rice. Place the fried eggs on top. Garnish with the crispy fried garlic and sliced scallions, if using.

Daytime Is the Right Time to Party

As told to by ZoeFoodParty chef **Zoë Komarin**, who regularly creates pop-ups, food-centered art installations, and private events—and loves cooking for friends at home.

Cooking and hosting a large meal can be tiring. Preparing dinner, cleaning it up, and getting a good night's rest can be overwhelming. With a brunch party, on the other hand, you can really go all-out because you have the rest of the day to bounce back.

Hosting during the day means I can enjoy it more. I find daytime entertaining to be more inclusive, too. If someone has kids, they can bring them, no babysitters needed, and it's easy to not drink.

When you're cooking food for friends in your home, involve them in the process. When people ask what they can bring, don't say nothing. You don't have to demand a specific thing. I like offering a general prompt like "bring a vegetable." Maybe they'll bring something lovely from the farmers' market. Then when they arrive, get them cracking eggs, chopping vegetables, or mixing up the salad dressing. Put your friends to work and hang out at the same time. Making the meal *is* the party.

Go Ahead, Make Punch

When asked what they would serve for a big brunch party at home, many of the country's top bartenders offered the same resounding reply: "Punch!" Punch, by definition, is both large format—who wants to mix individual cocktails in the morning?—and fun. This basic formula comes courtesy of **Alex Anderson**, a lover of historic cocktails and bartender at Portland's

Takibi. Switch up the components based on the season or your mood. In the summer, for example, you could do gin, sparkling wine, pineapple syrup (make it yourself by adding equal parts sugar to pineapple juice and heating until the sugar dissolves), plus mint tea instead of water, garnished with some lemon wedges.

BASIC FORMULA

Makes about 30 drinks

1 (750 ml) bottle spirit

1 (750 ml) bottle wine

2 cups (480 ml) fresh lemon or lime juice

2 cups (480 ml) simple syrup

Ice, for serving

Combine all the ingredients with 4 cups (960 ml) water. Serve over pebble ice or standard ice cubes.

Create a Cafe-Style Creamer Station

"Any coffee bar in the country is mostly selling milk with coffee in it; everywhere is a latte factory," jokes Yes Plz Coffee founder **Sumi Ali**. He and his wife, Christine, realized they could easily bring that spirit to their LA home, too, and devised this creative coffee service for when friends come over: In pitchers, set out iced coffee (you could do hot, if you prefer, but iced is easier) and a few options for creamers, and, as Ali puts it: "Give the people what they want!"

Above all else, Ali recommends not letting any residual barista "theater" get in the way of enjoying what you've made. "You don't have to enjoy your coffee less just because you worked less to make it," he says. That goes for enjoying a sweeter coffee drink, too. "Even though there's some stigma with sweetening coffee, for a brunch, as a complement to sweet and savory foods, I'd still do a sweet drink."

THE COFFEE: "Cold brew has great body and natural sweetness, however it takes the uniqueness out of some coffees," Ali explains. Brewing coffee with hot water ahead of time preserves more of the flavor, so Ali prefers to make it ahead and chill it in the fridge overnight (or for about 90 seconds in a Coldwave pitcher). Don't overthink it. Use the beans you like, brew it with the technique you're most comfortable with, and don't take it too seriously. ("Really, just brew it in an automatic drip and put the carafe in the fridge overnight.")

THE CREAMER: Taking a page from coffee shop trends, Ali often opts for oat milk, which accommodates most guests' dietary restrictions. Confectioners' sugar will dissolve easily in cold oat milk, and from there you can also add good vanilla extract for a vanilla creamer or high-quality cocoa powder for chocolate creamer. If you want to include dairy options, try sweetened condensed milk plus coconut cream; sweetened heavy cream plus almond extract; sweetened whole milk plus lavender simple syrup. If you want to go the extra mile, you could create labels for your pitchers or set out cards explaining what's in each creamer.

ONE-PAN MIGAS TACOS and Pink Panther Smoothie

VERACRUZ ALL NATURAL
Austin, Texas

Sisters and co-owners Maritza and Reyna Vazquez run a veritable breakfast-taco empire in Austin, but they began with a much humbler vision, serving fresh juices and smoothies. The Veracruz migas taco may well be the single most recommended food from across the Eater universe. You'd be hard-pressed to find an Eater staffer in or out of Austin who wouldn't rave about the special alchemy that comes from combining pan-fried tortilla strips, eggs, and avocado. To put it plainly: We love it, and we think you will, too. Here, Reyna offers up a recipe to do everything in one pan, as well as a smoothie, to keep it true to the original Veracruz way.

Serves **6**

¼ cup (60 ml) vegetable oil

4 corn tortillas, cut into squares

1 teaspoon minced garlic

1 cup (180 g) diced tomato

1 cup (125 g) diced red onion

1 cup (40 g) chopped fresh cilantro

1 tablespoon minced jalapeño chile

5 eggs

Salt and freshly ground black pepper

6 taco-size tortillas (corn or flour), heated

1 cup (120 g) crumbled queso fresco

1 avocado, sliced

Salsa of your choice

Pink Panther Smoothie (recipe follows)

Heat a large skillet over medium-high heat and add the vegetable oil. Once the oil is hot, add the tortilla squares and fry them until crispy. Add the garlic and stir to incorporate with the tortilla chips. Add the tomato, onion, cilantro, and jalapeño and stir to incorporate all the ingredients.

Add the eggs to the pan and stir to cook until scrambled. Season with salt and pepper and mix to incorporate all the ingredients.

To serve, take a heated tortilla and fill with the migas. Garnish with a sprinkling of queso fresco, a slice of avocado, and salsa and serve with a Pink Panther Smoothie.

The Pink Panther Smoothie

Serves 4
(makes 3 cups/720 ml)

1 cup (165 g) frozen mango chunks

1 cup (150 g) frozen strawberries

1 whole banana, peeled

2 cups (480 ml) orange juice

Put all the ingredients in a high-powered blender. Blend on high speed for about 1 minute, until a thick, smooth consistency is reached.

BREAKFAST CONGEE
with Cinnamon-Bacon Croutons, Portuguese Sausage, and Chili Oil

KOKO HEAD CAFE
Honolulu, Hawai'i

◇◇◇

Koko Head Cafe is a Honolulu brunch destination that embraces Hawai'i flavors but steers clear of touristy cliché. With a sprawling menu that brings together poke omelets, cornflake French toast, and pork dumplings, chef Lee Anne Wong has won the hearts of chefs, out-of-towners, and locals alike. Her breakfast congee, a longtime staple of the menu, takes a maximalist approach: cheddar cheese, ham, scallions, Portuguese sausage, chili oil, and cinnamon-bacon croutons all contribute to a soulful, comforting bowl that is more than the sum of its parts. Embracing those contrasting flavors and textures is key to nailing that Honolulu vibe at home.

Serves **4** to **6**

◇◇◇◇◇◇◇◇◇◇◇◇◇◇◇◇◇◇◇◇◇◇◇◇◇◇◇◇◇◇   ◇◇

For the cinnamon-bacon croutons:

1 (8-ounce/226 g) package bacon (about 8 slices)

2 tablespoons sugar

1 teaspoon ground cinnamon

1 teaspoon salt

2 cups baguette (diced or torn into 1-inch/2.5 cm pieces), left uncovered to dry out at room temperature overnight

For the congee:

1 cup (195 g) medium- or long-grain white rice

2 quarts (2 L) chicken stock, vegetable stock, or water

Salt

½ cup (68 g) diced ham

½ cup (115 g) diced Portuguese sausage

½ cup (115 g) diced Szechuan preserved vegetables/shredded preserved mustard stems

½ cup (115 g) diced cooked bacon (from the croutons above)

3 tablespoons maple syrup

3 tablespoons Indonesian sweet soy sauce (ABC brand is ideal)

1 cup (115 g) grated cheddar cheese

4 eggs, soft poached

2 tablespoons chili oil

½ cup sliced scallions, green parts only, for garnish

To make the cinnamon-bacon croutons, first, cook the bacon in a large skillet over medium heat until it is just cooked through (it will cook again, so don't over-crisp it). While the bacon cooks, combine the sugar, cinnamon, and salt in a large heatproof bowl. Remove the bacon from the pan and set aside. Toss the fat into the bowl with the cinnamon-sugar and torn baguette. Stir to evenly coat.

Preheat the oven to 325°F (165°C) and line a baking sheet with parchment paper.

Place the coated bread on the prepared baking sheet and bake for about 20 minutes, until golden; you can give the croutons a stir or shake the pan halfway through. Cool the croutons to room temperature and store in an airtight container up to overnight.

To make the congee, combine the rice and stock in a heavy-bottomed pot. Bring to a boil, then reduce the heat to maintain a simmer and cook, stirring often, for 1 hour, or until the rice has broken down and the mixture is creamy. Season with salt.

Heat a large skillet over medium-high heat and add the ham, Portuguese sausage, and Szechuan preserved vegetables. Cook for 5 minutes, then add the cooked bacon and continue to cook until everything is crisped, about 10 minutes, stirring as you go.

Meanwhile, in a small bowl, combine the maple syrup and sweet soy sauce.

Divide the hot congee into 4 to 6 bowls. Sprinkle with the grated cheese and cooked breakfast meats. Top with a poached egg and drizzle with chili oil and maple sweet soy. Garnish with sliced scallions and bacon-cinnamon croutons.

LUNCH

2

ON POWER LUNCHING

A good restaurant lunch in the middle of the workday is a small rebellion. Maybe you keep it to an hour, but maybe it's more like two. Maybe you're discussing work; maybe you're actually just catching up with a friend. It's energizing, and, for the extroverts among us anyway, restorative.

The term *power lunch* was coined by *Esquire* in the 1970s, describing the meals in New York City over which deals were brokered. Getting a seat at the table was half the battle. These days, the definition of a power lunch is, mercifully, less narrow—and what might constitute a power lunch spot for one community might not make sense for another. But the aspirational appeal of it rings as true as ever. So sure, a three-martini lunch to win an account is a power lunch, but so is queuing up for a must-try pop-up or settling in for a meal at one of the country's most famous cafes. Above all else, a power lunch is one in which we declare loud and clear that even during the workweek, we are allowed to have fun and enjoy ourselves—that we can make an escape out of a necessary meal.

At home, you can get the same thrill by having a supremely delicious lunch, whether you prep it in advance, bring it in with you to eat on break, or luxuriate in taking time in a work-from-home day to cook something nourishing and satisfying for yourself. Of course, all of these recipes also make for great dinners or day-off lunches, too. The main objective here is finding ways to bring more pleasure and intentionality to the plate when our days are so easily consumed with other things.

Stock a Lunch-Ready Kitchen

After talking with chefs who make some of the best lunches in the business, one thing is clear: Making a great lunch at home is 95 percent about what you're keeping in your pantry and fridge. The other 5 percent is thinking just a bit more strategically about what you're doing with that inventory.

Here's what you need for excellent lunches at home *without a recipe.*

FLAVOR BOOSTERS

That's what Yangban chef-owner Katianna Hong calls things like Kewpie mayo and Yondu, a plant-based seasoning liquid she uses instead of soy sauce to "add depth, round everything out, and make things taste professional." A bit of tinned fish can be combined with Kewpie mayo and served with rice, a dash of Yondu, and nori sheets for a DIY hand roll.

She puts roasted, salted almonds in the flavor-booster category, too. "Just chop them, and add them to anything: half an avocado, even meat. Restaurants use a lot of nuts—adding a sprinkle elevates your plate." She also always has furikake on hand, which, along with adding umami flavor, has

the added bonus of looking like a fancy garnish on the plate. Other easy flavor boosters include chili crisp (see page 54 for more ideas on what to do with it), lemons, fresh herbs, and spice mixes.

PICKLES AND KIMCHI

Along with the sandwich pickles and spears you can buy at any grocery store, consider keeping some homemade quick pickles in the fridge (see page 55) as a way to use up leftover vegetables and have crunchy, bright additions to your lunch at the ready. You can also use the pickle brine from your favorite jar as part of a vinaigrette or marinade. Monteverde chef Sarah Grueneberg relies on Mrs. Renfro's pickled jalapeños to add "zip and spice, to munch on with crackers, to level up a burrito, a taco, a sandwich." Hong always keeps cabbage *and* radish kimchi on hand—but if you don't have access to the good stuff, don't despair. She learned this tip from her husband and Yangban co-chef John Hong's mom: "If you thin out your just-okay kimchi with a splash of sesame oil and a splash of soy sauce, and some toasted

sesame seeds, it will taste much better and even a bit more aged." From there, chopped kimchi is an excellent sandwich topping, or you can turn your kimchi into a vinaigrette like Hong does by adding some avocado or sesame oil, a rice wine or white wine vinegar, and a smashed clove of garlic. Add liberally to any part of your lunch, from salads to shredded chicken.

GRAINS AND BEANS

JJ Johnson, the chef-restaurateur behind FieldTrip, a mini-chain of fast-casual rice bowl shops in New York, recommends starting with farro, millet, fonio, and, of course, quinoa—then when you're ready to level up, seek out a grain vendor at the farmers' market and try something you've never cooked before. Make your grains ahead (Johnson recommends a grain cooking session with multiple pots going on the stove) and store them in your fridge to have quick

bases for grain bowls or to add to salads. Ditto for big batches of dried beans, but there's no shame in using canned. "Having grains you can then cook, or fry, or roast, or puff will up your ante for lunch at home," the chef says. Johnson loves subbing grains in for rice, or frying them with leafy greens, diced veggies, and a protein on top.

BREADS

Sandwich bread can be fun to bake if you're looking for a project, or you can seek out a good local bakery for crusty baguettes and hearty sourdoughs. Peter Lemos, chef-owner of the LA sandwich shop Wax Paper Co., notes that if you buy a whole loaf and slice as you need it, the loaf will stay fresher longer. (You can also slice and then freeze to get more mileage out of buying a large loaf.) Pita is also great to have on hand for dipping into hummus and creating layered sandwiches. Flatbreads like lavash and naan are welcome additions, too. Tortillas aren't bread, of course, but they are your friend when it comes to helping you reimagine what's in your fridge.

LEFTOVERS

Armed with all of the above, you'll see leftovers as your secret weapon rather than your chore. Plan dinners with lunch leftovers in mind. "When I'm at home cooking for my family, I always cook in abundance. Make more chicken than you need—that way you have food for the week," says Johnson. Hong makes sure to always save leftover rice, which can be crisped up in a pan ("sort of like the top of a tahdig") or microwaved and rolled into balls and topped with sesame oil and furikake. A bit of leftover chicken can be shredded, seasoned, and layered into a salad or grain bowl (see page 171 for more ideas); thinly slice leftover steak and add it to a green salad; a hunk of leftover salmon can be smashed with sriracha and mayo and put on top of rice for a quick donburi; leftover ground beef can be quickly tossed with salsa and thrown into a quesadilla.

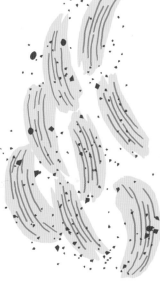

TARTARE FRITES

FRENCHETTE
New York City

Chefs Riad Nasr and Lee Hanson are veterans of Minetta Tavern and Balthazar, two of New York City's most storied power lunch spots. At their perpetually packed restaurant Frenchette, the duo knows exactly what it takes to enthrall Tribeca's chic lunch crowd. The tartare frites, nearly always on the menu, reward guests who want to stick with a classic with one of the finest versions in the country. At home, consider this the only from-scratch French fry recipe you'll ever need; and making the tartare is like getting a lesson on knife work from a pro (a butcher can help source a good tenderloin for this one; see page 182). When paired with a funky natural wine, this is French bistro fare at its coolest.

Serves 4

For the fries:

5 large (4 pounds/1.8 kg) Idaho potatoes

2 quarts (2 L) peanut oil or other neutral oil

Salt and freshly ground black pepper

For the tartare:

4 ounces (110 g) beef tenderloin

1 tablespoon chopped cornichon

1 tablespoon chopped capers

1 tablespoon minced shallots

1 teaspoon Worcestershire sauce

1 teaspoon ketchup

1 teaspoon Dijon mustard

½ teaspoon Tabasco sauce

¾ teaspoon egg yolk

2 tablespoons minced fresh chives, cut just before serving

Salt and freshly ground black pepper

1 teaspoon grated fresh horseradish

Start your fries at least one night, if not two, before you plan on serving. Peel the potatoes and place them into a bowl full of cold water. Cut each one into ½ × ½-inch (1.25 × 1.25 cm) strips and place them back into the cold water. Cover with a kitchen towel and soak the fries overnight. The following day, heat the peanut oil over high heat in a large flat-bottomed pot to 300°F (148°C) according to a deep-frying thermometer. Working in batches, blanch the fries for 4 minutes, or until slightly soft. Remove the fries from the oil and place on a platter lined with paper towels to blot excess oil. When done blanching and blotting, transfer the fries to a sheet pan and chill in the fridge until you are ready for the second fry, up to the next day.

The day you plan on serving, partially freeze the beef tenderloin, about 45 minutes, to make the beef easier to dice. Fill a medium bowl with ice and water and place a smaller bowl inside it. This is where you'll put the meat after you cut it to keep it cold and, therefore, as red as possible. Working in batches, cut the fillet into small dice (¼ × ¼-inch/6 × 6 mm cubes): To do this, using a very sharp knife, cut against the grain, crosswise, into ¼-inch (6 mm) slices. Then stack the slices and dice them, aiming to create even, consistent cubes. Place the diced meat inside the small bowl on ice.

Mix the beef, cornichons, capers, and shallots in a large bowl (a chilled metal bowl would be ideal here). Add the Worcestershire sauce, ketchup, mustard, Tabasco, and egg yolk. Finally, add the freshly cut chives and mix well. Season with salt and pepper. Using a large spoon, scoop the tartare onto one side of a large serving plate. Pat the tartare down with the back of the spoon to flatten it a bit. Transfer the plate to the fridge while you finish the French fries.

For the second fry, use the same flat-bottomed pot over high heat and bring the same oil up to 350°F (175°C). Fry the fries for 3 to 5 minutes, until they are crispy. Transfer to a baking sheet lined with power towels to blot excess oil.

Remove the plate of tartare from the fridge and, using a Microplane, grate the horseradish over the top. Serve immediately with the fries.

CURRY CHANNA DOUBLES

BRIDGETOWN ROTI
Los Angeles, California

After years of cooking in hip LA restaurants, chef Rashida Holmes turned her attention to the Caribbean fare she grew up eating with her pandemic-born pop-up Bridgetown Roti. As she hosted events across the city, she quickly found an audience for her patties, the turmeric-colored pastries hiding the most delicious stewed oxtail, and for her impossibly flaky rotis, another Caribbean staple carb. But Bridgetown's biggest fans know that Sundays mean doubles, the famous Trinidadian dish of curried chickpeas nestled into a fried flatbread called *bara* (the name *doubles* refers to the pieces of fried bara, typically two per order). As with much of the Bridgetown menu, Holmes's curry channa doubles, which she serves with a kicky green sofrito, are vegan, but almost incidentally. Holmes also uses the sofrito to top her fan-favorite goat curry, and at home, you'll find it a versatile addition to anything in need of more flavor—use it in soups and marinades and on grilled meats and sandwiches. Just like diners need a plan to snag their doubles before Bridgetown sells out, home cooks need to think ahead here, too: Make sure to start soaking your dried chickpeas the night before and plan for at least a two-hour second proof (or an overnight rest in the fridge) for your bara dough.

For the chickpeas:

2 cups (370 g) dried chickpeas (see Note)

½ cup (13 g) fresh curry leaves

¾ teaspoon baking soda

Salt

For the bara:

1 cup (240 ml) warm water

2 teaspoons sugar

1 teaspoon instant dry yeast

2 cups (250 g) all-purpose flour

½ teaspoon baking powder

1 teaspoon salt

¼ teaspoon ground turmeric

2 quarts (2 L) frying oil, such as vegetable or canola

For the green pepper sofrito:

2 green bell peppers, roughly chopped

2 Anaheim chiles, roughly chopped

1 large white onion, roughly chopped

2 bunches scallions, green and white parts, roughly chopped

4 cloves garlic, roughly chopped

2 tablespoons plus 2 teaspoons peeled and diced fresh ginger

1 habanero chile, seeds removed, chopped

3½ teaspoons ground fenugreek

1½ teaspoons salt

To assemble:

Optional garnishes: grated cucumbers seasoned with lime juice and salt, Scotch bonnet pepper sauce, tamarind sauce, fermented mango

→ NOTE: While Holmes prefers to use dried chickpeas, if you want to sub in canned chickpeas, don't let them get mushy. In a medium pot, bring 4 cups (960 ml) water to a boil, add the curry leaves, and simmer for 30 minutes. Rinse and drain 4 (15-ounce/425 g) cans of chickpeas and add them to the simmering water. Turn off the heat and let sit for at least an hour to allow the chickpeas to get warm and flavorful.

To make the chickpeas, soak them in a bowl with water to cover by a few inches overnight. Drain, then place in a pot with 4 quarts (4 L) water, the curry leaves, and baking soda. Bring to a simmer over medium-high heat, then lower the heat to low and cook for 30 minutes, or until soft. Season with salt. If making ahead, store the chickpeas in their cooking liquid in an airtight container in the fridge for up to 5 days. When ready to serve, warm the chickpeas in a pot over low heat.

To make the bara, in a small bowl, mix the warm water, sugar, and yeast together and let sit for about 5 minutes to proof. Meanwhile, whisk together the flour, baking powder, salt, and turmeric in a large bowl. Add the yeast mixture and combine just until a soft, sticky dough forms. Do not over-knead.

Cover the dough and let rise for 1½ hours, or until doubled. Punch down the dough, divide into 6 equal pieces (about 2½ ounces/70 g each), and place on a sheet tray. Cover with plastic wrap and let rest again for another 2 hours at room temperature or overnight in the fridge, until doubled.

Heat the frying oil in a large heavy-bottomed pot or Dutch oven to 375°F (190°C) according to a deep-frying thermometer. Flatten the dough balls and fry for about 30 seconds on each side, until puffed.

Transfer the fried bara to a paper towel–lined baking sheet and set aside until ready to use. You can serve them at room temperature.

To make the sofrito, combine the green peppers, Anaheim chiles, onion, scallions, garlic, ginger, and habanero chile in a food processer or blender and process until finely diced. Transfer to a medium saucepan, place over high heat, and cook the vegetable mixture until soft, 8 to 10 minutes. In a small pan, swirl the ground fenugreek over medium heat until fragrant. Add to the vegetable mixture, with the salt. If the mixture is watery, strain some of the liquid out. You should serve the sofrito the same day you make it, and it can be enjoyed warm or at room temperature.

To assemble the doubles, take a fried bara and spoon some green pepper sofrito on it. Fill the bara with the warm chickpeas, then drizzle with a little more sofrito. Top with as many garnishes as you like. Repeat with the remaining bara and serve.

PIZZA BAGELS

Call Your Mother is D.C.'s most exciting deli. Co-owner and executive chef Daniela Moreira brings her live-fire expertise to the genre's staples—and then takes things to the next level with high-octane flavor combos and old-fashioned nineties nostalgia. Enter the pizza bagel: In Moreira's hands, the beloved after-school snack is a technical wonder built upon a housemade wood-fired bagel with just the right amount of chew. At the restaurant, Moreira makes her own sauce by blending San Marzano tomatoes with fresh basil and salt. You can do that, too, or, since making bagels at home is impressive enough, go ahead and just use your favorite store-bought sauce.

Makes **12** bagels

For the dough:
8 cups (1 kg) high-gluten or bread flour, plus more for dusting

2 (¼-ounce/7 g) envelopes instant dry yeast

1½ tablespoons (20 g) salt

⅓ cup (50 g) malt powder

¾ cup (100 g) honey

2 teaspoons (10 g) malt syrup

For the boil:
¼ cup (60 ml) malt syrup

1 teaspoon baking soda

To assemble, per bagel (12 bagels total):
1 bagel, sliced in half

¼ cup (60 ml) pizza sauce

¼ cup (30 g) shredded low-moisture mozzarella cheese

¼ cup (30 g) shredded sharp aged provolone

Small pepperoni slices (ideally cup and char style)

Fresh basil leaves, for garnish

To make the dough, in a medium to large mixing bowl, combine the flour, yeast, salt, malt powder, honey, malt syrup, and 2 cups plus 2 tablespoons (500 ml) water. Mix slowly until the ingredients are completely combined and create a dough-like texture. Turn the dough out on a flat surface and knead for 5 to 7 minutes, until the dough is soft and smooth. (If you prefer to use a stand mixer, mix the water, yeast, honey, and malt syrup with a paddle attachment until all the wet ingredients are combined. Then add the dry ingredients and continue to mix until a dough is formed. Switch to the dough hook attachment and knead on medium speed for 10 minutes, or until the dough is smooth.)

Sprinkle a sheet tray with flour. Cut the dough into 5-ounce (140 g) portions (or 12 equal pieces if you don't have a scale) and roll each piece into a small ball. Using your thumb, press down in the center of each piece until there's a hole, then smooth the disc into a bagel-like shape and repeat until all of your dough is shaped. Place each bagel on the floured tray, leaving room in between so they don't stick together. Cover with plastic wrap and let proof for about 30 minutes. From there, place the tray in the refrigerator overnight.

The next day, in a large pot, combine 6 quarts (6 L) water with the malt syrup and baking soda and bring to a boil. Cook your bagels in the boiling water for about 1 minute on each side, then place on a lightly greased baking sheet.

Preheat the oven to 500°F (260°C). Place your tray of bagels into the oven and bake for 15 to 25 minutes, until they're golden brown. Remove from the oven and cool completely. Once fully cooled, the bagels can be sliced and stored in a plastic bag in the freezer for up to 2 months.

To assemble the pizza bagels, preheat the oven to 450°F (230°C), or lower it to that temperature if you're making the pizza bagels right away.

Place the bagels (thawed if frozen) in the oven for 2 to 3 minutes to lightly toast. Remove the bagels from the oven and spread 2 tablespoons sauce on each side. Sprinkle on the mozzarella and provolone and top with pepperoni slices. Bake the bagels for 6 to 8 minutes, until the cheese is bubbling and the pepperoni is crisp. Garnish with basil leaves and enjoy immediately.

PITA PARTY
with Roasted Broccoli and Beet Salad

ZOEFOODPARTY
Los Angeles, California

◇◇◇◇◇◇◇◇◇◇◇◇◇◇◇◇◇◇◇◇◇◇◇◇◇◇◇◇◇◇◇◇◇◇◇◇◇◇ ◇◇◇◇◇◇◇◇◇◇◇◇◇◇◇◇◇◇◇◇◇◇◇◇◇

After years cooking at some of Tel Aviv's hottest restaurants, chef and artist Zoë Komarin found her groove hosting pop-ups and parties from Brooklyn to Berlin to Berkeley. When Komarin moved to LA in 2019, she brought her pop-ups with her, installing herself in Collage Coffee's Highland Park backyard and serving fluffy pitas stuffed to the brim with an ever-changing array of salads, spreads, and fillings. The night before one pita party, Komarin meant to dust her roasted broccoli and beets in baharat but mistakenly grabbed curry powder—she loved this result. Komarin devised each of these components to be stuffed into a pita, but they are infinitely adaptable: The broccoli and beet salad is wonderful on its own and the dill labneh is a great dip; the potato chip "dukkah" spices up any salad or sandwich. And setting up your own pita filling station is an excellent party trick.

For the roasted vegetables:

1 (1-pound/455 g) head broccoli, cut into florets

1 large beet, cut into ¼-inch (6 mm) slices (peeled or unpeeled)

1 orange, cut into ¼-inch (6 mm) slices, rind and pith included

Olive oil

Salt and freshly ground black pepper

1½ teaspoons curry powder, or more to taste

For the dill labneh:

1 cup (240 g) labneh

10 or so sprigs fresh dill

Zest of 1 lemon

Salt

Serves 4 to 6

For the potato chip dukkah:

¼ teaspoon cumin seeds

1 tablespoon fennel seeds

1 teaspoon coriander seeds

¼ cup (28 g) sesame seeds

¼ cup (28 g) pumpkin seeds or sunflower seeds

2 tablespoons shelled pistachios or another nut

Salt

Red chile flakes

2 big handfuls ruffled potato chips

For the sandwiches:

4 to 6 pita bread halves

◇◇

To make the roasted vegetables, preheat the oven to 375°F (190°C) and line a baking sheet with parchment paper.

In a large bowl, toss the broccoli florets, beet slices, and orange slices in a few glugs of olive oil and season with salt and pepper. Space everything out on the baking sheet as much as you can. Roast for 25 to 35 minutes, until the broccoli crowns start to look nicely browned and you can easily pierce the beets with a knife.

Slide the roasted vegetables into a big bowl and dust with the curry powder. Taste, adjust the seasonings to your liking, and let cool a bit before eating. You can make the remaining components while the vegetables are roasting.

To make the dill labneh, put the labneh in a medium bowl. Finely chop the dill, stems and all. Add the dill and lemon zest to the labneh and season with salt. Mix to combine and use immediately or store in an airtight container in the fridge for up to 1 week.

To make the potato chip dukkah, start by toasting the cumin, fennel, and coriander seeds together in a small skillet over medium-low heat until fragrant, 1 to 2 minutes, keeping the pan moving so nothing burns. Transfer to a bowl and set aside.

Add the sesame seeds and pumpkin seeds to the same pan and swirl until the sesame seeds are nicely golden. This can happen quickly, so keep a watchful eye. Add to the same bowl as the toasted spices. Finally, toast the pistachios in the same way and toss them into the same bowl.

Continued

Place all of the toasted ingredients in a small food processor and add a generous pinch of salt and the right amount of chile for you. Pulse a few times, until the mixture is broken down but not too fine—you want to maintain some texture and crunch. Put it back into the bowl and process the potato chips. They should still be coarse, and obviously potato chips, so don't overprocess. If you're not assembling the sandwiches right away, store the dukkah in an airtight container for up to 2 weeks.

To make your sandwiches, warm one pita at a time in a pan over medium heat. Spread about 2 tablespoons of the dill labneh inside the pita, then layer in as many roasted vegetables as you can fit without overstuffing. Sprinkle the vegetables with potato chip dukkah. Repeat the process for the other pita breads and serve.

Make Magic with a Jar of Chili Crisp

"Chili crisp is a cheat code for easy, flavorful home cooking," says LA-based pastry chef and Boon Sauce maker Max Boonthanakit. "It's so versatile."

Typically made with red chile flakes, shallots, garlic, and an array of spices frizzled in oil, chili crisp is a must for a well-stocked, restaurant-worthy pantry. Some brands are easy to find in grocery stores: Lao Gan Ma is the old-school gold standard, Trader Joe's has a mild one called Crunchy Chili Onion, and Whole Foods stocks food-world obsession Fly by Jing Sichuan Chili Crisp as well as Momofuku Chili Crunch. Plenty of restaurants and chefs have gotten into the game as well, releasing small batches on their websites—Xi'an Famous Foods, 886, Junzi, Nowon, Pagu, Mei Lin, and Melissa King all offer their own take.

Once you have a jar at home, you can use it to top fried eggs, noodles, pizza, and any leftovers that need a bit of punch. Reach for it when you want to zhuzh up congee, stir-fries, and avocado toast, too.

But chili crisp is more than just a condiment—in the hands of chefs and creative cooks, it's an *ingredient*. Here's how heat-seeking experts recommend cooking with a jar of the good stuff.

- Make **CHILLED NOODLES** with chili crisp, sesame oil, and soy sauce.
  Recommended by: Majordomo chef Jude Parra-Sickels
  Go-to chili crisp: Momofuku Chili Crunch

- Sub it in for anything that calls for olive oil, such as **BRUSCHETTA**, and add it to anything with mayo for a crunchy kick, like a soft **EGG SALAD**.
  Recommended by: Boon Sauce creator and Camphor co-chef Max Boonthanakit
  Go-to chili crisp: Boon Sauce

- Bake with it—try it in flourless **PEANUT BUTTER COOKIES** with white or yellow miso.
  Recommended by: Zoë's Doughies baker Zoë Kanan
  Go-to chili crisp: Fly by Jing Sichuan Chili Crisp

- Step up your lunch game with chili crisp **SALAD VINAIGRETTE**—combine chili crisp, whatever acid you like (lemon juice, vinegar), and season at will.
  Recommended by: 886 chef-owner and Sze Daddy creator Eric Sze
  Go-to chili crisp: Sze Daddy & Fly by Jing Sichuan Chili Crisp

- Create a dipping sauce for dumplings with chili crisp, aged black vinegar, soy sauce, honey, and garlic, or use chili crisp for a shortcut to homemade **MAPO TOFU**. You can also drink it—make a **COCKTAIL**, like a chili crisp mezcal paloma.
  Recommended by: Fly by Jing founder Jing Gao
  Go-to chili crisp: Fly by Jing Sichuan Chili Crisp

Anatomy of a Veggie Sandwich

Each sandwich at **LA's Wax Paper Co.** is named after an NPR host. With its mountain of alfalfa sprouts and cheery shredded cheddar, the Ira Glass is a fan favorite. It's also a brilliant template for how to build a better sandwich at home.

THE BREAD
Co-owners Lauren and Peter Lemos use Bub and Grandma's bread. Look for a local baker making a moist sourdough with good chew and sturdy crust—it needs to be strong enough to support your sandwich.

THE SPREAD
Instead of plain mayo, the Ira Glass has a garlic aioli. Make your own at home by adding garlic powder, onion powder, and salt to a neutral mayo like Best Foods.

THE CHEDDAR CHEESE
Shredded means even more texture, sharp means more flavor.

THE CUCUMBER
Wide slices of cucumber add crunch and act as a sturdy base for the shredded cheese.

THE ONION
Combining pickled red onion with raw onion offers brine and bite.

THE ALFALFA SPROUTS
Be generous; the goal is for the sprouts to create a lot of texture.

THE AVOCADOS
Every component in a sandwich should be flavorful and seasoned. Sprinkling flaky sea salt on slices of creamy avocado does the trick.

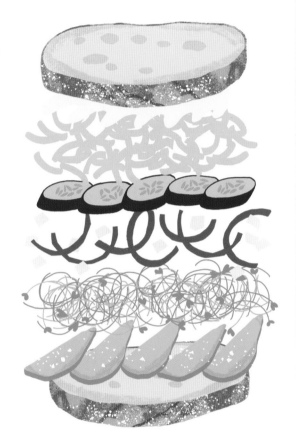

Wax Paper Co.'s Quick Pickle
2 cups (110 g) thinly sliced red onion
½ cup (100 g) sugar
½ cup (120 ml) red wine vinegar

Place the onions in a small heatproof bowl. In a small pot, combine ½ cup (120 ml) water, the sugar, and vinegar and bring to a boil. Remove from the heat, immediately pour the mixture over the onions, and let them sit until totally cooled. This can be made in advance and kept in the refrigerator for up to 2 weeks.

Chilled Zucchini Soup,
Baked Goat Cheese
with Garden Lettuce,
Big Salad with Kale,
Carrot Chips and
Pumpkin Seeds

CHILLED ZUCCHINI SOUP

It's one thing to be one of New York City's restaurant icons; it's another to be an icon that has itself spawned other icons. The crown jewel in veteran restaurateur Danny Meyer's hospitality empire, Gramercy Tavern was the launching pad for big names like Tom Colicchio, Jim Meehan, Claudia Fleming, and so many more. For decades, New Yorkers have flocked to the restaurant to splurge on a tasting menu in the dining room or be regulars in the tavern, which occupies the window-clad front half of the spacious restaurant. The tavern opens for lunch and stays open until the restaurant closes, serving up comfortably sophisticated takes on American classics. In the warmer months, chef Michael Anthony usually has a chilled vegetable soup on the menu to show off the bounty of the nearby Union Square farmers' market and offer an antidote to the city heat. It's what you cook when summer overflows with squash and freeze to treat yourself to the season's taste once the weather turns. Enjoy it with crusty bread, good butter, and a crisp salad.

Serves **4** as a starter or side

For the soup:
1½ teaspoons olive oil

½ medium onion, thinly sliced

3 shallots, thinly sliced

½ leek, white part only, halved lengthwise and thinly sliced

2 cloves garlic, thinly sliced

3 sprigs lemon thyme

3 cups (720 ml) vegetable broth or water

1 pound zucchini (455 g), halved lengthwise, seeded, and sliced (about 6 cups)

Salt

1½ cups (50 g) packed baby spinach

Handful of fresh Italian parsley leaves

5 fresh basil leaves

For the garnish:
Salt

4 baby turnips, peeled and quartered

6 Sungold or other small cherry tomatoes, halved

⅓ cup (44 g) seeded and finely diced cucumber

Fresh lemon juice

Freshly ground black pepper

Extra-virgin olive oil

In a large pot, heat the olive oil over medium heat. Add the onion, shallots, leek, and garlic and cook, stirring occasionally, until the onion is softened, about 6 minutes. Add the lemon thyme and cook, stirring, for 1 minute, then add the broth and bring to a simmer. Raise the heat to high, add the zucchini, season with salt, and bring to a boil.

Cook until the zucchini is tender, about 3 minutes. Add the spinach, parsley, and basil. As soon as the greens are wilted, no more than a minute, pour the mixture into a large bowl, set it in an ice bath, and stir to cool it quickly and preserve the color. Discard the lemon thyme.

Transfer the solids to a blender in batches and blend until very smooth and creamy, adding enough of the liquid to the blender to achieve a thin consistency. Pass through a fine-mesh strainer into a container. Season with salt, cover, and refrigerate.

Reserve any remaining broth. The soup should thicken as it chills, so thin with a bit of the reserved liquid or water before serving.

To prepare the garnish, fill a bowl with ice and water. Bring a small pot of water to a boil over medium-high heat and salt it. Add the turnips and cook until tender, about 5 minutes. Drain, shock in the ice water, then drain again. In a small bowl, combine the turnips, tomatoes, and cucumber and toss with lemon juice, salt, and pepper to taste.

To serve, ladle the soup into bowls and top with the garnish and a drizzle of extra-virgin olive oil.

BAKED GOAT CHEESE
with Garden Lettuces

CHEZ PANISSE
Berkeley, California

◇◇

Before chains proclaimed their organic bona fides, before chic restaurants listed farms in their menu descriptions, before TikTokers made chopped green goddess salads go viral, the legendary chef and restaurateur Alice Waters was celebrating fresh, local vegetables at her iconic Berkeley, California, restaurant Chez Panisse, which she opened in 1971. The downstairs restaurant is a formal but still homey affair; the upstairs cafe is more laid-back, attracting a busy lunch crowd, delighting in a meal at one of the country's most famous restaurants and enjoying the bounty of one of the country's most delicious regions. This team has offered baked, herb-crusted disks of locally made chèvre alongside a salad of small-farm lettuces for more than forty years. The medium really is the message with this recipe: A simple salad, made from the finest tender lettuces you can find, enhanced with a properly balanced vinaigrette, toasty breadcrumbs, and a creamy, warm cheese is all you need to make a beautiful meal.

Serves **4**

◇◇

1 (8-ounce/225 g) fresh goat cheese log (about 2 inches/5 cm wide and 5 inches/ 12 cm long)

¾ cup (180 ml) extra-virgin olive oil

½ teaspoon chopped fresh thyme

½ teaspoon chopped fresh marjoram

½ teaspoon chopped fresh Italian parsley

½ sourdough baguette, preferably a day old

1 tablespoon red wine vinegar

1 teaspoon Banyuls vinegar

Salt and freshly ground black pepper

8 ounces (225 g) garden lettuces (wild arugula, chervil, young red and green lettuces, baby speckled lettuce, or frisée), trimmed (about 16 cups)

Carefully slice the goat cheese into 8 disks. Pour ½ cup (120 ml) of the olive oil over the disks, fully coating all the surfaces, and sprinkle with the chopped herbs. Cover and refrigerate for several hours or up to 1 week.

To make the breadcrumbs, preheat the oven to 300°F (150°C).

Cut the baguette in half lengthwise and pop it in the oven to dry out for 20 minutes or so, until the color appears to have faded. Using a box grater or a food processor, grate it into fine crumbs.

When you're ready to assemble and serve the salad, preheat the oven to 400°F (205°C) and line a baking sheet with parchment paper.

Spread the breadcrumbs on a plate. Remove the cheese disks from the marinade and roll them in the breadcrumbs, coating them thoroughly. Place the crumb-coated cheese on the prepared baking sheet and bake for 6 minutes, or until the cheese is warm and the crust is browned.

Place the vinegars in a small bowl and season with salt and pepper. Whisk in the remaining ¼ cup (60 ml) olive oil. Taste for seasoning and adjust. Toss the lettuces lightly with the vinaigrette and arrange on 4 salad plates. With a spatula, carefully place 2 disks of the baked cheese on each plate, next to the greens, and serve.

BIG SALAD
with Kale, Carrot Chips, and Pumpkin Seeds

DIMES
New York City

When chef-owners Alissa Wagner and Sabrina De Sousa opened their Canal Street cafe in 2014, they named it Dimes, after the beautiful—10s on a scale of 1 to 10—crowd they planned to serve. Here, grain bowls, salads, and mains from the oven become oddball, Technicolored flavor bombs. Thanks to the riotous energy on every plate, what started as a daytime cafe with an appealing health-food sensibility has become an essential downtown spot; their corner of the city is now known as Dimes Square. If your trendiest friend is talking about having a "big salad" for lunch, chances are they're not quoting *Seinfeld*—they're talking about wanting to dig into Dimes's signature kale salad. The recipe is a blueprint for better salads: It's a reminder to season every component going in, to consider coaxing multiple textures out of one ingredient, and to master an upgraded-but-still-easy vinaigrette you can make every weekend and use throughout the week. The carrot chips are optional, and you can use store-bought roasted pumpkin seeds, if you don't want to make them yourself. To make it a bit more filling, add some protein; De Sousa recommends pickled eggs, roasted salmon, or tinned fish.

◇◇◇◇◇◇◇◇◇◇◇◇◇◇◇◇◇◇◇◇◇◇◇◇◇ ◇◇◇

For the dressing:
2 cloves garlic, peeled

1 shallot, peeled

1 cup (240 ml) olive oil, plus more for roasting the garlic and shallot

¾ tablespoon Dijon mustard

¼ cup (60 ml) white wine vinegar

Zest and juice of 1 orange

Juice of ½ lemon

Salt and freshly ground black pepper

For the spiced, roasted pumpkin seeds:
½ cup (60 g) hulled pumpkin seeds

2 tablespoons olive oil

½ teaspoon smoked paprika

Salt and freshly ground black pepper

For the carrot chips (optional):
2 cups (480 ml) vegetable oil

1½ carrots, julienned into matchsticks

1 tablespoon cornstarch

For the roasted carrots:
2 carrots (210 g), cut into 2-inch (5 cm) pieces and halved or quartered, if large

1½ teaspoons sumac

1½ teaspoons Aleppo pepper

2 tablespoons olive oil

For the salad:
2 bunches lacinato kale, stemmed and thinly sliced

¼ red cabbage, thinly sliced (about 2 cups/195 g)

1 Cubanelle pepper, seeds removed and julienned

Salt and freshly ground black pepper

To make the dressing, preheat the oven to 250°F (120°C).

In a deep roasting dish, cover the garlic and shallot with olive oil, cover with aluminum foil, and roast for 2 hours. You could also do this on the stovetop—put everything in a small pot and simmer for 20 to 30 minutes. When cooled, put the garlic and shallot in a food processor or blender with the remaining olive oil from the roasting dish, and blend to combine. Add the mustard, vinegar, orange zest, orange juice, and lemon juice and then drizzle in the 1 cup (240 ml) olive oil through the hole in the top, continuing to process until the dressing is smooth. Season with salt and pepper. You can store this in an airtight container in the refrigerator for up to 1 week.

To make the pumpkin seeds, preheat the oven to 200°F (90°C).

Place the pumpkin seeds on a small baking sheet and roast for about 1 hour, until golden brown. Set aside to cool, then toss with the olive oil and paprika and season with salt and pepper. You can store the pumpkin seeds in an airtight container for up to 2 weeks.

If you're going to include the carrot chips, heat the vegetable oil in a medium saucepan to 450°F (230°C) on a deep-frying thermometer. Toss the julienned carrots with the cornstarch and fry for 5 minutes, or until crispy. Remove from the oil and let cool on a paper towel–lined plate to blot the oil.

To make the roasted carrots, preheat the oven to 350°F (175°C).

In a medium bowl, toss the carrots with the sumac, Aleppo pepper, and olive oil and roast for 40 minutes, or until soft. These can be made and stored in fridge for up to 1 day. Bring the carrots to room temperature before serving.

When you're ready to eat, toss the kale, cabbage, Cubanelle pepper, and roasted carrots in a large bowl with 1 cup (240 ml) of the dressing (about half of what you've made). Season with salt and pepper. Portion out to individual serving dishes and garnish with pumpkin seeds and, if using, carrot chips.

How to Build a Salad with Pizzazz

Why is it so hard to make a great salad at home? "A salad is all about textural contrast and balance of flavors," says chef Steven Satterfield of Atlanta's vegetable-centric Miller Union. You need something creamy, something crunchy, good acidity, and proper seasoning (yes, salads need seasoning, too).

Chefs get there by paying close attention to what every single component of the salad brings to the whole. Of course, restaurant kitchens also have loads of fresh produce and surprising ingredients on hand. Cooks are whisking freshly made dressings by hand and using whatever popped up at the farmers' market that morning, not pulling a plastic bag off the shelf.

LETTUCE

Think beyond romaine. Satterfield loves using arugula, mizuna, escarole, cabbage, and little gems. Or skip the leafy greens entirely. "Some of my favorites are field peas and boiled peanuts with ricotta, mint, tomato, and pepper. Or blanched green beans with cherry tomatoes, shallot vinaigrette, and basil." You can also use fruit as your base, as in a papaya salad (see page 67).

HERBS

Fresh herbs bring life and flavor to a salad. Luis Martinez, the chef behind Atlanta's hit Puerto Rican food pop-up My Abuelas Food, suggests starting with dill, chives, mint, or basil. And don't be afraid to "be generous with them," says ZoeFoodParty chef Zoë Komarin. "Sometimes the only green in my salad will be herbs."

VEGGIES

If you're only using cucumbers, tomatoes, and bell peppers, of course, you'll get bored. Vary it up. Martinez relies on his mandoline for getting paper-thin veggies into his bowl, and Satterfield recommends roasted potatoes. Try using a vegetable two ways—cooked and raw. For example, if you've got a zucchini, toss raw, thin slices with some olive oil and lemon and pan-sear the rest. Komarin likes how this brings warm components into a salad and really shows off what each vegetable is all about.

Most important: Each element you put into your salad should be individually seasoned as you go. Don't make the dressing do all the work.

PROTEINS AND GRAINS

Any leftover chicken or salmon you've got in your fridge can help round out your salad; so can tinned fish. Consider oil-packed tuna belly as a topper, and use a bit of the flavor-packed oil in your dressing. Leftover quinoa, farro, barley, or beans add welcome texture.

CREAMY

Soft cheeses like feta and fresh mozzarella turn salad decadent. Satterfield especially likes chevre (you can bake it first, too, like the iconic Chez Panisse salad on page 59). Komarin relies on tahini to bring richness; avocado also fits the bill here, as would the egg yolk from a jammy soft-boiled egg or a still-runny fried egg. Lil Deb's Oasis chef Carla Perez-Gallardo often starts building a salad with a schmear of Greek yogurt at the bottom of the bowl or plate.

BRIGHT

To balance everything out, you'll need something with acid; think vinegar and citrus pieces and/or juice. Komarin likes thin slices of Meyer lemons (skin on! not-too-waxy!). Dimes co-chef Sabrina De Sousa opts for

pickles, and notes that she always has "a jar of something pickling in the fridge. It's a nice way to use up veggies that might be on their way out and add pizzazz."

CRUNCHY

Salty, crunchy add-ins like nuts, seeds, croutons, tortilla strips, or rice crackers take any salad to the next level. For a real surprise, crush up potato chips like Komarin does, use a little fried chicken skin or breadcrumbs like Satterfield, or go with crispy onions like Martinez.

FINISHING TOUCHES

If after all of this your salad is not sufficiently dressed, you can make a vinaigrette, ideally with cold-pressed olive oil, or just finish things off with a squeeze of lemon. Use a vegetable peeler to get long, beautiful strips of a hard cheese like pecorino. Taste your salad, and season at will: Cracked pepper and flaky sea salt will take you far, but you could also add some furikake or dukkah. Komarin recommends seasoning, dressing, and tossing salad not so early

that it gets soggy, but ten or so minutes before you plan on eating. "Salt will draw flavor out from the vegetables you're eating and make them more palatable. Even if they leach liquid, that's yummy—and the juice is great for grains or bread."

Last, if you see any edible flowers at the farmers' market, pick some up. HAGS chef Telly Justice likes how they "showcase your gentleness in the kitchen." She recommends you add them in "right at the end, after the rest of the salad has been dressed, nestled delicately as a garnish for a pop of florality. Take care not to damage or bruise them, as this will make their contribution to the dish less fresh and vibrant."

THREE SISTERS' VEGGIE BOWL

WAHPEPAH'S KITCHEN
Oakland, California

Crystal Wahpepah's restaurant, Wahpepah's Kitchen, picks up where her work as a Bay Area caterer left off: making and serving Native American cuisine that both nourishes and educates diners, with the goal of fostering Indigenous food sovereignty. Her menu is intimately tied to the provenance of the Ohlone land she grew up on in Oakland, California, and the food traditions of her multi-tribe community there (Wahpehpah is an enrolled member of the Kickapoo nation of Oklahoma). Tribes throughout North America tell the legend of "the three sisters," the story of how corn, beans, and squash help each other to grow and sustain the community. Wahpepah's eponymous nod to these Indigenous staple crops is a fixture on her menu: This veggie bowl leaves plenty of room for you to adapt, just as the restaurant does. Use whatever fruit is in season or suits your preference, if not strawberry, try blueberry or pomegranate seeds; use the nuts you like best; feel free to play with the greens you use. It's essential, however, to use corn, beans, and squash. Even better if you take a page from Wahpepah's book and also use this recipe as a chance to seek out connections with your region's Indigenous farmers.

Serves **4**

For the dressing:
¼ cup (60 ml) agave

¼ cup (60 ml) olive oil

¼ cup (60 ml) apple cider vinegar

Salt and freshly ground black pepper

For the bowl:
1 cup (115 g) diced winter squash, such as pumpkin, spaghetti, or butternut

3 tablespoons olive oil

Salt and freshly ground black pepper

1 cup (20 to 30 g) fresh spinach

1 cup (200 g) cooked quinoa, warm

½ cup cooked (175 g) white beans

1 cup (145 g) cooked yellow corn kernels

1 cup (165 g) diced strawberries
(or another seasonal fruit)

⅔ cup (85 g) diced purple onion

⅔ cup (75 g) shredded carrots

⅔ cup (80 g) chopped nuts, such as walnuts or pecans

Edible flowers (optional)

To make the dressing, combine all ingredients in a bowl and mix well to incorporate. If making ahead, store in an airtight container in the fridge for up to 4 days.

To assemble the bowls, preheat the oven to 350°F (175°C). Toss the diced squash with 1 tablespoon of olive oil and season with salt and pepper. Transfer to a baking sheet, cut sides down, and roast, without turning, for 10 to 15 minutes, until lightly browned. Set aside.

Meanwhile, set a pan over medium-low heat and add the remaining 2 tablespoons olive oil. Add the spinach and sauté until it wilts, 3 to 5 minutes. Season with salt and set aside.

To serve, mix the dressing again if separated and then pour into 4 individual small ramekins or small bowls. To assemble each serving, plate the warm, cooked quinoa in the center of a large, shallow bowl or plate-bowl. Place a portion of the squash, beans, corn, strawberries, onion, spinach, carrots, and chopped nuts around the quinoa, leaving space to place the ramekin of dressing. Garnish with edible flowers, if using.

"VERY SPICY" PAPAYA SALAD

EEM
Portland, Oregon

Portland is spoiled for choice when it comes to excellent Thai food, thanks in no small part to chef Earl Ninsom's work at Langbaan, Paadee, and Hat Yai. At his restaurant Eem, Ninsom joined forces with pitmaster Matt Vicedomini and barman Eric Nelson to serve a menu of Thai barbecue mashups and inventive drinks for an all-day party vibe. The "Very Spicy" Papaya Salad is a fairly straightforward example of som tum, so to do it justice, make sure you're using palm sugar in your dressing, green papaya, and a large mortar and pestle if you've got it. Sweet, sour, and fiery, it pairs perfectly with the smoky meats on the Eem menu—try it at home alongside anything grilled or fried, or even just sticky rice.

Serves **4**

For the dressing:

2 tablespoons palm sugar

¼ cup (60 ml) fish sauce

¼ cup (60 ml) lime juice

For the salad:

4 to 6 cloves garlic, peeled

2 to 3 Thai chiles, less if you don't love spice

2 cups (250 g) sliced long beans, cut into 2-inch (5 cm) pieces

4 cups (500 g) shredded green papaya (see Note)

1 cup (145 g) cherry tomatoes, halved

¼ cup (37 g) roasted peanuts

Lime wedges

→ **NOTE:** You can typically find green, unripened papaya at Asian grocery stores, or you can find a vendor online. To shred a green papaya, peel and seed it. Then shred it using a cleaver, a kiwi peeler, a julienne Y-peeler, or even a box grater.

Use a mortar and pestle (or food processor, or even a mixing bowl) to combine the palm sugar, fish sauce, and lime juice until the sugar is completely dissolved. Set aside.

Using the mortar and pestle, gently smash the garlic, then add the chiles and gently smash until they're broken down but not yet a paste. Add the long beans and continue to gently smash. Add the shredded papaya, cherry tomatoes, and the dressing and gently smash and stir together. If your mortar and pestle is not big enough, you can transfer the garlic-chile-bean mixture to a large bowl and then add the shredded papaya and cherry tomatoes and toss with the prepared dressing.

After the salad is dressed, portion it out or transfer to a large platter. Top with the roasted peanuts and serve with lime wedges.

CARNE ASADA BURRITO

In a Spanish-style building on bustling Mission Street, La Taqueria beckons diners through its front arches with promises of iconic burritos and a taste of San Francisco history. Miguel Jara opened the restaurant in 1973 and can still be seen chatting up guests today—though he leaves more of the operations to his children now. His legacy in the city is undeniable: When it comes to Mission-style burritos, Jara's creation is both the pinnacle and an outlier, since he famously doesn't add rice. What he does include: vibrant housemade salsa; pinto beans that are never, ever smashed; guacamole so simple it's actually just plain avocado; and carne asada that he really wants you not to overcook, ever. As with any good long-standing family restaurant, the Jaras hold the recipe for their "sabor" (signature flavor) a close secret—but what they've shared here will get you close, and do feel free to experiment to create your own family blend. Most guests ask for their burrito dorado, crisped up until golden on the flat top. (You can also toast it with a grill pan, as shown here, depending on what you have on hand.) La Taqueria staff are expected to be able to roll a burrito in no more than seven seconds. It might take you a bit more practice, but that's okay—more practice means more burritos. It's a win win.

For the beans:

3 cups (579 g) dried pinto beans

Salt

¼ cup (57 g) lard

For the carne asada:

2 pounds (910 g) beef sirloin steak

2 tablespoons garlic powder

1 tablespoon salt

2 teaspoons ground black pepper

¼ cup (60 ml) cottonseed or other neutral oil

1 (24-ounce/790 ml) can light beer, for basting

For the pico de gallo:

2 cups (330 g) seeded and finely diced tomatoes

2 cups (250 g) finely diced white onions

1 cup (40 g) fresh cilantro leaves

Salt

To assemble:

4 cups (460 g) shredded Monterey Jack or Mexican blend cheese

6 to 8 (10-inch/25 cm) flour tortillas

3 to 4 avocados, flesh scooped out and smashed

Cottonseed or other neutral oil for griddling

To make the beans, soak the dried beans in water to cover by a few inches overnight. Discard any beans that float to the top. On the day of cooking, drain and rinse the beans and transfer them to a medium pot filled with salted water.

Boil the beans for 1 to 3 hours, tasting every so often for taste and texture. If the water level is running low, add more so the beans don't stick to the bottom of the pot. When the beans are tender, add the lard and gently stir until the fat is absorbed. Taste again and adjust for salt.

To make the carne asada, run the beef through a tenderizer or pound it with the bumpy side of a meat mallet. Season with the garlic powder, salt, and pepper and coat with the oil, then put it in a container and let it marinate in the refrigerator for about 2 hours. Prepare a charcoal grill. When the coals are hot, grill the beef, basting with the beer and flipping once after the first side has some char. Char the other side and then remove to rest. The cooking will be fast, potentially only a minute per side, depending on how thin your pieces are. Transfer to a cutting board and rest for 10 minutes to allow the

meat to come up to temperature, then slice across the grain into bite-size pieces.

To make the pico de gallo, mix the tomatoes, onions, and cilantro in a medium bowl. Season with salt and set aside in an airtight container in the fridge for no more than 2 hours.

To assemble, layer a generous portion of beans (drain with a slotted spoon to get rid of any excess liquid), carne asada, cheese, and pico de gallo on a flour burrito. Add some smashed avocado. Fold the sides in and roll the burrito to seal it. Repeat the process to assemble the rest of the burritos.

In the meantime, get a griddle or large sauté pan hot. Add some oil, then griddle the burrito seam side down to seal. Turn it over to ensure browning on both sides and to make sure that the cheese is melted. Wrap the burritos in foil to preserve the heat and serve warm.

6 Ways to Level Up a Homemade Burrito

1. CHANGE UP THE CHEESE
Pondicheri chef Anita Jaisinghani likes adding Amul, a processed cheddar from India that's creamy, tangy, and, for everyone who grew up eating it, extremely nostalgic.

2. FREEZE GOOD SAUSAGE
Here's Looking at You chef Jonathan Whitener recommends keeping portions of chopped sausage in the freezer in sandwich bags—try longganisa or chorizo, or take home some smoked links from your local barbecue spot.

3. GET THE BEST TORTILLA
Sonoratown co-owner Jennifer Feltham says tortillas are the most important part of any burrito; her favorite store-bought option is flour tortillas from Super A Foods (an LA grocery chain). From there, the key to nailing the rolling is practice, practice, practice.

4. OR TRY A DIFFERENT WRAP
My Abuelas Food chef Luis Martinez promises subbing in phyllo dough for a tortilla will change your life.

5. AIR-FRY IT
Dhamaka chef Chintan Pandya likes air-frying burritos at home and then finishing in a pan; it reliably revives leftover and frozen burritos.

6. SEAR IT
Take a cue from La Taqueria's Miguel Jara and sear both sides on a griddle or cast-iron pan with a little oil for a nicely browned, slightly crisp burrito.

"HALF-AND-HALF" LOBSTER ROLLS

MCLOONS LOBSTER SHACK
South Thomaston, Maine

A quintessential Maine lobster shack, complete with red siding and its own dock on a working lobster wharf, McLoons sits on the coast of Spruce Head Island with picnic tables overlooking Seal Harbor. The setting is postcard-ready Maine, but for diners who can't decide between a Maine-style or a Connecticut-style lobster roll, the Douty family splits the difference and finds perfection with their iconic "half-and-half." Where a typical Maine lobster roll features meat that's been tossed with mayo, McLoons opts for spreading mayo on the roll so that the sweet flavors of freshly steamed lobster meat shine through, which are then enhanced by the drizzle of butter that comes from the Connecticut tradition. It's a lobster roll to convince you that a road trip is in order. At home, it's your ticket to a New England summer escape: You're steaming lobsters, you're toasting split-top buns, you're drizzling melted butter on hand-picked knuckle, tail, and claw pieces. Serve your rolls with a bag of Cape Cod potato chips and eat them outside to really get into the New England spirit.

Serves **4**

4 large lobsters, about 1¼ pounds (570 g) each

½ cup (1 stick/113 g) salted butter, softened

4 New England–style split-top rolls (see Note)

4 teaspoons mayonnaise, or to taste

Chopped fresh herbs, such as chives, tarragon, and/or parsley, for Connecticut style

Fresh lemon juice, for Connecticut style

→ **NOTE:** If your local grocery store doesn't sell split-top buns, you can find them online or use regular hot dog buns.

To get your lobster meat, prepare both an ice bath and your large steaming setup. Quickly plunge a sharp knife into the head of the lobsters and add the lobsters to a large pot of boiling water fitted with a steamer rack. Steam for 10 to 15 minutes, until they're bright red and cooked through. Immediately chill the cooked lobsters in your ice bath. Once cool, pick out the tail, claw, and knuckle meat. Start assembling sandwiches immediately, or store the lobster meat in the refrigerator until you're ready to use.

To prepare the sandwiches, spread softened butter onto both sides of each split-top roll. Toast in a skillet over medium heat until golden. Spread 1 teaspoon mayonnaise on the inside of each roll and fill with ½ cup (about 4 ounces/113 g) lobster meat. Make sure to give each roll an equal share of tail, knuckle, and claw meat. Melt the remaining butter and drizzle it over the top of the rolls. Enjoy immediately.

Alternatively, if you'd rather have a warm, Connecticut-style roll, heat the lobster in a pan over low heat with melted butter until warmed through. Fill the toasted rolls with the warmed meat and sprinkle with fresh herbs and a squeeze of lemon on top.

STEAK JIBARITOS

Chicago is a sandwich town, and it rewards diners who look beyond the Italian beef combo (the Chicago delicacy showcasing thinly sliced roast beef dipped in jus and layered over a link of Italian sausage, topped with giardiniera peppers on a cut French roll). To be more precise, it rewards them with jibaritos, which combine thinly sliced or shredded steak and fixin's between two crunchy fried plantains. Credit for the delicacy goes to Borinquen, a Puerto Rican restaurant that introduced the sandwich to the city in 1996. These days, Chicago food lovers head to Jibaritos y Más, where owners Jesus Arrieta and his wife, Tatianny Urdaneta, serve some of the city's finest at their four locations. They take green (very green) plantains, which they smash and fry. Then they assemble their jibaritos à la minute to keep them crispy—that garlicky sauce and juicy beef could make the sandwich soggy otherwise. And a soggy jibarito just isn't a true Chicago-style jibarito.

Serves **4**

For the garlic mojo:
1 cup (240 ml) olive oil

½ cup (112 g) garlic cloves, peeled

3 tablespoons distilled white vinegar

For the steak jibarito:
1½ pounds (680 g) beef sirloin, thinly sliced

½ cup (120 ml) olive oil

1 tablespoon adobo seasoning

2 quarts (2 L) vegetable or other frying oil

4 large green plantains

1 cup (55 g) sliced white onion

To assemble:
½ cup (114 g) mayonnaise

1 head romaine lettuce, leaves chopped

8 slices tomato

8 slices American cheese or any cheese you prefer

To make the garlic mojo, in a blender, combine the olive oil, garlic, and vinegar and blend until the ingredients are well combined.

To marinate the steak, place the sirloin in a baking dish or a medium bowl, add the olive oil and adobo seasoning, toss to coat, cover, and refrigerate for a minimum of 2 hours or up to overnight.

Meanwhile, start to prepare the plantains: Heat the vegetable oil in a large pot over medium-high heat to 325°F (162°C) according to a deep-frying thermometer. Run the plantains under hot water so it's easier to peel the skins off, which you'll do with a paring knife. Split the plantains in half and fry them in the hot oil for about 10 minutes. Transfer to a paper towel–lined sheet pan to blot out excess oil. Then smash both sides of the plantains using a heavy cutting board or a tortilla press.

Heat a griddle or pan over high heat, and then add the steak and the oil it was marinated in. As soon as the steak starts to brown, add the sliced onions and cook until onions are golden and the sirloin is cooked to your preference. Remove from heat and set aside.

While the steak and onions are cooking, deep-fry the plantains again in the same hot oil for 8 to 10 minutes, until crispy. Use tongs or a slotted spoon to remove them from the oil.

To assemble, spread some mayonnaise on one side of each piece of fried plantain. Layer the lettuce, tomato, steak, and cheese and place the other plantain on top. Drizzle the assembled steak jibarito with garlic mojo and serve immediately.

WITH THE RIGHT GEAR, YOU CAN MAKE GREAT PIZZA AT HOME

Part of the fun of getting extremely into pizza making is the research and shopping. We talked to chefs and pizzaiolos to figure out what tools home cooks really need to achieve pizza worth staying home for.

STAND MIXER
A stand mixer with a hook attachment will simplify making any dough, as the machine will do the kneading for you. Chef Curtis Stone also recommends getting a good food processor; outfitted with the proper blades, that one tool can make the dough, puree the sauce, grate the cheese, and slice toppings! (Or consider getting the food processor attachment for your stand mixer to reap the same benefits.)

PROOFING BOXES
If you get into making pizza dough, you'll want these. Perfectly designed for the job, pizza proofing boxes maintain an airtight seal to prevent the dough from drying out, and they're spacious enough to store multiple portions without letting them touch. Daniele Uditi, the pizzaiolo behind LA's Pizzana, recommends the brand DoughMate.

PIZZA OVENS
Most chefs name-checked Ooni and Gozney—both brands create a range of outdoor pizza ovens designed to burn at more than 900°F (480°C), allowing you to create Neapolitan-style pizzas at home, complete with leopard-spotted crusts. They're an investment, but Ooni does have a few models that clock in under $500.

Pizza Party

- **"Flipside" Pizza with Barbecue Sauce, Beef Bacon, Caramelized Pineapple, and Pickled Jalapeños**
  DOWN NORTH · PHILADELPHIA, PA

- **Cosacca Pizza with San Marzano Tomatoes, Pecorino Romano, and Basil**
  UNA PIZZA NAPOLETANA, NYC

- **Grilled Pizza with Asparagus Pesto, Prosciutto, and Burrata**
  AL FORNO · PROVIDENCE, RI

- **"The Lola" Pizza with Tomato, Crushed Red Chile, Pecorino, and Sicilian Anchovy**
  JON & VINNY'S · LOS ANGELES, CA

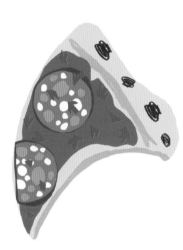

PIZZA STONE

If getting a dedicated pizza oven isn't realistic for your space or budget, consider a pizza stone. These ceramic slabs absorb and retain the heat from your oven, ultimately raising the oven's temperature and acting as a super-hot surface for your pizza to cook on, similar to how it would cook in a pizzeria's brick oven. It quickly cooks your crust without overcooking the toppings. Bonus: A pizza stone is great for crisping up leftover slices.

PEEL

Whether you're using a specialized oven or a pizza stone, you'll want a peel to help you get the pie in and out. These surfaces are hot; the peel means your hands won't be too close.

PIZZA CUTTER

Slicing your pizza in front of your guests with a rolling pizza cutter will add that final pizzeria touch. Chef Ashley Christensen likes the ones that have replaceable blades; so, if a blade is not doing its job properly, swap in a new, sharper blade. Sharp kitchen scissors will do the trick quite nicely, too (opt for gold ones to look more restaurant-y).

Recommendations by: Curtis Stone, Ashley Christensen, David Wilcox, Anthony Mangieri, Jamie Bissonnette, Mike Carter, Daniele Uditi, and Sarah Grueneberg

"Lola" Pizza, Grilled Pizza,
Cosacca Pizza, "Flipside" Pizza

"FLIPSIDE" PIZZA with Barbecue Sauce, Beef Bacon, Caramelized Pineapple, and Pickled Jalapeños

DOWN NORTH
Philadelphia, PA

Origin stories are always murky, but Detroit-style pizza started at the legendary Motor City pizzeria Buddy's. Its crispy edges and "square" shape (geometry buffs would call the pizza a rectangle, with individual slices cut into squares) come from being baked in deep pans, and from baking the cheese directly on top of the dough, not the sauce. Detroit-style pies started trending nationwide in the mid 2010s and can now be found in cities across the country. Down North is slinging this style in North Philly, going brick-and-mortar after a successful pop-up that introduced the city to chef-co-founders Mike Carter and Muhammad Abdul-Hadi, their no-holds-barred pies, and their mission of breaking down barriers to employment for formerly incarcerated people. The pizzeria's popular Flipside pizza is an umami bomb (Worcestershire-laced barbecue sauce and heady beef bacon will do that), but it's balanced with bracing acidity, too, from the pickled jalapeños and caramelized pineapple. To save home cooks a bit of work, we've gone ahead and subbed in bottled sauce here (Carter's favorite is Bull's-Eye), but if you're local, you could buy the Down North sauce right from the shop. Pro tip: Do not gloss over the instructions to keep your hands well-oiled (this is a very hydrated dough, which means it can be sticky), and do your best to press it all the way into the corners to achieve a defined "square" shape.

Makes 1 (9 x 13-inch/22 x 33 cm) pizza

For the dough:

3½ teaspoons (10 g) active dry yeast

2 teaspoons (8 g) sugar

5 cups (600 g) high-gluten flour

2 tablespoons (26 g) vegetable oil, plus more for your hands and the pan

1 tablespoon (18 g) salt

To assemble:

4 ounces (115 g) beef bacon, chopped

1¼ cups (284 g) canned crushed pineapple, drained

2 tablespoons (24 g) sugar

1½ teaspoons lemon juice

1¼ cups (227 g) shredded low-moisture mozzarella cheese

Barbecue sauce

½ cup (120 g) pickled jalapeños

To make the dough, in a stand mixer, whisk 2 cups plus 2 tablespoons (503 ml) water with the yeast and sugar. Combine the flour and salt, then add to the yeast mixture along with the vegetable oil. Using a dough hook, run the mixer on low speed until a dough is formed, about 5 minutes. Scrape down the sides of the bowl, then increase the speed to medium. Knead the dough in the mixer until it is smooth, elastic, and consistently hydrated, about 10 minutes.

Oil your hands before handling the dough to ensure it doesn't stick. Oil a 9 × 13-inch (22 × 33 cm) baking pan and transfer the dough to the pan. Cover the pan with plastic wrap and proof the dough for at least 20 minutes, until it expands to cover most of the pan.

Again, with oiled hands, press the proofed dough into the corners of the pan and proof uncovered for another 20 minutes.

Preheat the oven to 500°F (260°C) or the highest possible setting.

Once the dough is finished proofing, bake it in the oven for 2 to 5 minutes. Pull the pan from the oven and, with a metal spatula, carefully check to see if the bottom is golden brown.

Transfer the partially baked dough onto a cooling rack. If not proceeding to assembly, cool completely and store the parbaked crust in plastic wrap at room temperature for no more than 1 day.

To assemble and cook your pizza, preheat the oven to 400°F (205°C).

Heat a medium saucepan over medium-high and add the bacon. Stir and be careful not to sear. Cook down until a nice amount (1 tablespoon or more) of fat is rendered, about 5 minutes.

Remove the bacon from the pan and leave the rendered fat behind. Reduce the heat to low, add the crushed pineapple and sugar to the bacon fat, and mix thoroughly. Cook until somewhere in between caramelized and candied and the pineapple looks bronze, about 10 minutes. Stir in the lemon juice, remove from the heat, and set aside.

Return the partially baked pizza dough to a 9 × 13-inch (22 × 33 cm) baking pan. Evenly spread the cheese over the par-baked dough. Sprinkle the cooked bacon on top. Spoon the pineapple in the spaces between the bacon pieces.

Bake the pizza for 10 to 15 minutes, until the edges are browned. Remove from the pan with a metal spatula and slice into 8 pieces. Generously drizzle the barbecue sauce in a zigzag pattern across the pizza and finish with a big sprinkle of pickled jalapeños.

COSACCA PIZZA with San Marzano Tomatoes, Pecorino Romano, and Basil

UNA PIZZA NAPOLETANA
New York City

Anthony Mangieri is a pizzaiolo's pizzaiolo: obsessive, tinkering, and unquestionably committed to the craft. He makes Neapolitan-style pizzas with naturally leavened, never refrigerated dough that bakes in a custom-built Stefano Ferrara wood-burning oven. Cooking the pizza takes only one minute (it's about 900°F/480°C in there) but represents a lifetime of planning. He's been making pizza since the mid-90s, and up until only recently made every single pie Una Pizza Napoletana sold as he moved the shop from New Jersey to New York to San Francisco, only sharing the work when he moved the restaurant back to New York City in 2018. Pizza cosacca is a staple in Naples and at Una. Mangieri revels in its simplicity: San Marzano tomatoes, a drizzle of good olive oil, a smattering of basil, freshly grated pecorino Romano, and a sprinkle of salt are all it takes to make a divine pie. The devil is in the details when a dish is so unadorned, which is why Mangieri is always experimenting at the restaurant: with which flours make the best dough (see Notes), which purveyors sell the best cheese, and daily specials that allow him to stretch beyond his traditional Neapolitan offerings.

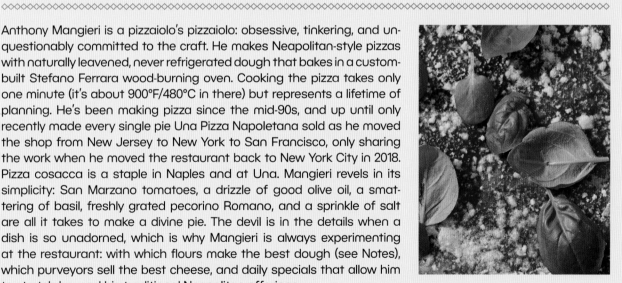

Continued

For the dough:

1½ cups (360 ml) warm water

1½ teaspoons fine sea salt

4 cups (550 g) flour (see Notes)

½ teaspoon dry yeast

2 tablespoons olive oil (optional; see Notes)

To assemble:

1 (28-ounce/794 g) can San Marzano DOP peeled tomatoes, blended

Coarse Sicilian sea salt

2 cups (80 g) fresh Italian basil leaves

Italian extra-virgin olive oil (preferably from Sorrento or Liguria)

Pecorino Romano cheese, for grating

→ NOTES: Mangieri recommends experimenting with your flour to find what you like best. At the pizzeria he uses "oo" King Arthur or Central Milling flour and blends it with Italian flour, like Marino or Caputo. Experiment!

The olive oil facilitates browning and also makes the dough a bit easier to work with. If you are using a pizza oven, you might want to omit the oil; if you are baking in a home oven, you will want to add it.

If you plan on making pizza with some regularity, you can save a golf-ball-size portion from your current batch of dough in a lidded glass jar in the refrigerator and add it into your next batch of dough to add flavor and complexity. Alternatively, you can use sourdough starter, if you have one.

To make the dough, in a small bowl, take 3 tablespoons of the warm water and add the salt. Mix well and set aside. Place the flour in a large bowl and make a well. Put the remaining water in the center of the flour well. Add the yeast to the water and mix. Let the mixed yeast water sit for 5 minutes.

Add the olive oil to the dough, if using, and start mixing the flour into the water-yeast mixture by hand. Once you have about two-thirds of the flour incorporated, stop mixing and cover the bowl. Let the dough rest in a warm place for 20 to 30 minutes, until it starts getting puffy.

Add the salt and water mixture and resume mixing the dough by hand. Continue to incorporate flour into the dough if it is incorporated easily, but don't force it in, if it's not needed. The resulting dough should be soft and smooth.

Place the dough in an oiled bowl, cover with a lid or plastic wrap, and let it rest in a warm place for 1 hour, or until doubled in size, then gently do a four-sided envelope fold: Put the dough back onto your floured surface, pat the dough, and then fold the right side to the middle. Then fold the left side to the middle and over the first fold. Finally, fold the top side over to the middle, then fold the bottom up to cover it all.

Let the dough rise in a warm place for another hour, or until doubled in size. Then do the four-sided envelope fold again and let the dough rest, covered, in a warm place for 30 minutes. The dough will not double in size this time, but it will start to have a lot of elasticity.

Divide the dough into 4 balls and shape into smooth rounds with the seam on the bottom. Place on a floured sheet pan and loosely cover with plastic wrap. Let the dough rest in a warm place for 1 to 3 hours, depending on the temperature of the room, until they've doubled in size. They are ready to bake (and the longer the rise, the more flavorful your dough will be).

To assemble and cook your pizza, preheat your oven with a pizza stone or preheat your pizza oven to the hottest setting (ideally 800°F/425°C or higher). Shape the dough by delicately stretching it out with your fingertips. Press down on the center to stretch into a 10- to 12-inch (25 to 30 cm) pizza, but be careful not to deflate the crust.

Transfer the dough to a floured pizza peel or flat tray top. (If you are par-baking the crust on a sheet tray instead of using a peel or flat tray top, do that before adding the toppings.) Evenly spread the blended tomato sauce over the flattened dough, but leave the crust untouched. Sprinkle the pizza with coarse sea salt and place 6 to 8 leaves of basil on top. Drizzle generously with Italian olive oil.

Slide the pizza into the floor of your pizza oven or onto a pizza stone. Bake for 1 to 2 minutes in a pizza oven (longer if you're using a stone in a standard oven), rotating regularly for an even crust. When done, take the pizza out of the oven using a peel and grate pecorino Romano cheese on top using a Microplane.

Cut the pizza into portions and serve immediately.

What Makes a Pizza Wine?

As told to by **Helen Johannesen**, founder-owner of Helen's Wines, the LA wine shop inside Jon & Vinny's.

A pizza wine is on the juicy side. It can be chilled. It drinks easily on its own. When you taste it with a bite of pizza, there shouldn't be a clash; it should be a harmonious up-splash. You want to be able to drink it before the pizza arrives, while it's there, and after. You don't need to wait for this wine to breathe or open up in the glass. It should be ready to roll. A pizza wine isn't about an extended dining experience. We're in the now: Pizza is a quick food to eat; it's not like a lobster.

There are some classic Italian varietals that are fun and accessible: Sangiovese, Bombino Nero, these have some earthiness but with a lot of fruit notes, and they're not too heavy. Gamay can be delicious with pizza, too, and there are some wines from the Jura that aren't too light-bodied (look for Jura-grown Pinot Noir). For sparkling options, try a pét-nat or piquette.

Skin-contact white wines—orange wines—lend themselves well to the amount of different flavor notes a pizza can deliver. There's the slight char, the dough, the cheese, the sauce, the fresh garlic. A darker-hued rosato or rosé would be great. Skin-macerated wines do well because they're chilled and refreshing and bring a clean feel to what is usually considered an indulgent food.

MORE GREAT PIZZA DRINKS

- **Lambrusco**
- **Rossese di Dolceacqua**
- **Gragnano**
- **Chianti**
- **Barolo**
- **Barbera d'Alba**
- **Tempranillo**
- **Brachetto**
- **Syrah**
- **Beaujolais**
- **Nero d'Avola**
- **Junmai Ginjo**
- **Junmai Kimoto**
- **Pilsner**

Recommended by: Camille Lindsley, Anthony Mangieri, Caroline Styne, Chintan Pandya, Seung Hee Lee, Molly Austad, Liz Martinez, Luis Martinez, Rob Mosher, Sabrina De Sousa, Miguel de Leon, Sarina Garibović, Mike Carter, Natasha Bermudez, Alyssa Mikiko DiPasquale, Michael Roper

GRILLED PIZZA
with Asparagus Pesto, Prosciutto, and Burrata

AL FORNO
Providence, Rhode Island

Grilled pizza is what happens when you take the "cook it hot and cook it fast" ethos of Neapolitan pizza but basically throw all its rules out the window. By making their pizza on a hot grill, chefs Johanne Killeen and her late husband, George Germon, quickly realized they'd get a freeform crust that was crispy on the outside, chewy on the inside, no pizza oven required. And so, for more than thirty years, grilled pizza has been a staple starter at their beloved Providence restaurant Al Forno. Even today, when basically every table orders at least one grilled pizza, the restaurant is not a pizzeria. For home cooks, that means this is a pizza recipe that doesn't require you turn your home into a pizzeria, either. This dough requires some proofing, sure, but not nearly as much as a Neapolitan dough. You shape it using a cookie sheet. And when it comes to toppings, the grill-marked crust is a wonderful base for the classic margherita that's always on the Al Forno menu, as well as grilled corn and tomatoes in the summer, or this one, with verdant asparagus pesto that shouts the arrival of spring. Which is all to say: Consider this combination a starting point on your own grilled pizza journey, not the only destination.

Makes 1 (10- to 12-inch/25 to 30 cm) pizza

For the dough:
¼ cup (60 ml) warm water (105 to 110°F/40 to 43°C)

1½ teaspoons instant dry yeast

3 cups (360 g) all-purpose flour

1¼ teaspoons kosher salt or sea salt

Extra-virgin olive oil

For the roasted asparagus pesto:
1 pound (455 g) fresh asparagus

3 tablespoons plus ⅓ cup (113 g) extra-virgin olive oil

¼ teaspoon salt

To assemble:
Extra-virgin olive oil

½ cup (115 g) shredded fontina cheese

3 tablespoons freshly grated pecorino Romano cheese

½ cup (175 g) asparagus pesto

6 pieces thinly cut prosciutto

1 (4-ounce/115 g) ball burrata cheese

2 tablespoons chopped roasted pistachios

1 tablespoon chopped fresh Italian parsley

To make the dough, pour the warm water into a small bowl, sprinkle the yeast over it, and set aside to dissolve and activate, about 5 minutes.

Combine the flour and salt on a cool work surface and mound it, creating a high-walled well in the center.

Combine the yeast mixture with 1¼ cups (300 ml) cool water and pour into the well. Slowly mix the water and flour, a little at a time, moving your fingers in short, counterclockwise circles around the border of the water.

When the dough is firm enough to hold its shape, scrape the remaining flour over it and knead until the mass is smooth and shiny, about 7 minutes. It may not require all the flour.

Brush a large bowl with olive oil and transfer the dough to the bowl. Brush the top of the dough with oil to prevent a skin from forming, cover the bowl with plastic wrap, and let rise in a warm place away from drafts until doubled in bulk, about 2 hours.

Punch down the dough and knead once more. Let the dough rise again for about 40 minutes. Punch down the dough again and form into two 14-ounce (400 g) dough balls. This recipe is for one pizza, but keep the second dough ball around in case something goes wrong during your stretching or grilling. If nothing goes wrong, wrap the second pizza dough ball in plastic wrap and freeze it for up to 3 months for future pizza making.

To make the roasted asparagus pesto, preheat the oven to 500°F (260°C).

Trim off and discard any tough, woody ends of the asparagus spears. Spread the asparagus out on a baking sheet in a single layer and brush with 3 tablespoons of the olive oil. Sprinkle with salt and roast the asparagus in the upper third of the oven until the spears are tender when pierced with the tip of a knife, 8 to 12 minutes, depending on their thickness. Set aside to cool for 5 minutes.

Transfer the asparagus to a cutting board and coarsely chop it. Put the asparagus and any oil left on the baking sheet in a blender. Add the remaining ⅓ cup (80 ml) olive oil and blend until smooth. Set aside, allowing to cool to room temperature before use, or make ahead and store in an airtight container in the fridge for up to 3 days (use any extra to top more grilled pizzas or toast, or as the starting point for a pasta sauce).

To assemble and cook the pizza, prepare a charcoal fire, setting the grill rack 3 to 4 inches (7 to 10 cm) above the coals.

Oil a large inverted cookie sheet, and on the cookie sheet, spread and flatten the pizza dough with your hands into a 10- to 12-inch (25 to 30 cm) free-form circle, ⅛ inch (3 mm) thick. Do not make a lip for a crust. You could form a rectangle rather than a circle, if preferred; the shape is unimportant, but do take care to maintain even thickness.

When the fire is medium-hot, use your fingertips to gently lift the dough by the two corners closest to you and drape it onto the grill. Catch the loose edge on the grill first and guide the remaining dough into place over the fire. Within a minute the dough will puff slightly, the underside will stiffen, and grill marks will appear.

Using tongs, immediately flip the crust onto the coolest part of the grill. Quickly brush the cooked surface with olive oil. Top with a thin layer of fontina and pecorino Romano cheese. Place a few slices of prosciutto in decorative mounds around the pizza's surface interspersed with chunks of burrata cheese and dollops of asparagus pesto. Scatter the pistachios and parsley on top and drizzle with olive oil.

Slide the pizza back toward the hot coals but not directly over them. Using tongs, rotate the pizza frequently so that different sections receive high heat; check the underside often to see that it is not burning. The pizza is done when the top is bubbly and the cheese is melted, 2 to 4 minutes. Serve at once topped with additional olive oil, if desired.

"THE LOLA" PIZZA with Tomato, Crushed Red Chile, Pecorino, and Sicilian Anchovy

JON & VINNY'S
Los Angeles, California

Chef-restaurateurs Jon Shook and Vinny Dotolo are LA hitmakers: Their restaurant empire extends well beyond the Fairfax neighborhood they began in with perpetually packed spots like Animal and Son of a Gun. Their Italian restaurant Jon & Vinny's is where scenesters go for comforting red sauce classics made with care. The menu delivers hit after hit: shockingly good mozzarella sticks, a plate-size chicken parm, and a whole array of pizzas that run the gamut from classic to over-the-top. The Lola leans classic: It's a spicy, salty, and bright pie that gets its punch from anchovies (Sicilian at the restaurant, but use your favorite) and an impressive nine cloves of garlic. To make things as easy as possible for you at home, Shook and Dotolo's recipe calls for store-bought dough and focusing your energy on your toppings. Pro tip: Before checking the grocery store, ask your local pizzeria if they sell balls of dough, and if so, you're really in for a treat.

Makes 1 (10-inch/25 cm) pizza

All-purpose flour

8 ounces (225 g) store-bought pizza dough

⅓ cup (85 g) canned crushed tomatoes, blended smooth

½ cup (50 g) grated pecorino cheese

9 cloves garlic, sliced

1 teaspoon dried oregano

½ teaspoon crushed red chile

10 fresh basil leaves, torn

Extra-virgin olive oil

6 anchovies

→ NOTE: If you don't have a pizza stone, you can build the pizza on a baking sheet and bake it in a hot oven.

Place a pizza stone in the oven and preheat the oven to 450°F (230°C) or the highest possible setting.

Sprinkle a little flour onto the peel and stretch, toss, or roll out the dough into a circle on the peel. You can use a rolling pin or a wine bottle to work the dough from the center toward the outer edge and maintain a circular shape. The resulting dough should be thin. Shake the pizza on the peel to ensure that it will slide effortlessly onto the pizza stone.

Spread the blended tomatoes evenly across the dough and sprinkle on the cheese. Add the garlic, dried oregano, crushed red chile, and half of the torn basil leaves and drizzle with olive oil.

Slide the pizza onto the stone and bake for 8 to 10 minutes. Remove the pizza from the oven and brush the crust with olive oil. Cut the pizza into 6 slices and garnish each slice with an anchovy, the remaining fresh basil, and a drizzle of olive oil. Serve immediately.

3

SNACK LIKE A PRO

Yes, "small plates made for sharing" is a total cliché, but the reality is, at restaurants and bars, the snacks and starters section of the menu is often the most exciting. Here are the dishes—since they're tasked with priming the palate rather than satiating the belly—that contain the biggest flavors, where chefs can take big swings and experiment with their most creative ideas. They reflect the changing seasons, the day's market haul, or simply a line cook's whims.

The top of the menu boasts funky cured meats, beautifully composed salads, and playful fried surprises. The salty, crunchy signature bites paired perfectly with a cocktail or glass of wine and the jaw-dropping presentations are meant to awe you— they're the restaurant's first impression.

These high-impact, high-flavor recipes and serving ideas are even more impressive at home. Considering drink pairing and presentation will turn your snacks into a *moment*. In fact, we'd suggest a whole dinner built from snacks. That's what happens after the "small plates meant for sharing" spiel anyway.

Fried "Dollar Bills," Gilda Pinxto, Five-Minute Hummus, Crawfish and Jalapeño Hushpuppies

FIVE-MINUTE HUMMUS
with Crispy Cremini Mushrooms

ZAHAV
Philadelphia, Pennsylvania

If Eater had a hall of fame, Zahav would be a shoo-in: It's where our Philly and national staff will send you, if you have only one meal in town *or* if you're a local just looking for a special night out. Where Zahav's hummus recipe relies on soaking dried chickpeas overnight, chef Michael Solomonov and partner Steve Cook have outlined how to achieve a Zahav-worthy rendition in mere minutes using canned chickpeas and a full jar of tahini. Feel free to just make the hummus and use it on sandwiches or in salads, spread it on meats, dip your vegetables in it, and blow the mind of anyone who drops by for a snack. Once you start making the "quick tehina," a combination of tahini, lemon, garlic, and seasonings, you'll find it infinitely useful, too: Add it to salads for a creamy element or drizzle it over grilled kabobs, chops, or fish; toss roasted veggies in it for a side. You'll be happy for the extra shawarma spice mix, too—sprinkle it on veggies or meats before grilling or roasting (or use it to revive leftovers, page 45).

Makes about 4 cups (1,000 g)

To make the shawarma spice, combine the turmeric, cumin, fenugreek, cinnamon, allspice, and black pepper in a small bowl and mix well.

To make the hummus, first make a quick tehina sauce. Slice off a quarter piece of the garlic clove and drop it into the bowl of a food processor. Squeeze the lemon juice into the bowl. Pour the tahini on top, making sure to scrape it all out of the container. Add the cumin and salt. Process until the mixture resembles peanut butter, then stream in the ice water through the hole in the lid a little at a time with the motor running. Run the food processor until the mixture is smooth and creamy and lightens to the color of dry sand.

Remove 2 tablespoons of the tehina sauce from the food processor and set aside to drizzle on top of your final dish. Add the chickpeas to the food processor and run it for about 3 minutes, periodically stopping to scrape down the sides. Keep going until the hummus is smooth and uniform in color.

To make the crispy mushrooms, preheat the oven to 350°F (175°C). Drizzle 1 tablespoon of the canola oil on the pine nuts and toss to coat. Roast for 5 to 10 minutes, until golden brown, then remove from the oven and set aside.

Heat a large skillet over medium-high heat and add the remaining 2 tablespoons canola oil. Add the sliced mushrooms to the hot pan and cook, undisturbed, for about 5 minutes. Add the slivered garlic and season with salt. Cook for another 2 minutes without stirring, then season with 1 tablespoon of the shawarma spice and toss. Remove the pan from the heat, add the vinegar and parsley, swirl it a bit, and return it to the heat. Cook for about 1 more minute, until all the liquid has evaporated. Serve the crispy mushrooms over the hummus and top with the toasted pine nuts and a drizzle of tehina sauce.

For the shawarma spice:
2 tablespoons ground turmeric

2 tablespoons ground cumin

2 tablespoons ground fenugreek

2 tablespoons ground cinnamon

1½ teaspoons ground allspice

1½ teaspoons ground black pepper

For the hummus:
1 clove garlic, peeled

Juice of 1 lemon

1 (16-ounce/454 g) jar tahini

1 teaspoon ground cumin

1 tablespoon salt

½ to 1 cup (120 to 240 ml) ice water

2 (15.5-ounce/440 g) cans chickpeas, drained and rinsed

For the crispy mushrooms:
3 tablespoons canola oil

¼ cup (35 g) pine nuts

1½ pounds (680 g) cremini mushrooms, sliced

4 cloves garlic, slivered

1 teaspoon salt

1 tablespoon shawarma spice (see above)

2 tablespoons sherry vinegar

½ cup (31 g) fresh Italian parsley leaves, chopped

CRAWFISH AND JALAPEÑO HUSHPUPPIES

COMPÈRE LAPIN
New Orleans, Louisiana

Compère Lapin is where chef Nina Compton combines her personal take on Caribbean flavors, channeling her childhood in St. Lucia, with her fine-dining pedigree, making her restaurant a New Orleans essential. When crawfish are in season, Compton makes her own take on a local favorite: crawfish hushpuppies, with sweet crawfish tails folded into a traditional hushpuppy dough that's amped up with jalapeño. She serves them with a remoulade-adjacent cilantro aioli, laced with iconic Louisiana hot sauce Crystal as well as Spanish smoked pimentón from La Dalia. You'll want to use it for everything from dipping chips and crudité to spreading on sandwiches. And don't worry if you don't have access to crawfish—you can still get delicious results by subbing in crabmeat or shrimp.

Makes **28** hushpuppies

To make the aioli, combine the cilantro, jalapeños, pimentón, hot sauce, capers, and one-third of the mayonnaise in a medium bowl. Fold in the rest of the mayonnaise and add the salt.

To make the hushpuppies, in a large bowl, combine the flour, cornmeal, sugar, baking powder, and salt. Add the jalapeños, scallions, paprika, grated garlic, and crawfish tails. In a separate bowl, whisk the eggs, buttermilk, and melted butter. Fold the wet ingredients into the dry ingredients just until combined—don't overwork the batter.

In a heavy-bottomed pot or Dutch oven, heat the frying oil over high heat to 350°F (175°C) according to a deep-frying thermometer. Use one teaspoon to scoop a spoonful of batter and another teaspoon to push it off the first and into the hot oil. Fry until golden brown and use a slotted spoon to remove from the hot oil onto a paper towel–lined plate. Serve with cilantro aioli and lemon wedges.

→ **NOTES:** Depending on where you're located, you can find fresh crawfish meat at some fishmongers and grocery stores. Frozen crawfish will work here, too; availability at stores will vary regionally, but it's easy to find online.

Any smoked paprika will work, but if you find yourself reaching for it often, consider springing for La Dalia or another Spanish brand.

For the cornmeal, Compton uses Anson Mills at the restaurant, but you can use any fine cornmeal you prefer.

For the cilantro aioli:

¾ cup (30 g) chopped fresh cilantro

2 tablespoons seeded and finely chopped jalapeño chiles

1 teaspoon smoked pimentón, preferably La Dalia (see Notes)

1 tablespoon Crystal hot sauce

2 tablespoons capers, chopped

2 cups (448 g) mayonnaise

1 teaspoon salt

For the hushpuppies:

1¼ cups (144 g) all-purpose flour

¾ cup plus 3 tablespoons (144 g) fine cornmeal (see Notes)

1 tablespoon sugar

2¾ teaspoons baking powder

2¼ teaspoons salt

3 tablespoons minced jalapeño chiles

1 cup (50 g) minced scallions, green and white parts

2 teaspoons paprika

1 clove garlic, grated

½ cup (72 g) cooked crawfish tails (thawed if frozen; see Notes)

2 large eggs, beaten

1 cup (240 ml) buttermilk

3 tablespoons butter, melted

Neutral oil such as vegetable or canola, for frying

Lemon wedges, for serving

GILDA PINTXO
with Olive, Pepper, and Anchovy

CÚRATE
Asheville, North Carolina

Three shoppable ingredients—okay, a bit more if you count the skewers and olive oil—are all you need to create an elegant drinking snack: This tidy stack of olive, pickled piparra pepper, and a fancy anchovy is called the Gilda. (Legend has it that Rita Hayworth's star turn in the movie *Gilda* inspired the name.) At Cúrate, Asheville's acclaimed Spanish tapas restaurant, chef-owner Katie Button serves her Gildas on colorful East Fork ceramic plates—try using your nicest serving plates to bring some pro style. With so few ingredients, it's worth it to splurge where you can: Look for salt-cured oil-packed, Spanish or Basque anchovies, nice olives, and exceptional extra-virgin olive oil like O-Med Picual or Finca la Torre. There's no cooking involved, but Button's recipe below is chock-full of tips for nailing this iconic Basque pintxo; she especially loves pairing these with negronis, spritzes, and gin and tonics. They also make for an impressive martini garnish. See page 206 for more martini ideas and page 113 for more on anchovies.

Makes 16 skewers

1 (3.3-ounce/95 g) jar anchovies

1 (6.4-ounce/180 g) jar pickled piparra peppers

1 (12-ounce/340 g) jar pitted manzanilla or Castelvetrano olives

1½ cups (360 ml) extra-virgin olive oil

16 cocktail skewers (wood or metal)

Soak the anchovies in a bowl of warm water for 5 minutes after they come out of the jar or can. Remove them from the water, pat dry, and then put them in a medium bowl with the peppers and olives and pour over the olive oil. Let sit for at least 30 minutes or up to 2 hours at room temperature.

Drain the olives, anchovies, and piparra peppers from the olive oil. Reserve the oil and use it to dress up a salad, pasta, or vegetables. Thread one end of an anchovy onto one skewer, followed by an olive and pepper, and then weave the anchovy back onto the skewer followed by another olive and pepper, and finally thread back the other end of the anchovy, creating an S shape.

Each skewer should have a total of 2 olives, 2 peppers, and 1 nice long anchovy, or 2 if they are smaller. Repeat the steps for the rest of the skewers and serve at room temperature.

How to Make a Great Aperitivo

A pre-dinner drink should be relatively low proof, with some bubbles to prime your palate, and a touch of bitterness. Consider the spritz your starting point and play with the components: 2 ounces (60 ml) aperitif, 2 ounces (60ml) sparkling wine, and 1½ ounces (44 ml) soda water. "That ratio has worked throughout time," says Sam Miller, the bar manager of Salt Lake City's Water Witch and one-half of the hit tiki pop-up Island Time. "It's printed right on the Aperol bottle." Aperol, Amaro, Campari, and other liqueurs can all work in the spritz format.

Here are more aperitivo ideas from the pros.

VERMOUTH AND GRAPEFRUIT SODA
Recommended by: Llama Inn bar director Natasha Bermudez

Start by sipping sweet vermouth with a bit of soda and see how you like it. To build a more composed aperitivo, try 2 ounces (60 ml) sweet vermouth with 4 ounces (120 ml) grapefruit soda. The grapefruit soda will add some necessary bitterness and keep things lower proof. Add a twist if you're feeling fancy.

SAKE SPRITZ
Recommended by: Koji Club owner Alyssa Mikiko DiPasquale

Genshu (undiluted) and Namazake (unpasteurized) both have big, robust flavor profiles. They are great to spritz out by adding club soda or tonic water.

GIN AND TONIC
Recommended by: Cocktail expert John deBary

A gin and tonic is a perfect pre-dinner drink. It's bubbly and there's some bitterness, but it won't blow your palate.

NEGRONI
Recommended by: Marrow wine director Liz Martinez

A negroni has nice bitterness as well as juiciness to get the taste buds going. Go for one part gin, one part red vermouth, and one part Campari, and serve with an orange twist.

LILLET BLANC AND SODA WITH GRAPEFRUIT
Recommended by: Bludorn wine director Molly Austad

Lillet Blanc with soda water and a grapefruit slice is delicious. You can adjust the ratio to suit your taste, but 50-50 is a great place to start.

MIMOSA
Recommended by: Pinch Chinese wine director Miguel de Leon

For a low lift option, pour some of your favorite bubbly (Champagne, pét-nat, prosecco) and add in some fruit juice. Who doesn't love a mimosa?

FRENCH 75
Recommended by: Takibi bartender Alex Anderson

Try the original recipe, which uses cognac. The chocolate notes of the cognac pair beautifully with the lemon and Champagne, but if you prefer the more herbal flavor of gin, go for it. Pro tip: Pour your sparkling wine into the serving glass (ideally a coup) first, about 3 ounces (88 ml). Then in a cocktail shaker, combine 1 ounce (30 ml) cognac or gin, ½ ounce (15 ml) fresh lemon juice and ½ ounce (15 ml) simple syrup. Add ice, shake, add the strainer, and then pour through a fine-mesh strainer directly into the coup.

FRIED "DOLLAR BILLS"
(Collard Greens)

CHEF & THE FARMER
Kinston, North Carolina

You might know Vivian Howard from her beloved TV show, *A Chef's Life*. You might know her from her popular cookbooks, *Deep Run Roots* and *This Will Make It Taste Good*. But the luckiest diners know her from her work at her restaurants throughout the Carolinas, including her longtime flagship, Chef & the Farmer, in Kinston, North Carolina. These crispy fried collards, which Howard calls "dollar bills," are a staple. The recipe below is the simplest version of her signature collards: just the greens, the frying, and as much salt as you like. Since these stay crisp for a long time, they can be made ahead and set out in a bowl for snacking or even used as a topping for a grain bowl. (See page 44 for more grain bowl ideas.) A word of advice from Howard: "Although the process is simple, the collards pop and act the fool when they fry, so if you have too much oil, it can bubble over the rim, and that's a bad situation. If you don't have your wits about you, this can be dangerous. By which I mean: Don't drink and fry Dollar Bills!"

Serves **4**

2 bunches collard greens

2 quarts (2 L) peanut or vegetable oil, for deep-frying

Salt

Take the stems off the collard greens and cut the leaves into 1-inch (2.5 cm) strips.

In a Dutch oven or a large heavy-bottomed pot, heat the peanut oil over medium heat to 350°F (175°C) according to a deep-fry thermometer. While waiting for the oil to come to temperature, line a baking sheet with paper towels.

Using tongs to handle the collards, do a test fry by adding one or two leaves into the oil and immediately cover with a lid. When the oil stops crackling, the collards are cooked. The leaves should be crisp, dark green, and a little translucent. Keep an eye on the temperature of the oil, so as not to allow it to drop.

Repeat the process for the rest of the collard greens, working in small batches (the more you add, the more violently the collards will crackle and pop). Transfer the fried collards to the prepared baking sheet and season with salt. If fried correctly, the fried dollar bills will remain crisp at room temperature for hours.

CAULIFLOWER TOTS
with Beet Ketchup

BETTER HALF COFFEE & COCKTAILS
Austin, Texas

◇◇◇

Better Half is a coffee shop, a restaurant, and a bar—it's a place where you can bring a laptop and get some work done and stay for happy hour, or have a date night, or close out an evening downtown with a nightcap. And at nearly every one of the Better Half's many outdoor picnic tables, you'll spot friends digging into a plate of these cauliflower tots. With this dish, chef Rich Reimbolt has hit all the must-haves for a drinking snack: The tots are a salty, shareable finger food with a decidedly grownup twist thanks to the vegetal cauliflower and the earthy beet ketchup he serves. While these tots are definitely more effort than opening up a bag of frozen Ore-Ida (no shade intended; Ore-Ida tater tots are a great drinking snack, too), the beet ketchup is a lower lift and a fun way to make the most of a fall CSA haul. It will be your new favorite condiment; try it as a dip with chicken nuggets and fries and as a spread on burgers or egg sandwiches. You'll want to fry the tots right before serving, so if you'd like to serve them together, make and chill the beet ketchup first.

Makes about 100 tots

◇◇◇◇◇◇◇◇◇◇◇◇◇◇◇◇◇◇◇◇◇◇◇◇◇◇◇ ◇◇◇◇◇◇◇◇◇◇◇◇◇◇◇◇◇◇◇◇◇◇◇◇◇◇◇◇◇◇◇◇◇◇◇◇◇

3 large heads cauliflower

8 egg whites (250 g), beaten

1 cup plus 2 tablespoons (150 g) cornstarch

1½ teaspoons salt

Cooking spray

2 quarts (2 L) vegetable oil, for frying

Beet Ketchup (recipe follows)

Preheat the oven to 325°F (165°C).

Chop the cauliflower, discarding the stems. Working in batches, pulse the chopped cauliflower in a food processor until it is the texture of rice, then wrap it in cheesecloth to wring out as much water as possible. After the water is wrung out, measure 10 cups (1 kg) cauliflower rice. (If you have extra, freeze it for another use.) Place the cauliflower rice in a large bowl, add the egg whites, cornstarch, and salt, and mix until thoroughly combined.

Line a baking sheet with a silicone mat and liberally spray with cooking spray. Alternatively, line a 9 × 13-inch (22 × 33 cm) baking dish with foil and liberally spray with cooking spray. Use a spatula to pack the rice mixture into a layer that's ¾ inch to 1 inch (2 to 2.5 cm) in height and bake for 30 minutes until golden brown. Allow to cool completely, then unmold and cut into bite-size pieces.

You'll have about 100 cauliflower tots, so if you're not throwing a party, this is the point at which you want to freeze whatever you're not using for another day. (The tots can be fried or air-fried from frozen.)

In a heavy-bottomed pot or a Dutch oven, heat the frying oil to 350°F (175°C) according to a deep-frying thermometer. Working in batches, fry the cauliflower tots for 5 minutes, or until golden. Remove and transfer the fried tots to a paper towel–lined tray to blot the oil. Serve with beet ketchup.

Beet Ketchup

Makes 2 cups (480 ml)

1 pound (455 g) beets
1 tablespoon canola oil
½ medium yellow onion, diced
1 cup (240 ml) apple cider vinegar
½ cup (110 g) packed brown sugar
¼ teaspoon ground cloves
¼ teaspoon ground coriander
Salt and freshly ground black pepper

Preheat the oven to 400°F (205°C).

Put the beets on a baking sheet and roast until tender when pierced with a fork, about 45 minutes. Allow to cool, then peel and cut into medium dice.

In a large saucepan, heat the canola oil over medium heat. Add the onion and cook until translucent, 7 to 9 minutes, then add the cooked beets, vinegar, brown sugar, cloves, and coriander and season with salt and pepper. Cook the beet mixture until the beets are soft.

Allow the mixture to cool a bit, so it will be easier to handle. Transfer to a blender and blend until smooth, then strain through a fine-mesh strainer. Chill the beet ketchup before serving. It will keep in an airtight container in the refrigerator for up to 1 week.

Shopping List: Bar Snacks

Here's what chefs and bartenders like to set out when they're serving drinks:

- **Wasabi peas**
- **Trader Joe's Giant Peruvian Inca Corn**
- **Chicharrones**
- **Potato chips**
- **Tater tots**

"Tater tots and caviar is super easy and fun but feels a little fancy. We serve with chives, crème fraîche, and brunoise (finely diced) red onion"
—KINDRED CHEF-OWNER JOE KINDRED AND KINDRED AND SOMMELIER-OWNER KATY KINDRED

- **Caviar**
- **Flamin' Hot Cheetos**
- **Sabritas Adobada Chips**
- **Nacho Cheese Doritos**
- **Salted shelled pistachios**

"Pistachios are classy, and getting them shelled means easier cleanup and it's more considerate for your guests, too."
—COCKTAIL EXPERT JOHN DEBARY

- **Marcona almonds**
- **Castelvetrano olives**
- **Chakli (Indian fried rice- and wheat-flour snacks)**

Recommended by: Mike Carter, Sam Yoo, Charly Pierre, Joe and Katy Kindred, Jennifer Feltham, Sarina Garibović, John deBary, Caroline Styne, Chintan Pandya

EGG TOAST
with Caviar and Dill

In a serene dining room on Columbus Avenue, well-heeled diners look out through floor-to-ceiling windows and marvel at their comfortable distance from the bustle of Columbus Circle. This is Jean-Georges, the most famous restaurant of chef Jean-Georges Vongerichten's empire, and it's known for an exacting yet playful menu that's a bit French, a bit Japanese, and all the way luxurious. The egg toast with caviar is one of the most high-end expressions of comfort food in the business, sending typically humble eggs and toast through the fine-dining looking glass. The grilled-cheese-like bite typically appears within the first four courses in a tasting menu of ten dishes; it's a bit more filling than a typical amuse bouche, thanks to the rich egg yolk and the salty punch of a caviar quenelle. A gorgeous dinner starter, it would also fit right in at a celebratory daytime brunch or a New Year's Eve party.

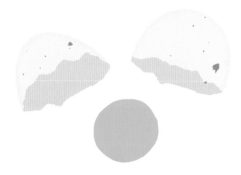

Serves **4**

4 eggs, at room temperature

½ loaf brioche, ideally dried out, uncovered, in the refrigerator overnight

¼ cup (½ stick/57 g) butter, at room temperature

Kosher salt and freshly ground black pepper

Flaky sea salt

1 tablespoon minced fresh chives

1 tablespoon chopped fresh dill

3 tablespoons (40 g) Ossetra caviar (for less of a splurge, try trout or salmon roe)

Sous-vide the eggs in a 149°F (65°C) water bath for 1 hour (alternatively, boil for about 6 minutes). When done, cool them down in an ice bath. Peel and separate the yolk from the white. Be sure to clean all the white off the egg yolk. You can discard the whites or use them for another dish.

Cut the dried brioche into ⅛-inch (3 mm) thick slices, then into 2½-inch (6 cm) long and 1½-inch (3.5 cm) wide pieces.

Spread a thin layer of butter on each piece of bread. Heat the remaining butter in a large skillet over medium heat and toast each strip for about 1 minute on each side, until golden brown. Remove the toasts from the pan onto a tray lined with paper towels.

Cut each yolk in half and set 2 halves on each piece of bread, cut side up. Season well with salt and pepper, then top with another piece of bread. Sprinkle the top of each sandwich with flaky sea salt, the chives, and dill, then top each with a small scoop of caviar. Eat immediately.

How to Build a Seafood Tower

A tower of chilled shellfish and some bubbles make any night out feel like a celebration. To go all out at home, prioritize—maybe you want to shuck your own oysters or poach your own shrimp—and then fill out the rest of your platter with smartly shopped items and condiments.

OYSTERS

The most iconic part of a chilled seafood tower, oysters should be fresh and alive when you purchase them. Plenty of farms ship directly to customers—Island Creek in Massachusetts, Taylor Shellfish in Washington, Murder Point in Alabama—or you can talk to your local fishmonger about what's local and delicious. "Oysters direct from a farm will typically come in bags of one hundred," says chef James McNeal, who charms Miami diners with his "not too fancy" seafood towers at hotspot Over Under. "So if you don't quite get it at first, by the time you shuck a hundred you'll be a pro." Alternatively, make it a group activity at your cocktail party!

Plan for a mess. Chef Chris Pandel sends out plenty of seafood towers to diners at Chicago steak house Swift & Sons. His biggest tip for keeping your kitchen clean is to do your shucking over a sheet pan on a paper towel–lined countertop. There will still be cleanup, but the pan should collect a lot of the liquid and any shell scraps. And be safe. If you're anything but confident, use a cut glove, along with a dry towel to hold the oyster

and a proper oyster knife. "If you miss and hit your hand with the brute force and leverage needed to open an oyster, it's not fun," says Pandel. Wear the glove.

SHRIMP

Chilled shrimp are always welcome on a seafood tower. For basic cocktail shrimp, gently poach them in water with aromatics (like some chopped carrots, celery, onion, herbs, and a bay leaf) and chill before serving. For a casual, fun touch, set out bowls and let your guests peel their own. (Prepared cocktail shrimp are also widely available at grocery stores; just make sure you're getting a fresh batch.) For a more inventive twist, Pandel suggests doing a Southern-style pickled shrimp or baby shrimp salad tossed with mayonnaise and celery.

OTHER FISH

McNeal likes highlighting "the cleanest, freshest seafood we can get our hands on without manipulating it too much." At home, that might mean talking to your fishmonger and then

going with "thinly sliced tuna, salmon, or scallops with some nice olive oil, capers, and flaky sea salt." Thin slices of good smoked salmon garnished with herbs can fill space to make your platter feel more bountiful, and a smoked fish dip is also a welcome addition. Escabeche or ceviche would also work well.

Pandel suggests making crab salad: Get some nice lump crabmeat (like peekytoe) and dress simply with lemon, olive oil, and fresh tarragon. You can also steam littleneck clams and make a clam salad, using the shells as a serving vessel. If you want lobster or crab claws, consider ordering online from a purveyor that will send them cooked.

And if you're spending big, go for caviar. "High impact, zero work," says Pandel.

ACCOUTREMENTS

"The key is to have each item served with some kind of sauce or something to go with it," says Cameron Rolka, the executive chef of Detroit's fish-focused restaurant Mink. "You can always

bulk up a seafood tower with ramekins of sauces and pickles." Lemon wedges and cocktail sauce are traditional, but Rolka recommends chimichurri and chili crisp. Pandel's favorite is vadouvan Dijonnaise: Combine equal parts mayonnaise and Dijon mustard and season with curry powder or a vadouvan spice mix. McNeal likes lemony aioli, and Over Under serves seafood towers with fried saltines, spicy pickled peppers, and hot sauce.

ICE

Skip cubed ice—"it melts quickly and doesn't keep the food sitting on top of it cold," says Rolka—and go for crushed. Rolka recommends asking your fishmonger for an extra bag or two, but if you've got a sturdy blender, you can make your own. To give it a real restaurant look, see if they will also sell you some seaweed. Blanch it and use it to decorate your platter. Store in your freezer until you're ready to set up. Then, Pandel recommends wetting a linen napkin and using that as a buffer between the ice and the fish so that the ice won't end up sloshing over your table as it melts.

PLATTERS

Tiered seafood trays are available at restaurant supply stores. If you entertain regularly, you'll find other uses for them—setting out desserts, pastries, fruit, or anything else you want to serve

cornucopia-style. But you don't need them. Any deep serving platter will do, especially if it's a long one. Even a large salad bowl could work. Pandel recommends filling the bowl three-quarters full of ice and then plating in circles toward the center. Or serve things separately. "Serve shrimp cocktail next to shucked oysters next to clams on the half shell," says Pandel. "Nobody's going to complain if it's not in a tower."

FINES LAMELLES D'AVOCAT ET TOURTEAU
with Avocado and Crab

Bar Crenn
San Francisco, California

◇◇

After wowing critics and diners alike with her tasting menu at Atelier Crenn, chef Dominique Crenn wanted to offer up something a bit more like a salon. At Bar Crenn, she welcomes guests into a romantic den of plush velvet couches where they sip wine paired with "small bites" like a bone marrow–filled eggshell topped with caviar and fines lamelles d'avocat et tourteau, literally thinly sliced avocado and crab. The stack is made from layers of creamy avocado sandwiching delicate Dungeness crab, finished with a drizzle of sweet almond oil and studded with Marcona almonds and edible flowers like nasturtium. Delicate and impossibly elegant, it's like a dolled-up Crab Louie, the crab-and-avocado salad that originated on the West Coast. This being a Crenn spot, the cooking is as technical as the end product is beautiful. For your effort, you'll be rewarded with a heck of a gorgeous way to kick off dinner.

Serves **4**

For the court bouillon (to cook the whole crab):

1 bouquet garni (use premade, or assemble your own by combining fresh parsley, thyme, and bay leaf in a sachet)

2 cups (256 g) cubed carrots

2 cups (200 g) cubed celery

1 tablespoon kosher salt

10 black peppercorns

1 Dungeness crab (about 1¾ pounds/ 800 g)

To serve:
Flaky sea salt

Zest of 1 lime, plus 2 tablespoons fresh lime juice

Zest of ½ orange

2 teaspoons finely chopped fresh chives, plus more for garnish

6 tablespoons (90 ml) sweet almond oil

Freshly ground black pepper

4 ripe avocados

Lime wedges, Marcona almond halves, and edible flowers (optional), for serving

To make the court bouillon, in which you will cook the whole crab, in a stockpot, combine 4 quarts (4 L) water with the bouquet garni, carrots, celery, salt, and peppercorns. Bring to a boil, then reduce the heat and simmer for about 30 minutes. Let stand for 10 minutes, then strain.

While the court bouillon is simmering, clean the crab by rinsing and brushing it well under cold water, then place it in a large pot. Bring the court bouillon back to a boil and pour it over the crab. Let the crab sit for 6 minutes in the broth and prepare an ice bath while you wait. Remove the crab from the liquid, remove the legs, and place them directly into the ice bath. Return the body of the crab to the hot liquid and cook for an additional 5 minutes, then transfer it to the ice bath. Once everything's cooled, remove the crab meat.

To serve, in a small bowl, season the crab with the flaky salt, add the lime and orange zest, lime juice, chives, 3 tablespoons of the sweet almond oil, and pepper to taste. Mix gently with a fork and set aside.

Using a mandoline, cut the unpeeled avocados (including the pit) lengthwise into thin slices. Remove the skin and any pit from each slice, which will leave some slices with holes in the center.

To serve, set aside the smaller slices of avocado (preferably these do not have holes); these will be used to top each portion. On each of the 4 plates, lay down 2 slices of avocado, side by side, creating a long strip of avocado to serve as the base. Then divide the seasoned crabmeat into 4 portions and gently place them on top of the plated avocados. Top each portion with a small slice of avocado. Sprinkle with flaky sea salt and pepper, followed by a gentle squeeze of lime juice and a drizzle of the remaining sweet almond oil. Garnish with Marcona almonds, chives, and, if you have them, edible flowers.

SAFFRON TOMATO DIP
with Goat Cheese and Spiced Pita Chips

SAFFRON DE TWAH
Detroit, Michigan

After getting his start as a restaurateur in Detroit with his two food trucks, chef Omar Anani went brick-and-mortar with Saffron De Twah back in 2019. On his Moroccan menu you'll also see nods to his family's Egyptian and Palestinian heritage. The casual bistro has quickly become one of Detroit's essential spots, in no small part because dishes like this saffron tomato dip and the perfectly seasoned pita chips alongside it are just so darn craveable. With jalapeños and plenty of saffron, garlic, and preserved lemon, this tomato dip packs a savory punch; the whipped goat cheese underneath cools things down and brings some tang. Keep the recipe for these spiced pita chips on file anytime you're looking to elevate a simple dip or wanting to add crunch to a salad.

Serves **4**

To make the pita chip seasoning, in a small bowl, combine the thyme, oregano, cumin, coriander, sesame seeds, sumac, salt, and Aleppo pepper.

Preheat the oven to 375°F (190°C).

Cut the pita into triangles and toss the pieces in the olive oil and pita chip seasoning mix. Place on a single layer on a baking sheet. Bake for 4 minutes, then turn the sheet and bake for another 3 minutes, or until the edges are golden brown. Do not cook the pita to your desired color, as they will continue to darken at least two shades once removed from the oven.

In a stand mixer with a whisk attachment, whip the goat cheese on medium speed to incorporate air until fluffy. Add the cream to thin it out and whip for another minute.

To make the sauce, in a medium sauté pan, heat the olive oil over medium heat. Add the garlic, onions, and chile and cook until fragrant, 5 to 7 minutes. Add the tomato puree, cumin, coriander, cinnamon, saffron, cayenne, and vegetable stock. Bring to a simmer and simmer for 20 minutes. Add the preserved lemon and simmer for an additional 10 minutes. Taste to see if the tomato sauce needs more salt. Preserved lemons are usually salty enough, so it's best to taste first. Remove the cinnamon stick.

To serve, put your desired amount of goat cheese onto a plate and ladle tomato sauce over it. Enjoy with toasted pita chips.

→ **NOTE:** Saffron De Twah sells bottles of its pita chip seasoning online for locals (and, hopefully soon, nationwide). If that's not an option and you want to go for a jarred spice mix, look for a high-quality za'atar.

4 pita breads

½ cup (120 ml) olive oil

For the pita chip seasoning:

1½ teaspoons dried thyme, crushed

1½ teaspoons dried oregano, crushed

1 tablespoon cumin seeds, toasted and ground

1 tablespoon coriander seeds, toasted and ground

2 tablespoons toasted sesame seeds

3 tablespoons sumac

1½ teaspoons salt

1½ teaspoons Aleppo pepper

For the goat cheese:

1 (8-ounce/227 g) log goat cheese, at room temperature

1 tablespoon heavy cream

For the saffron tomato sauce:

1 tablespoon olive oil

2 cloves garlic, minced

1½ medium yellow onions, cut into small dice

1 jalapeño chile, seeded and small diced

3 cups (495 g) chopped fresh tomatoes, pureed

½ teaspoon cumin seeds, toasted and ground

½ teaspoon coriander seeds, toasted and ground

1 cinnamon stick

7 threads saffron, ground either by hand or gently with a mortar and pestle

Pinch of cayenne pepper

1 cup (240 ml) vegetable stock

1½ teaspoons minced preserved lemon peel

Salt

KHACHAPURI

Restaurateur Rose Previte had a hunch her D.C. neighbors would love khachapuri just as much as she did when she lived in Russia with her husband and fell for the Georgian street food. When it was hard to find the typical Sulguni cheese, Compass Rose's first executive chef, John Paul Damato, devised a blend of mozzarella, ricotta, and feta that mimicked its creamy, slightly briny flavor—which (bonus!) is also easier for you at home. A sprinkling of za'atar balances the rich filling and nods to Previte's Lebanese heritage, and the silky, runny egg yolk takes it over the top. This reliable, impactful recipe is why after kicking off a khachapuri boom in D.C., Compass Rose's has been a must-order (and must-Instagram) for nearly a decade. Home bakers will rejoice that this cheesy bread boat is absolutely achievable, even for beginner bread bakers.

Serves 4 as a starter or snack

1¼ cups (155 g) all-purpose flour

1½ teaspoons salt

½ cup (120 ml) lukewarm water

1½ teaspoons active dry yeast

½ teaspoon honey

1 tablespoon olive oil

½ cup (30 g) sliced mozzarella cheese

¼ cup (40 g) crumbled feta cheese

¼ cup (60 g) ricotta cheese

2 large eggs

1 large egg yolk

1 tablespoon za'atar

1½ teaspoons butter

Place the flour and salt in the bowl of a stand mixer fitted with the dough hook. In a separate bowl, combine the lukewarm water, yeast, and honey and let proof for 3 minutes, or until the yeast mixture is frothy. Add it to the bowl of the stand mixer, then add the olive oil. Mix on low speed until all the flour is combined, then increase the speed to medium and mix until the dough forms an even ball that peels away from the bottom of the bowl. Transfer the dough to an oiled bowl, cover, and allow to proof at room temperature for about 90 minutes, until the dough has doubled in size.

When the dough is almost done proofing, combine the mozzarella, feta, and ricotta cheeses in the mixer bowl with the paddle attachment. Mix on medium speed until a spreadable consistency is achieved.

In a small bowl, whisk together the whole eggs and 1 tablespoon water to make an egg wash.

Preheat the oven to 425°F (220°C), line a baking sheet with parchment paper, and add a light layer of flour.

When the dough has doubled in size, roll it out on the parchment paper to create an oval shape. Fold over the edges of the oval to create a crust and brush the entire thing with egg wash. Add the cheese mixture to the middle and spread evenly to the crust of the dough.

Bake for about 15 minutes, until the edges are golden brown; the cheese should not be crispy. Take the khachapuri out of the oven and immediately add the egg yolk, za'atar, and butter. Break the yolk with a fork, spreading it around the hot cheese and gently mixing everything together. Let the khachapuri sit for 2 to 3 minutes while the egg yolk sets, then serve.

SHE-CRAB SOUP

From 1879 to 2004 Gage & Tollner was arguably Brooklyn's most famous restaurant. Then, despite its landmark status, it was a TGI Fridays. Luckily, the chain did not enjoy an equally long run—partners St. John Frizell, Ben Schneider, and Sohui Kim took over the space and shined it back to its original polish, reopening Gage & Tollner in 2021. The lively bar is always crowded and the dining room is always full, thanks to original dishes from Kim and executive chef Adam Shepard as well as recipes from the 1980s and '90s, when legendary chef Edna Lewis ran the kitchen; she brought her signature Southern cooking to Brooklyn with dishes like her famous she-crab soup, offering a taste of South Carolina. When you make this at home, ask your fishmonger for female crabs; their roe is an important part of what makes this creamy soup so flavorful. To make things easier at home, grab a package of good jumbo or lump crab meat, which you can pour the soup over to serve.

Serves **4 to 6**

To make the crab stock, wash the blue crabs under cold running water. Harvest all the roe and set aside in the refrigerator for later. Ideally you will have about 2 tablespoons (15 g) roe. Chop the crabs into pieces and place them in a stockpot along with the onion, carrot, celery, fennel trim, black peppercorns, bay leaf, and herb stems. Cover with water, about 4½ cups (1 L), bring to a simmer over medium heat, and simmer for 90 minutes, uncovered, skimming foam that floats to the surface. When done, if you want more flavor, process the shells through a food mill and add them back to the stock. Pass the stock through a fine-mesh strainer, pressing hard into the shells to extract the liquid. Set aside.

To make the soup, put two saucepans on the stovetop. Put the cream in one and the milk in the other. Reduce the cream by a quarter over low to medium heat—do not let it boil. Heat the milk until scalded, or until it almost boils; 180 to 185°F (82 to 85°C) is the sweet spot. Turn the heat off and put the lids on to keep them warm.

In a clean large pot, melt the butter over low heat. Add the onion, carrot, and celery and cook until tender and translucent, about 13 minutes. Stir in the crab roe and cook for another 2 to 3 minutes, giving it a chance to take on flavor. Add the wine and reduce by half. Stir in the rice flour and cook for an additional minute. Add the sherry and whisk the scalded milk into the rice flour roux until it's well incorporated. Add the reduced cream and 3½ cups (840 ml) crab stock and season with sugar, cayenne, and lemon. Bring to a simmer and simmer for 15 minutes.

Working in batches, puree the soup with a high-speed blender. Pass through a fine-mesh strainer and season with salt and pepper. Add 1 to 2 ounces (28 to 56 g) crab meat to the bottom of each bowl, then pour soup over. Garnish with chives and drizzle with sherry.

For the crab stock:

2 to 4 (9 ounces/250 g total) fresh female blue crabs

¾ cup (88 g) chopped white onion

¼ cup (38 g) chopped carrot

⅓ cup (38 g) chopped celery

¼ cup (25 g) chopped trimmed fennel bulb

½ teaspoon black peppercorns

1 dried bay leaf

1 bunch herb stems (aromatics, such as parsley, tarragon, and thyme)

For the soup:

1 cup (240 ml) heavy cream

4 cups (960 ml) milk

⅓ cup (68 g) butter

1 cup (125 g) minced white onion

½ cup (75 g) chopped carrot

¾ cup (75 g) chopped celery

½ cup (120 ml) white wine

½ cup (60 g) rice flour

1 dried bay leaf

3 tablespoons sherry, fino, or Manzanilla, plus more for garnish

1 teaspoon sugar

Cayenne pepper

Fresh lemon juice

Salt and freshly ground black pepper

1 8-ounce (227 g) container of jumbo or lump crab meat

Chopped fresh chives, for garnish

→ **NOTE:** If your fishmonger can't sell you she-crabs specifically, ask if you can purchase some supplemental roe, about 2 tablespoons (15 g).

"PEANUT BUTTER Y LENGUA"
Beef Tongue with Salsa de Cacahuate

MI TOCAYA ANTOJERÍA
Chicago, Illinois

◇◇◇

When chef Diana Dávila was ready to open her own restaurant, she named it for herself, *tocaya* (means "namesake"), and for *antojitos*. More on the former: Dávila is a restaurant kid who grew up working in the Mexican restaurants her parents ran in the Chicago suburbs and then honing her craft in high-end Chicago kitchens and through travels in Mexico. Antojitos are literally "little cravings," the snacks and small plates that comprise some of the country's favorite dishes—everything from tacos to sopes fits into the antojito category. This dish has been on her menu since the earliest days. The peanut butter is an exceptional salsa de cacahuate. Where a typical recipe would combine peanuts, arbol chiles, and garlic cloves, Dávila uses roasted garlic oil, herbs like epazote and bay leaf, as well as plum tomatoes to create a creamy, layered peanut sauce that would be as great with steak as it is with this savory, craveable lengua. You can achieve the restaurant-y look by using the back of your spoon to swoosh the sauce onto the plate before adding your lengua. But if it's more your style to offer the cubes of lengua with the sauce on the side for dipping, go with it.

Serves **8** to **10**

◇◇◇

To make the pickled onions, combine the vinegar, sugar, salt, jamaica, and bay leaf in a small pot and bring to a boil. Turn the heat off, cover, and let steep for 10 minutes. Strain the liquid and set aside to cool.

In a stainless steel bowl, toss the red onions with a touch of salt. Pour the cooled vinegar mixture over the onions and transfer to an airtight container. Refrigerate for at least 2 days before using, or up to 3 weeks.

To make the lengua, char the white and red onions and poblano chile on a grill or under the broiler until soft and blistered, making sure to turn to get both sides. Set aside.

Heavily season the scored and halved lengua with salt. Set aside for 20 minutes, then rinse the salt off thoroughly.

Place the lengua, charred vegetables, garlic, thyme, oregano, and bay leaves in a stockpot. Cover with water and bring to a boil. Season with salt, reduce the heat to maintain a rolling simmer, and cook until the lengua is tender, about 2½ hours, tasting for salt along the way.

Let the lengua cool in the stock, then strain the liquid, remove the lengua, and trim any unwanted parts such as the skin and additional membranes. Dice the lengua meat into 1-inch (2.5 cm) cubes and refrigerate until ready to use, for up to 2 days.

Continued

◇◇◇◇◇◇◇◇◇◇◇◇◇◇◇◇◇◇◇◇◇◇◇◇◇◇◇◇◇◇◇

For the pickled onions:

3 cups (720 ml) red wine vinegar

1 tablespoon sugar

2½ teaspoons salt, plus more for tossing the onions

1 cup (45 g) jamaica (dried hibiscus flowers)

1 dried bay leaf

2 medium red onions, thinly sliced

For the lengua:

⅓ small white onion, peeled (see Note)

⅓ small red onion, peeled

½ poblano chile

1 (2- to 3-pound/1,134 g) beef tongue, scored and cut in half widthwise

Salt

3 cloves garlic, peeled

⅓ cup (14 g) fresh thyme leaves

½ cup (14 g) fresh oregano leaves

2 bay leaves

For the salsa de cacahuate:

1 cup (240 ml) vegetable oil

1 head garlic, cloves chopped

1 cup (140 g) raw peanuts

6 medium plum tomatoes, diced

Salt

1 cup (14 g) chopped epazote

3 arbol chiles

1½ teaspoons black peppercorns

2 bay leaves

3 avocado leaves

To serve:

1 bunch radishes, greens trimmed and radishes quartered

¼ cup (60 ml) vegetable oil

Torn fresh herbs, such as cilantro or epazote

→ **NOTE:** Beef tongue can be found at butcher shops and at grocery stores with a butcher.

To make the salsa, heat the vegetable oil in a small pot over medium heat, add the garlic, and fry until golden brown, about 3 minutes. Remove from the heat and strain the oil. Set aside the fried garlic for another use and let the oil cool down completely. Wipe the pan and toast the peanuts over medium heat until golden brown on all sides, 4 to 5 minutes.

Put the tomatoes in a separate pot and season with salt. Work in the epazote and let sit for 20 minutes. Then add the toasted peanuts, arbol chiles, black peppercorns, bay leaves, and avocado leaves. Bring to a boil over medium-high heat, then reduce the heat and simmer for 10 minutes. Remove the pot from heat and let it cool enough to be handled. Transfer to a blender or food processor and blend until smooth. Taste and season with salt as needed. You can store the salsa in an airtight container in the fridge for up to 2 days before serving.

To serve, preheat a grill to medium-high heat. Grill the quartered radishes until charred and slightly tender.

In a large sauté pan, heat the vegetable oil over medium-high heat. Brown the cubed lengua 1 to 2 minutes each side, then transfer to a paper towel–lined plate to absorb excess oil.

Spoon a good amount of the salsa de cacahuate on a serving platter. Artfully place the browned lengua cubes on top. Garnish with the pickled onions, torn herbs, and grilled radishes and serve immediately.

Warm Your Olives

As told to by **Reem Assil**, chef-founder of Arabic bakery and restaurant Reem's in San Francisco.

I love putting olives on a cheese plate with Spanish hard cheeses like Manchego and Iberico, dried fruits like apricots and figs, and walnuts. Here's a trick to make it more special: Drain your olives of their brine, then warm them in oil with chiles, herbs, or lemon zest. That quick marinade will give them a restaurant-y, finished feeling. Lemon zest in particular can make anything feel fancier. Normally I'd go for white wine or rosé, but olives also go well with hot tea on a morning mezze table.

A Good Tin of Fish Is a Ready-Made Appetizer

HOW TO FIND GOOD TINS

La Vara chef and conservas expert Alex Raij says to focus on Spanish products, in particular fish from the Cantabrian sea—small, oily fish thrive in its cold waters. Look for olive oil–packed tuna loin and belly, says Cúrate chef Katie Button. Sardines in olive oil are perfect for making simple snacks, and she relies on salt-cured anchovies in oil when making Gilda Pintxo (page 92).

Plenty of grocery stores have reputable brands. For specialized options, seek out gourmet markets, but know that it's sometimes easier to shop online if you've got your eye on something specific. The good stuff won't be cheap, but "it's better to spend a little money on it to get the higher quality," says Dame co-owner Patricia Howard.

BRANDS CHEFS LOVE

Don Bocarte, Güeyu Mar, Minnow, Fishwife, Ortiz, Jose Gourmet, La Brujula, Fangst, Scout, Matiz, Ekone, Mariscadora, Conservas de Cambados, iCan, Wildfish Cannery, Patagonia Provisions

WHAT TO DO WITH IT

When you've got the good stuff, you don't need to do much at all. Try Spanish cockles or muscles in escabeche with potato chips and hot sauce or top a baguette with a generous spread of salted butter and a good sardine or anchovy fillet and you're golden. Some pickles and juicier veggies like tomatoes and cucumbers will round out your snack. For rich, creamy cod liver, try it on top of rice with some furikake or grated daikon and ponzu.

If you're creating a larger spread, set the tins out with some bread, crackers, olives, cured meats, and hard cheese for a snacky dinner or a party appetizer. For the latter, take a page from Kachka's book and create composed bites by taking a bit of pumpernickel toast, spreading some parsley mayo on it, topping it with a bit of an oily tinned fish like a Latvian tinned sprat, and finishing it with a slice of pickled onion (see page 111).

The oily fish will pair especially well with refreshing wines like orange wines, txakoli, and pét-nat, as well as sherry, martinis, and, really, anything that you like pairing with salty foods.

While the fancier brands are great on their own, less expensive options are super useful. Raij recommends making bagna cauda (a hot garlicky dip for vegetables) with basic anchovies or adding them to a pasta sauce or vinaigrette, and, of course, for topping pizzas. Kamonegi chef Mutsuko Soma adds minced garlic and a splash of soy sauce to basic grocery store sardines before baking them in the toaster oven and then eating them with rice.

Recommendations by: Alex Raij, Cameron Rolka, Curtis Stone, Ed Szymanski, Patricia Howard, Sam Yoo, Katie Button, Luis Martinez, Mutsuko Soma, Bonnie Frumkin Morales, Sarah Welch, Jonathan Whitener, Sabrina De Sousa, Steven Satterfield

AGEDASHI SHISO AND EBI SHINJO
with Dashi Tsuyu Broth

N/NAKA
Los Angeles, California

One of Los Angeles's best-known restaurants is a place that very few get to see on any given night, by nature of its four-hundred-square-foot size. At n/naka, chef-owner Niki Nakayama introduced the city—and, really, the country—to a generous vision of the Japanese kaiseki tradition that makes plenty of space for her to explore her own story and point of view. There's room, too, for Nakayama to build a life for herself that includes cooking alongside wife Carole Iida-Nakayama. For this agedashi shiso and ebi shinjo, you'll fill a shiso leaf with shrimp and then tempura-fry it. You'll serve it in a shallow pool of dashi tsuyu; dashi is a staple Japanese stock typically made with dried bonito and konbu, which you can make yourself (see page 124) or use a store-bought instant-dashi (Nakayama recommends Ajinomoto Hondashi). This dish makes for a gorgeous starter. Kaiseki promises technical mastery, delicate balance, and an impeccably timed show of pristine ingredients; if that seems like the furthest thing from your home kitchen, remember that you, like Nakayama, can bring those you love most into the process. And, for some perspective, you may well become a home tempura master with this recipe before you get a reservation at n/naka.

Serves 4 (4 dumplings each)

For the dashi tsuyu:

1 cup (240 ml) dashi broth

¼ cup (60 ml) mirin

¼ cup (60 ml) soy sauce

½ cup (113 g) grated daikon radish

For the shiso and shrimp tempura dumpling:

2 cups (320 g) peeled and deveined black tiger shrimp

1 large egg white (26 g)

2 tablespoons (16 g) potato starch, preferably Katakuriko brand

2 teaspoons soy sauce

16 shiso leaves

For the tempura batter and frying:

2½ cups (600 ml) vegetable oil, for frying

1 cup (125 g) tempura flour

2 cups (480 ml) ice-cold water

To make the dashi tsuyu, place the dashi broth, mirin, soy sauce, and grated daikon in a small pot and bring to a light boil. Turn off the heat and put the lid on to keep it warm.

To make the dumplings, put the shrimp in a food processor and pulse to mince, then add the egg white, potato starch, and soy sauce. Continue pulsing until well minced.

Transfer the shrimp mixture to a medium bowl and use a spatula to scrape any remaining ingredients from the food processor bowl. Mix thoroughly to make sure all ingredients are well incorporated.

Place about 2 tablespoons (20 g) of the shrimp filling onto a shiso leaf and fold lengthwise in half. The shiso leaf should be big enough to fully cover the paste. Continue to do this for the remainder of the shiso leaves and shrimp mixture.

In a large frying pan, heat the oil over medium-high heat to 350°F (175°C). Prepare an ice bath. Make the tempura batter by mixing the ice-cold water into the tempura flour. Be careful not to over-mix or leave small lumps in the batter, and keep the tempura batter cold as you work by setting it atop a bowl filled with ice and water.

Dip the dumplings into the batter, then slowly drop them into the oil, no more than 4 at a time. Cook for 1 minute on each side, or until golden. Transfer the fried tempura to a paper towel–lined dish to blot out excess oil.

To serve, ladle the warm dashi tsuyu broth into 4 bowls. Place 4 dumplings into each broth-filled bowl and serve immediately.

CANDY CANE
BEET CARPACCIO

DIRT CANDY
New York City

Before there was widespread acceptance of buzzwords like *vegetable-forward* and *plant-based*, there was Dirt Candy, Amanda Cohen's groundbreaking vegetarian fine-dining spot in the East Village. Now located in a roomier space on the Lower East Side, the acclaimed restaurant is always evolving—at times it's been an all-day a la carte spot and now it's back to its tasting menu roots. But through all its many iterations, Cohen's restaurant is always at the cutting-edge of freewheeling vegetarian cooking. She loves a visual or a flavor pun: Her many past dishes include a broccoli hot dog, a Nashville hot carrot, and an eggplant foster. This candy cane beet carpaccio is a stunner: The salt-roasting technique is one Cohen has used for many of her beet dishes; the number of cups you need will depend on your pan, but your goal is to cover the beets entirely, allowing them to steam in their skins for maximum flavor. The presentation, with a shower of freshly grated pecorino and horseradish feels expensive and like a totally plausible dupe for beef carpaccio. Consider wearing gloves to avoid staining your hands, and definitely be sure you're comfortable with your mandoline before tackling this; the supremely thin slices a mandoline achieves are critical for this to look and eat like the tasting menu–worthy dish it is. There is a completely optional step that involves a dehydrator, but don't stress if you don't have one.

Serves **4 to 6**

Salt

6 small or 4 medium candy cane or Chioggia beets

1 cup (240 ml) beet juice

¼ cup (60 ml) lemon juice

¼ cup (60 ml) extra-virgin olive oil

¼ cup (13 g) thinly sliced red pearl onions

½ cup (40 g) grated pecorino Romano cheese (use a Microplane, if possible)

½ cup (120 g) freshly grated horseradish (use a Microplane, if possible)

¼ cup (5 g) very small arugula leaves

Preheat the oven to 425°F (220°C).

Pour the salt one-quarter of the way up a small baking pan. Place the beets evenly in the pan and cover with salt. Cover the pan with aluminum foil.

Roast the beets for 1 hour, or until tender when pierced with a small knife.

Meanwhile, in a small pot, simmer the beet juice over medium heat until it reduces to about 3 tablespoons and is syrupy. Set aside to cool.

Immediately remove the beets from the pan and wash off the salt. Set aside to cool, then remove the skins. They should just slip off. Slice the beets on a mandoline as thinly as possible.

If you have a dehydrator, dehydrate the sliced beets for 1 hour at 115°F (46°C) to concentrate the flavor.

Divide the beets among 4 plates, laying the slices flat on the plate touching each other. Garnish with the beet syrup, lemon juice, olive oil, pearl onions, cheese, horseradish, and arugula.

BURGUNDY ESCARGOTS

PETIT TROIS
Los Angeles, California

Sitting across from an open kitchen at a marble-topped bar, in a dark-wood-clad narrow dining room, you could think you're in Paris and not an LA strip mall. Ludo Lefebvre's cooking has electrified the city and the country at Petit Trois, one of the first in a wave of hip French restaurants that ushered in a renewed interest in traditional French fare. Buttery, garlicky, and picture-perfect tucked into their shells, Petit Trois escargots are as recognizable on your social feed as they are on the plate. At the restaurant, Lefebvre serves this appetizer with six snails to an order; we're going with twelve here because if you're taking the effort to source escargot (which you can do online and at some specialty grocers), you ought to make a bunch and give your guests the chance to have at least a few per person. Plus, more snails equals more garlicky butter to sop up with a hunk of baguette.

For the escargot butter:

¾ cup plus 2 tablespoons (199 g) butter, softened

1½ teaspoons white wine

½ teaspoon salt

¼ teaspoon freshly ground black pepper

Pinch of freshly grated nutmeg

2 tablespoons finely minced shallot

¼ cup (10 g) finely minced fresh Italian parsley

3½ teaspoons grated garlic (on a Microplane)

To assemble the dish:

12 escargots

12 escargot shells

Flaky salt

1 tablespoon chopped fresh Italian parsley

1 baguette, toasted

Makes 12 escargots

Preheat the oven to 500°F (260°F).

To make the garlic butter, combine the butter, wine, salt, pepper, and nutmeg in a stand mixer fitted with the paddle attachment and mix on low speed. Add the shallot, minced parsley, and garlic and continue to mix on low speed until everything is incorporated. Transfer to a pastry bag (or a zip-top bag with the corner snipped off).

To assemble, add each escargot to its shell and pipe in 15 g (about 1 tablespoon) of the escargot butter in each one. Place on an escargot tray (see Note) and bake until the butter melts and the escargots are hot all the way through, 3 to 5 minutes. Remove from the oven and season with flaky salt and the chopped parsley. Plate and serve with the toasted baguette.

→ NOTE: Escargot trays can be sourced pretty inexpensively from a restaurant supply store or website. If you don't want to purchase a specialty item, you can use a small, round, rimmed baking dish.

GAMBAS AL AJILLO
(Garlic Shrimp with Brava Sauce)

JALEO
Washington, D.C.

It's almost easy to forget that America first admired José Andrés—famous now for his humanitarian work feeding people in regions hit by natural disasters and war—for his cooking alone. His first restaurant, Jaleo, is still thriving today some thirty years after it opened, offering up a mix of Spanish favorites like tapas, paellas, jamón, and more that diners can order either à la carte or in a multicourse tasting menu. These shrimp are a staple of the menu. As Andrés explains it, "traditional gambas al ajillo is a simple tapa of shrimp cooked in garlic and olive oil." But he likes putting his own spin on things, so he adds a bit of brava sauce for heat. Let that same spirit guide how you approach making this at home. Want a spicier brava sauce? Add another arbol chile. This recipe will yield extra sauce; consider using it for patatas bravas, as a dip for fries, as a sub for ketchup on your next burger, as a base for shakshuka, or even as a pasta sauce. Final thoughts on this dish from Andrés: "Be sure to serve with good bread for everyone to soak up the last drops of this amazing sauce."

Serves **4** to **6**

For the brava sauce:

2 tablespoons vegetable oil

6 cloves garlic, sliced

2 arbol chiles

2 tablespoons sugar

2 tablespoons sherry vinegar

1 tablespoon tomato paste

1 (28-ounce/794 g) can crushed tomatoes

1 tablespoon sweet pimentón

Salt

For the shrimp:

4 cloves garlic, peeled

1 cup (240 ml) Spanish extra-virgin olive oil

5 arbol chiles

1 pound (455 g) large shrimp, peeled and deveined

5 tablespoons brandy, preferably from Spain

5 tablespoons fresh lemon juice

Salt

2 tablespoons chopped fresh Italian parsley

To make the brava sauce, combine the vegetable oil, garlic, and arbol chiles in a deep, wide pot and cook over medium heat until everything starts to brown, 3 to 5 minutes, then add the sugar and stir until it melts. Add the vinegar and tomato paste and cook for 3 minutes. Pour in the crushed tomatoes, bring to a simmer, then lower the heat to low, partially cover to avoid splattering, and simmer, stirring frequently, until it's reduced by half. Add the pimentón, taste, and add salt if necessary. Strain the sauce through a sieve. You'll have about 1½ cups (360 ml), so whatever you don't use can be kept in the fridge for up to 1 week or frozen for up to 3 months.

To make the shrimp, thinly slice the garlic cloves with a knife or mandoline. In a large skillet, heat the olive oil over medium heat and add the garlic. When garlic starts to sizzle, add the arbol chiles and cook for 1 minute, then turn the heat up to high and add the shrimp. When the shrimp starts to turn pink, remove the pan from the heat and add the brandy—if you don't remove the pan from the heat, you'll get flames! Return the pan to the heat and add the lemon juice and 2 tablespoons of the brava sauce. Stir to combine. Remove the pan from the heat and season with salt.

To serve, divide the shrimp and chiles evenly into shallow bowls and garnish with the parsley.

noodles noo
noodles noo
noodles noo
noodles noo
noodles noo
noodles noo
noodles noo
noodles noo

4

NOODLES ARE THE MOVE

Always order the noodles. The noodles tell you what a restaurant is all about: Is the kitchen taking the task seriously? Are the strands cooked perfectly—are they chewy enough? Is the dish a cheeky play on something familiar? A faithful example of a regional specialty? Is it a reason to come back? That's when chefs have a hit.

At home, many of us turn to noodles and pasta when we need a quick meal or an easy comfort food. There's no reason to stop doing that. Ever. But if you carve out some time to consider noodles the way chefs do, you can add some stunners to your repertoire.

To that end, it's worth making your own noodles at least once. Getting started is not as intimidating as a beginner might think. And with some practice, you can get pretty darn far with good flour, water, and patience. You may well fall in love with the process like the chefs featured here. And if you don't, rest assured plenty of chefs use store-bought at home (and even in their restaurants), thanks to some spectacular dried options.

SOBA WITH MUSHROOM SUKIYAKI SEIRO BROTH

KAMONEGI
Seattle, Washington

Mutsuko Soma credits watching her grandmother make soba for how quickly she herself learned the craft. Now, more than five years into running her acclaimed restaurant Kamonegi in Seattle's Fremont neighborhood, she's an undisputed master, balancing tradition with her own creative pursuits (her ever-changing menu has at times included umeboshi ratatouille soba, duck fat tuna tartare, and spicy pork belly soba). This dish comes from the seiro section of the menu, which refers to soba that's served alongside a dipping broth. At the restaurant, Soma makes her buckwheat noodles entirely from scratch: grinding the flour, mixing the dough with her fingertips before kneading it, and precisely cutting the noodles with a knife. She tapped Yael Peet, who cooks with Soma at their bar, Hannyatou, to create a more home-friendly version that uses a stand mixer and a pasta machine. Soma's mushroom sukiyaki, typically a one-pot meal of slowly simmered sliced beef and vegetables, is silkily earthy, a perfect complement to her delicately firm soba. You can substitute with store-bought dashi, or to make this vegetarian, omit the bonito flakes and double the amount of kombu and shiitake. Everything else is the same; still simmer your dashi for 20 minutes to reduce.

→ **NOTES:** If you want to sub in instant dashi, Soma recommends Ajinomoto Hondashi as a cheap and reliable go-to. If you can spring for the more upscale Kayanoya, do that instead (they offer more variety, including vegan options).

If you don't want to make your own soba, Soma recommends Hime or any other Japanese brand you can find (though don't expect it to taste like soba from a restaurant). Make sure you don't accidentally pick up yakisoba or Korean buckwheat noodles, as those are different from soba.

For the noodles:

2 cups (280 g) soba/buckwheat flour

1 cup (120 g) all-purpose flour

¾ teaspoon salt

4 large eggs

For the dashi:

1 dried shiitake mushroom

1 piece (1 square inch/2.5 sq cm) dried kombu kelp

4 ounces (114 g) dried bonito flakes

½ cup (120 ml) Japanese soy sauce

2 tablespoons light brown sugar

2 tablespoons mirin

For the mushroom sukiyaki:

4 cloves garlic, minced

2 tablespoons canola or other neutral oil

2 leeks, sliced (discard stringy roots and leafy upper portion)

2 pounds (910 g) mushrooms of your choice, ripped or sliced into bite-size pieces

To make the noodles, sift both flours and the salt into one bowl. Whisk the eggs in another. Either by hand or using a stand mixer with a dough hook, combine the eggs and flour until a dry dough forms. Knead the dough for a few minutes, then cover and let it rest for 1 hour in the refrigerator.

Using a pasta machine, roll to a medium thickness, about ¹⁄₁₆ inch (3 mm), which is setting 4. Use a noodle attachment to cut your dough into thin noodles (or do it by hand). Prepare an ice bath in a large bowl and bring a large pot of water to a boil. Cook the noodles for 2 minutes, then strain them over a second pot. Reserve the cooking water and keep it over low heat until ready to serve. Remove the noodles from the heat, immediately dipping the strainer into the ice water to shock noodles and stop their cooking.

Slap the strainer against the sink to remove as much water from the noodles as possible. Place onto a serving plate.

To make the dashi, combine 4 cups (960 ml) water with the shiitake and kombu in a pot. Let stand for at least 30 minutes, or overnight if possible. When you're ready, slowly bring it up to a simmer and remove the kombu as it begins to bubble. If you leave it in too long, the dashi will get kind of slimy. Add the bonito flakes and simmer for 20 minutes. Remove from the heat and strain out the bonito and shiitake.

Make the kaeshi by combining the soy sauce, sugar, and mirin together in a small bowl. Add this to the dashi while it is still hot and stir well to dissolve the sugar. You'll have more dashi than you need; reserve the rest for another time.

To make the mushroom sukiyaki, in a large sauté pan, heat the garlic in the canola oil over medium heat until fragrant. Add the leeks and mushrooms and cook until tender, about 9 minutes. Add the dashi and stir to combine, making a concentrated, salty broth. Divide the mushroom sukiyaki evenly in 4 bowls (about 1 cup/240 ml per person).

Serve the chilled buckwheat noodles on the side and encourage everyone to dip the noodles into the broth. For a warm sipping broth, add the reserved cooking water into the broth after you are done eating your noodles.

You Don't Need a Recipe to Make a Restaurant-Worthy Sauce

Taking noodles from standard to special doesn't need to be a major undertaking. Here's how chefs make easy noodles at home.

EASIEST COCONUT SAUCE:
Sauté cumin seeds in olive oil, and then add coconut milk, copious amounts of fresh ginger, and minced serrano chile, bring to a boil, then simmer for 5 minutes or so. Then add all the chopped vegetables you can get your hands on.

Recommended by: Pondicheri chef-owner Anita Jaisinghani

MASTER VINAIGRETTE:
Learn this formula: 30 percent oil + 20 to 30 percent acid + 30 to 40 percent soy sauce. From there you can play further with ratios (and with seasonings). For example, combine sesame oil with aged Chinese vinegar and soy sauce in a large bowl, and then add your noodles and toss to coat.

Recommended by: 886 chef-owner and Sze Daddy creator Eric Sze

CHEATER BOLOGNESE:
If you don't have hours to simmer your sauce, sauté your finely diced aromatics (onion, garlic, carrots, celery) in chili crisp to quickly add umami flavor and depth. Add your meat and brown it, then stir in canned tomatoes and cook until thickened.

Recommended by: Boon Sauce creator and Camphor co-chef Max Boonthanakit

SIMPLE CACIO E PEPE:
Add a splash of water and a tablespoon of high-quality butter to your pan. Stir it constantly and keep adding tablespoons of butter until you have enough to coat your noodles. Stir in cracked pepper and grated high-quality pecorino cheese, then add your pasta noodles directly from the pot.

Recommended by: Kindred chef-owner Joe Kindred and sommelier-owner Katy Kindred

NO-COOK TOMATO SAUCE:
Grate fresh tomatoes into a large bowl and toss with extra-virgin olive oil, toasted garlic, whatever herbs you have in the fridge, and dried pasta that's been cooked to al dente.

Recommended by: Poole's Diner chef-owner Ashley Christensen

Shopping List: Noodles

Here are the pasta brands and noodle shapes chefs love:

- **Garofalo:**
  Mezze Maniche Rigate

- **Sfoglini:**
  Semolina Reginetti

- **Setaro:**
  Strozzapreti

- **Rustichella d'Abruzzo:**
  Garganelli

- **De Cecco:**
  Rigatoni

- **Pasta Mancini:**
  Bucatini

- **Felicetti:**
  Spaghetti

- **Yuan Yi:**
  Knife-Cut Noodles

Recommended by: Luis Martinez, Joe and Katy Kindred, Sam Yoo, Sarah Grueneberg, Michael Tusk

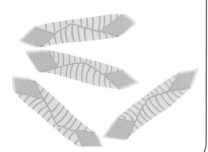

SPICY CUMIN LAMB with Biang-Biang Noodles

XI'AN FAMOUS FOODS
New York City

Restaurateur Jason Wang and his father, chef David Shi, have built a New York City restaurant empire one plate of spicy cumin lamb noodles at a time. For Wang, the dish is a nostalgic taste of childhood; for his father, it's proof that his cooking—his focus on the cuisine of Xi'an, China, but filtered through his family's own traditions—doesn't need to change to please New York City's palate. For diners, the dish might be a weekly lunch to look forward to in Midtown, an anchoring meal while out and about in Flushing, or a bucket-list stop when eating through New York as a visitor. Cooking with a jar of your favorite chili crisp at home is a smart shortcut here, and we'll use it in both the lamb preparation and to serve the finished noodle dish. The end result will be a bit milder and, depending on which brand you use, a variation on the restaurant's flavor profile. It's tempting to think of this recipe as its two key components (lamb and noodles)—and for sure, each on its own has plenty to offer. But if you're wanting to create the dish as a whole, plan ahead. Start your dough up to three days early. When you're ready to cook your lamb and pull your noodles, be fanatical about your mise en place. Once your noodles are pulled, it's a race to get them sauced so they can be served and slurped as quickly as possible. The slick, chewy noodles and the fragrant, fiery lamb are worth the effort!

Serves 2

10 ounces (280 g) boneless lamb leg, ideally partially frozen

1½ teaspoons cornstarch

2 teaspoons plus 2 tablespoons vegetable oil

1 green onion, trimmed and chopped

1-inch (2.5 cm) piece fresh ginger, peeled and finely chopped

1 clove garlic, sliced

1½ tablespoons ground cumin

1 teaspoon salt

½ medium red onion, sliced

1 longhorn pepper, diagonally sliced

1½ teaspoons jarred chili crisp, or more to taste, excess oil drained

To serve:
Biang-Biang Noodles (recipe follows) or store-bought fresh Chinese noodles, freshly cooked and drained

1 tablespoon chopped fresh chives

1 green onion, trimmed and chopped, whites and greens separated

¼ cup (60 ml) soy sauce

2 tablespoons black vinegar

2 tablespoons jarred chili crisp, or to taste, making sure to include both oil and crunchy bits

Carefully slice the lamb into ⅛-inch (3 mm) thick pieces (note: it's easier to cut when partially frozen).

Place the sliced lamb into a large bowl along with the cornstarch and 2 teaspoons of the vegetable oil. Mix together with your hands.

In a large skillet or wok, heat the remaining 2 tablespoons vegetable oil over high heat for 1 minute. Add the green onion, ginger, and garlic and cook for 30 seconds. Add the lamb and stir-fry for about 5 minutes, until the meat turns an even brown color. Turn the heat down to low, add the cumin and salt, and stir to combine. Add the red onion, longhorn pepper, and the 1½ teaspoons of chili crisp (drained of excess oil), stir to combine, and set aside.

To serve, put the noodles in a serving bowl and add the chives, the white parts of the green onion, the soy sauce, black vinegar, chili crisp, and the cooked lamb. Using tongs, toss gently to coat, being careful not to tear the noodles in the process. If desired, garnish with the green tops of the green onion and additional chili crisp. Serve immediately.

Continued

→ **NOTES:** While any chili crisp can work, Xi'an Famous Foods sells its own online that has the same secret spice blend used at the restaurant.

If you want to make the lamb but don't want to make your own noodles, Wang recommends seeking out fresh noodles from the refrigerated section of a Chinese grocery store. Or serve with white rice.

If there is leftover lamb, it can be saved for up to 2 days in the fridge. Reheat in a skillet.

Biang-Biang (Hand-Ripped) Noodles

Serves 2 to 3

3½ cups (405 g) all-purpose flour or high-gluten flour

½ teaspoon salt

¾ cup (180 ml) room-temperature water

Vegetable oil, to keep the dough from sticking

* * * * *

To make the dough, place the flour in a stand mixer with the dough hook attachment. In a Pyrex measuring cup or a container that has a mouth to pour, stir the salt into the room-temperature water until dissolved.

Start the mixer at low speed. Slowly add the salt water at the side of the mixer until all of the water is evenly incorporated. Keep running the mixer until the sides of the mixing bowl are flour-free and the dough is smooth. If the dough doesn't seem to be coming together, you can add up to ¼ cup (60 ml) more water, a little at a time.

Alternatively, if mixing by hand in a bowl, add the salt water ¼ cup (60 ml) at a time, using your hands to knead the mixture into a ball of dough. Knead until a dough is formed, 8 to 10 minutes.

Remove the dough from the mixing bowl and knead on a floured board. You'll need to use a bit of muscle, as the dough will be quite tough at first, but it will get smoother and springier the longer you work it. Knead until relatively smooth and springy. Cover with a moist towel

and let rest for 5 minutes. Then uncover and with clean hands knead the dough on a floured board for a minute or so. Repeat this rest-then-knead process twice more. In total, you should have rested the dough for 15 minutes and kneaded it three times.

After the final rest, flatten the dough into a rectangle to the best of your ability and cut the dough into 3½-ounce (100 g) pieces (about 6 pieces for one batch of dough). Use a rolling pin to roll each piece into a flat rectangle, a little over ¼ inch thick, 4 to 5 inches long, and about 1½ inches wide (6 mm thick, 10 to 12 cm long, and 4 cm wide).

Brush the dough with vegetable oil and store without stacking pieces on top of each other. In the stores, they pack the un-pulled pieces on their edge, like books, sideways in a container. Rest, covered with plastic wrap and refrigerated, for at least 1 hour and up to 3 days.

When ready to pull and cook the noodles, remember they cannot sit after being pulled and are best eaten fresh. Be prepared to immediately boil, sauce, and slurp them down. Take the pieces of dough out of the refrigerator and let them warm up to room temperature.

Bring a large pot of water to a boil. On a clean counter, warm up the pieces of dough by flattening them on the counter with your hands, until the dough feels stretchy and elastic. Evenly press the dough into a flat rectangular shape until it is about 6 inches long and 3 inches wide (15 cm and 7.5 cm).

Grab the ends of the rectangle with your thumbs and forefingers, as if you are checking if a bill is counterfeit in the light.

Pull the dough gently, stretching it until it is about shoulder-width long.

Start to slightly pull and bounce the noodle flat against the counter in an up-and-down motion. Pull and slap the dough against the counter until the dough is almost 4 feet (1.25 m) long. Be careful not to pull too quickly or grip too tight, as you'll break the noodle. If the noodle does break, just grab onto the broken part and try to pull from there.

When the noodle is the right length, pick it up at the middle and rip it into two pieces like string cheese. Pull until you almost reach the end, but don't pull all the way through. You'll end up with a giant noodle ring. Carefully press the ends of the strands to stretch and even them out if they are too thick.

Pull and rip the remaining noodles and throw all the strands into the pot of boiling water at the same time. Stir with tongs to make sure they do not stick. They should be "swimming" in the water.

Boil for 3 minutes. If the water is about to spill out, turn the heat down slightly but keep it at a boil. Add cold water to the pot if necessary.

Strain out the noodles and prepare to serve them immediately.

CINCINNATI CHILI "5-WAY"

CAMP WASHINGTON CHILI
Cincinnati, Ohio

For more than eighty years, Camp Washington Chili has been one of Cincinnati's favorite places to get its namesake dish, Cincinnati chili—a spiced meat sauce that typically tops spaghetti (that's known as a "2-way"). Unlike your average chili, this specialty marries savory seasonings like garlic and cumin with dessert-friendly flavors like cloves, cinnamon, and even chocolate. Bearing a faint resemblance to pastitsio, a Greek dish with noodles, meat, and cheese, this specific dish in this specific city is really the story of a particular immigrant group going all in on what sells. Greek-born John Johnson started working at his uncle's chili parlor back in 1951. Now, he runs it with his daughter Maria Papakirk, and while some things are different—they moved down the block, for example—mostly it's the same. The same stockpots, the same refusal to add chocolate to their chili, and the same secrets. The spice mix is kept under lock and key, and only family members are allowed to blend and add it to the simmering pots of chili at the restaurant. What Papakirk shared below is "a variation from the secret family recipe," she says, but with chili powder, cinnamon, cumin seeds, and other seasonings, you'll get pretty close. Make it a "5-way" by topping your spaghetti and chili with diced onions, red beans, and shredded cheddar (Wisconsin if you've got it). Serve with oyster crackers and hot sauce on the side to complete the Camp Washington setup.

1 tablespoon chile powder

¼ teaspoon ground cinnamon

¼ teaspoon ground cloves

1 teaspoon cumin seeds

¼ teaspoon powdered ginger

½ teaspoon powdered mustard

⅛ teaspoon ground nutmeg

1 teaspoon ground paprika

¼ cup (60 ml) olive oil

1½ cups peeled and finely chopped (or crushed) yellow onions

2 tablespoons minced garlic

1 tablespoon salt, plus more as needed

2 pounds (900 g) lean ground beef

2 (28-ounce/794 g) cans crushed tomatoes

1½ cups (360 ml) hot water

2 cubes beef bouillon

For serving:

1 pound (455 g) cooked spaghetti

1 cup (177 g) cooked red kidney beans

½ cup (71 g) diced white onions

4 cups (332 g) shredded cheddar cheese

Serves 6

In a small bowl, mix the chile powder, cinnamon, cloves, cumin seeds, ginger, mustard, nutmeg, and paprika.

Heat the olive oil in a large heavy-bottomed pot over medium heat. Add the onions and garlic and cook until soft and translucent, about 10 minutes, Then add the spice mixture and salt and cook, stirring, for 2 minutes. Add the ground beef to the pot and stir thoroughly until the ingredients are well combined. Continue cooking the beef until it is no longer pink. Add the crushed tomatoes and hot water to the pot and stir well.

Bring the mixture to a gentle simmer and add the beef bouillon cubes. Stir, then cover and simmer for 2 to 3 more hours. Taste and season with additional salt.

For a thicker and tastier chili, cook everything a day ahead, refrigerate overnight, and reheat the next day.

To serve, divide the spaghetti onto serving plates, then top each with a generous ladle of the chili. Layer the red beans, white onions, and a heaping mound of shredded cheddar on top.

FETTUCCINE WITH PORK RAGÙ

Hippo is where Los Angeles diners jockey for reservations and spots at the bar, waiting as patiently as they can for a taste of chef Matt Molina's expertly crafted pastas. Molina's something of a fixture in the LA restaurant scene, having helmed the kitchens at Nancy Silverton's iconic restaurants before striking out on his own. And while there is serious cooking happening, the atmosphere in the dining room is boisterous—more orange wine than chianti. Pork ragù is a menu staple, a saucy tangle of classic Italian comfort. At the restaurant, Molina serves this with fresh pasta, typically fettuccine or garganelli. At home, you can use whatever pasta you have on hand. With an umami-packed sofrito and a hint of nutmeg, Molina's ragù is a savory master class in the form, and peppered throughout his recipe are plenty of tips and tricks that will make you a better all-around pasta cook. Besides a celebration-worthy dinner, this ragù will also leave you with extra to freeze, gifting future-you a tremendously flavorful, low-lift meal.

For the soffritto:
½ cup (120 ml) extra-virgin olive oil

1 cup (113 g) diced white onion

1 cup (100 g) chopped celery

¾ cup (96 g) chopped carrot

For the ragù:
1 tablespoon extra-virgin olive oil

4 cloves garlic, peeled

2½ tablespoons chopped pancetta

2½ tablespoons double-concentrated tomato paste

1 pound (455 g) ground pork

Salt and freshly ground black pepper

⅛ teaspoon freshly grated nutmeg

½ cup (120 ml) dry white wine

2 cups (480 ml) chicken stock

6 tablespoons (90 ml) whole milk

To serve:
Salt

1½ teaspoons butter

Chicken stock, if needed

1 pound (455 g) fettuccine noodles

Extra-virgin olive oil, a high-quality finishing oil if available

1½ tablespoons freshly grated pecorino Romano cheese

1½ tablespoons freshly grated Parmigiano-Reggiano cheese, plus more for topping

Freshly ground black pepper

To make the soffrito, heat the olive oil in a medium sauté pan over medium-high heat until the oil is almost smoking and slides easily in the pan, 2 to 3 minutes. Add the onions and cook until they are tender and translucent, about 9 minutes. Add the celery and carrot and reduce the heat to low. Cook, stirring often, for about 1 hour, until the sofrito is a deep brown caramel color and the vegetables are almost melted. Try to keep the mixture from sticking to the bottom of the pot so it doesn't burn.

You can use the soffritto immediately or cool it to room temperature and transfer to an airtight container. It will keep in the refrigerator for up to 1 week or frozen for up to several months.

To make the ragù, combine the olive oil and garlic in the bowl of a food processor or blender and process to a puree. Add the pancetta and continue to process, stopping to scrape down the sides of the bowl a few times, until the ingredients form a homogenous paste.

Transfer the pancetta-garlic paste to a large sauté pan and cook over medium heat until the fat from the pancetta is rendered, about 5 minutes, stirring constantly to prevent the garlic from browning. Stir in the soffritto and cook for about 1 minute. Move the vegetables to create a bare spot in the pan, add the tomato paste to that spot, and cook for 1 minute, stirring, to slightly caramelize the tomato paste.

Add the pork, season with salt, pepper, and the nutmeg, and cook, stirring occasionally, until all the juices released from the meat have cooked off and the pan is almost dry, about 10 minutes. Add the wine, increase the heat to medium-high, and cook until the wine has evaporated and the pan is almost dry, about 10 minutes.

Add the chicken stock, bring it to a simmer, then reduce the heat and simmer for about an hour, stirring occasionally to prevent the meat from sticking to the bottom of the pan, until the stock has almost all cooked off but the pan is not completely dry. Add the milk and simmer until the ragù returns to a thick, saucy consistency, 15 to 20 minutes.

When you are ready to serve, bring a large pot of salted water to a boil.

While the water is coming to a boil, combine the ragù and butter in a large sauté pan over medium heat. Stir the ingredients to combine and heat, stirring occasionally, until the butter is melted and the sauce is warmed through, adding more chicken stock, if necessary, to obtain a loose sauce-like consistency.

Cook the fettuccine until just al dente, 2 to 3 minutes less than what the package says. Drain the pasta, reserving 1 cup (240 ml) pasta water. Immediately add the pasta to the pan with ragù. Do not let your drained pasta sit. Cook the pasta with sauce for about 2 minutes, being careful not to break the pasta. Add the reserved pasta water as needed to prevent the pasta from drying, sticking, or breaking. It should look slippery and glistening.

Turn off the heat and finish with some olive oil, stirring vigorously and shaking the pan to emulsify the sauce. Add the grated pecorino Romano and Parmigiano-Reggiano cheeses and stir to combine. Add salt and pepper to taste.

Divide evenly, adding any remaining sauce on top and finishing with Parmigiano-Reggiano cheese.

RIGATONI DIAVOLA

LILIA
New York City

Chef Missy Robbins knows pasta. At her restaurant Lilia, her menu of filled and extruded pastas levels up red-sauce-joint classics; at her follow-up spot, Misi, she and her team work in a glass pasta room; and her cookbook is literally titled *Pasta*. Rigatoni Diavola is a fixture of the Lilia menu and is simple enough to become one at home, thanks to a recipe that calls for pantry staples like canned tomatoes (San Marzano wins every time), a good tomato paste (Robbins likes Mutti Double Concentrated), and crushed Calabrian chiles. Combining slow-cooked whole garlic cloves with slivered garlic brings caramelized sweetness and punch to this spicy and oh-so-satisfying dish, and the sauce yields extra, leaving your freezer better stocked for next time.

→ NOTE: Robbins makes her fresh rigatoni with semolina flour and water only; look for the same ingredients when you shop and keep an eye out for Robbins's favorite dried pasta brands: De Cecco, Rustichella D'Abruzzo, Faella, and Monograno Felicetti. If you do want to tackle making your own rigatoni, Robbins lays out her process in her cookbook *Pasta: The Spirit and Craft of Italy's Greatest Food*.

Serves **4 to 6**

For the diavola sauce:
½ cup (120 ml) olive oil

10 cloves garlic, peeled

4 cloves garlic, thinly sliced

¼ cup plus 3 tablespoons (113 g) tomato paste

1 tablespoon crushed Calabrian chiles

2 teaspoons red chile flakes

1 tablespoon plus ½ teaspoon fennel seeds

2 (28-ounce/794 g) cans whole San Marzano tomatoes, crushed by hand

Salt

To serve:
Salt

22 ounces (624 g) rigatoni

¼ cup (22 g) finely grated pecorino Romano cheese

3 sprigs marjoram, leaves removed from stems

1 tablespoon olive oil

Freshly ground black pepper

To make the diavola sauce, place a large heavy saucepan or Dutch oven over medium-low heat. Add the olive oil and whole garlic cloves and cook until the garlic is light golden brown, caramelized, and soft enough to mash, 7 to 10 minutes. Gently mash the garlic in the pot with a fork or the back of a wooden spoon. Add the sliced garlic to the pot, decrease the heat to low, and cook until aromatic but without color, 30 seconds to 1 minute. Add the tomato paste and cook, stirring, until the mixture starts to turn a deeper red and is well combined with the oil and garlic, 3 to 5 minutes.

Add the Calabrian chiles, chile flakes, and fennel seeds, then add the tomatoes and their juice. Stir to incorporate the ingredients and cook until the flavors have blended, 30 to 45 minutes. Season with salt.

Remove from the heat and set aside until you're ready to use. (Or cool, transfer to an airtight container, and refrigerate for up to 5 days or freeze for up to 1 month. You will have about 6½ cups (1,690 g) sauce, which is more than you will need for this recipe.)

To serve, place a large pot of water over high heat and bring to a boil. Generously salt the water. Add the rigatoni to the water and cook until al dente (at least 2 minutes less than what the package says).

Meanwhile, place a large sauté pan over low heat. Add 2¼ cups (585 g) diavola sauce and 1 ladle (¼ cup/60 ml) pasta cooking water and stir to combine.

Using a spider or pasta basket, remove the pasta from the pot and transfer to the sauté pan. Turn the heat up to medium. Toss for 1 to 2 minutes to marry the pasta and sauce. If the sauce begins to tighten, add a splash of pasta cooking water to loosen and continue tossing. When properly married, the pasta should absorb the sauce and glide easily when tossed, and there should be little sauce left at the bottom of the pan. Divide into serving bowls and garnish with the cheese, marjoram, olive oil, and black pepper.

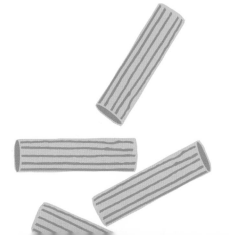

CACIO WHEY PEPE

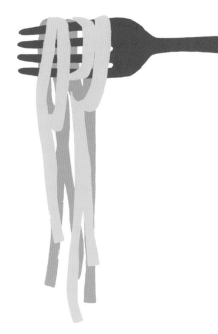

Cacio e pepe is a Roman classic, "a perfect example of simplicity and technique," says Monteverde chef Sarah Grueneberg. Her Cacio Whey Pepe is a Chicago classic, embracing traditional pasta-making and exuberant innovation. Instead of sticking to butter, cheese, and black pepper, Grueneberg blends cheese with whey from the restaurant's house-made ricotta to emulsify the cheese, allowing it to melt into the creamiest pasta sauce you can imagine that is still, somehow, lighter than typical cacio e pepe. At home, you'll make a mock whey with the help of milk and lemon juice (or you could get whey from buying *a lot* of whole-milk mozzarella or burrata and draining their liquids). To really be true to the Monteverde experience, use Pasta Mancini bucatini (you can buy it online).

Serves **4** to **6**

For the mock whey:
1½ cups (360 ml) milk

3 tablespoons lemon juice

For the pecorino pesto:
2 cups (200 g) grated aged pecorino cheese

2 cups (200 g) grated Parmigiano-Reggiano cheese

2 cups (480 ml) mock whey (see above)

For the pasta:
1 pound (455 g) bucatini pasta

2 tablespoons extra-virgin olive oil

2 teaspoons freshly cracked black pepper, plus more for serving

1 cup (240 ml) mock whey (see above), cooled

1 cup (100 g) pecorino pesto (see above)

2 tablespoons butter

To make the mock whey, combine 3 cups (711 g) water, the milk, and lemon juice in a pot and bring to a simmer. Turn off the heat, remove 1 cup (240 ml) from the pot to cool down for the pasta, and cover the other 2 cups (480 ml) to keep warm for the pecorino pesto.

To make the pecorino pesto, place the grated cheeses in the bowl of a food processor and process until fine. Keep it running and drizzle in the warm mock whey through the hole in the lid; it will help melt the cheese. Continue to process for 4 to 5 minutes, until the pesto is smooth and slightly thickened. Cool, transfer to an airtight container, and refrigerate until ready to make your pasta; it will keep refrigerated for up to 3 days.

To make the pasta, bring a large pot of salted water to a boil. Cook the pasta for the shortest amount of time specified on the packaging.

Meanwhile, in a large nonstick pan, heat the olive oil over medium-high heat. Add the black pepper and toast until fragrant, about 1 minute. Turn off the heat until your pasta is ready, then drain the pasta and add to the pepper, then add the mock whey.

Turn the heat back up to medium-high and cook the pasta and mock whey until reduced by half. Reduce the heat to low, then slowly stir the pecorino pesto into the pasta with a rubber spatula until everything is blended. Add the butter and a touch of water to the sauce if it feels too thick.

Garnish with a generous amount of black pepper and serve immediately.

STRANGOLAPRETI
with Brown Butter and Sage

FELIX
Venice, California

◇◇◇

Dinners at Felix start with puffy focaccia and end with tiramisu—when you can snag a reservation, that is. Evan Funke is one of LA's pasta heavyweights, a nerd's nerd who, along with his team, cranks out pastas not often seen on LA menus: trofie, foglie d'ulivo, and strangolapreti, a ricotta dumpling from Italy's mountainous north that's similar to gnudi. These strangolapreti di spinaci (spinach) are a mainstay on the fall and winter menu—coated in warm, nutty brown butter and sage, they make for a comforting dinner on a chilly night. Home cooks can rejoice that this particular pasta doesn't require a pasta machine or an extruder. (Funke prefers handmade shapes—the restaurant has a sign that says, "Fuck your pasta machine.")

Serves **4**

◇◇◇◇◇◇◇◇◇◇◇◇◇◇◇◇◇◇◇◇◇◇◇◇◇◇◇◇◇◇◇ ◇◇◇

Salt

10½ ounces (300 g) fresh spinach

1 extra-large egg

Scant 10 tablespoons (150 g) cow's milk ricotta cheese

½ cup (50 g) grated Parmigiano-Reggiano cheese (plus the rest of the block for serving)

½ cup (50 g) toasted breadcrumbs

5 strokes of whole nutmeg (on a Microplane)

2 tablespoons (15 g) "00" flour

1 cup plus 2 tablespoons (200 g) semolina flour

7 tablespoons (100 g) butter

16 to 20 fresh sage leaves

Fill a large bowl with ice and water. In a large heavy-bottom pot, bring salted water to a rapid boil. Cook the spinach for approximately 1 minute, then immediately transfer to the prepared ice bath.

Remove the spinach from the ice bath and wring in an absorbent terry-cloth towel until very dry. Note: 10½ ounces (300 g) of spinach will yield approximately 3½ ounces (100 g) after it's wrung dry. Put half the spinach in a blender, add the egg, and blend until very smooth. Finely chop the remaining spinach and set aside.

In a medium mixing bowl, combine the ricotta cheese, grated Parmigiano-Reggiano cheese, ¾ teaspoon salt, breadcrumbs, and blended spinach. Grate in the nutmeg, add a quarter of the "00" flour (about 1½ teaspoons), and mix with a whisk until smooth. Then fold the remaining "00" flour into the mixture with a rubber spatula until combined. Cover with plastic wrap and refrigerate for 1 hour.

Spread the semolina on a sheet pan, and line another sheet pan with parchment paper. With a small ice cream scoop or spoon, portion the cheese mixture into round or oval pieces, about ¾ ounces (20 g each). This should yield 40 pieces. Coat each with the semolina flour and place on the parchment-lined sheet pan. Cover and refrigerate for at least 30 minutes or up to 2 days.

When you're ready to cook your strangolapreti, bring a large pot of salted water to a boil. On another burner, brown the butter in a sauté pan over medium heat, stirring often. Add the sage leaves, frying until crispy.

Meanwhile, cook the strangolapreti in rapidly boiling salted water for 1 minute 45 seconds, until they float. (If your pot is not large enough to do it all at once, work in batches.) Remove the strangolapreti using a slotted spoon or spider and drain all the water. Gently add the strangolapreti to the browned butter and swirl; do not toss. To serve, spoon the strangolapreti into 4 plates or low bowls, finishing each with brown butter, sage, and shaved strips of Parmigiano-Reggiano cheese, and serve immediately.

Bún Bowls Are a Weeknight Dream

"If you find a pho restaurant that excels at and is famous for it, it's worth seeking out and supporting that. The same thing goes for ramen," says Andrew Le, the chef-owner of Honolulu's always packed, always innovative Vietnamese restaurants the Pig and the Lady and Piggy Smalls. At home, he says, opt for a bún bowl instead. Sometimes called a noodle salad or a dry soup, Le explains this staple Vietnamese dish is "versatile and great for busy home cooks." Here are his tips for making a great bowl.

MARINATE YOUR PROTEIN

To nail the Vietnamese flavor profile, you need a balance of sweet and salty. In your marinade, sweet can come from sugar, honey, agave, or even maple syrup, and salty will come from fish sauce, oyster sauce, or Vietnamese preserved lemon. Then you complete what Le calls the "triangle of flavor" with sour: with lime juice, tamarind, calamansi juice, or yuzu juice. Round out your marinade with spices and customize it: Try black pepper, Chinese five-spice, turmeric, lemongrass, ginger, Thai chile, sambal, or sriracha. The result is a strong marinade that can quickly penetrate your protein of choice (pork, chicken, tofu) within 30 minutes. Cooking is quick, too: While your noodles cook (see below), just grill or pan-sear your protein.

MAKE YOUR NOODLES

When it comes to cooking Vietnamese rice vermicelli, Le says "al dente is a cardinal sin." For noodles with a soft center, bring water to a boil, add the noodles, and then turn it down to a low simmer. Cook the noodles slowly, and test along the way.

GET YOUR DRESSING READY

"I always go for a typical nuoc cham," says Le. His ratio: 2 parts fish sauce, 2 parts sugar, ¾ part lime juice. If you want to, go ahead and add garlic and chile. Serve this on the side.

BUILD YOUR BOWL

Lay down lettuce, then add your noodles on top. Next comes herbs "that can withstand these big flavors," as Le puts it. Opt for floral, aromatic options like shiso, mint, Thai basil, and even cilantro. Add your proteins. Then, finishing touches: something pickled (typically carrot or daikon, but you could also do a pickled seasonal veggie like ramps or kohlrabi), peanuts, and crunchy fried garlic or shallots.

Sake Goes with Everything

As told to by **Alyssa Mikiko DiPasquale**, certified advanced sake professional and owner of Boston's sake-focused bar, the Koji Club.

Sake is inherently savory, high in amino acids (just like food!), and therefore a natural cheerleader for your favorite dishes.

Its delicate tasting notes and graceful acidity play well with cuisines outside of sushi and ramen. Next time you're having Thai food, pair a warmly spiced Massaman curry with Junmai Ginjo, which can be a real show-off. It has huge range, with fruity, vegetable, and herbaceous qualities that will support the mild heat as well as the nuances of the dish. The robust, earthy flavors of a traditional Junmai Kimoto can stand up to the umami and salt of Spanish jamón, roast chicken, or even pizza. Learn what you like best of the varying categories and styles by trying different bottles when you see them on menus.

A pro move is going to a dope restaurant that cares about sake and instead of going for the 300-milliliter bottle, go for the 720, and then ask to take the rest home. You're getting the bonus of the expert guidance in selecting a bottle, plus you get to then keep discovering how it drinks with other food. Because unlike wine, you can keep an opened bottle of sake in your fridge for weeks. So, after your night out, screw the cap back on and keep revisiting the bottle. I'll keep a bottle open in my fridge for a month. Its flavors will change, but not to the severity of wine. And, if you've let it go too long and no longer like it, cook with it. That will extend the life and the value of the bottle. Never hesitate to cook with the good stuff.

When you're buying retail, level up. The marketing industry hasn't hit sake as hard as wine (there's no celebrity-made sake, for example). When you're spending more, you're usually getting a higher-labor, better-quality product.

Otoko (the tiny sake cups) are small for a reason. It's a non-verbal gesture of gratitude for who you're sharing with that you're always pouring for one another, not yourself. That said, don't sweat the glasses when you're just getting started on your sake journey: Whatever you love drinking out of works.

So, pair sake with your next good meal. Be fearless!

GO OUT FOR MAKI, STAY HOME FOR HAND ROLLS

As told to by **Nick Bognar**, veteran sushi chef and chef-owner of Indo in St. Louis.

If you're just getting started making sushi at home, hand rolls are the most fun. I love setting myself up on the couch for a movie with all my components on the coffee table. I have my seaweed, rice, my bottle of Kewpie mayo, eel sauce, ponzu, some crab, some avocado, some cucumber, some Japanese pickles, or even tofu. Cleanup is a cinch; I just lid up my Tupperware and then I can do it again tomorrow.

Hand rolls are great for a party, too. Lay out some dishes you know you make well along with good nori (look for seaweed labeled for sushi), sushi rice, fillings, and any condiments you like. Get your friends around the table to converse and make hand rolls all night long with some bottles of wine. Make them try what you made and vice versa. It's way more chill than trying to roll perfect maki.

When it comes to selecting fish, find a reliable fishmonger. If you've got a line on some good fish, make a sashimi platter and lay it out with your hand roll components. The sashimi can go right in there. You can also find good fish at the grocery store if you stick with mainstream options like salmon and tuna. A popular fish from a busy store won't have sat out for long. The fish should look good and smell clean. Ikura is a soigné upgrade, as is smoked trout roe, which is sometimes easier to find. Don't forget vegetables, like avocado and cucumber. (If you do want to do proper maki rolls, practice with cucumber.)

If you find that even hand rolls are too much trouble, just direct all your ingredients and energy into a rice bowl.

A Sushi Moment

- **Far East Side**
  BAR GOTO · NEW YORK, NY

- **Sushi Rice**
  SUSHI NOZ · NEW YORK, NY

- **Kanpachi Sashimi with Shiro Ponzu Sauce and Sesame Brittle**
  INDO · ST. LOUIS, MO

Sake Is Great for Cocktails

There are a few things to think about when you're building a cocktail with sake. It's umami-rich, which means it can stand up to other flavorful ingredients, but it's not terribly acidic, which means you'll want to either balance your drink with something like citrus or lean all the way into the smoothness. It's lower ABV, too, which means sake is great for session drinks like spritzes (page 93). You can swap sake in for gin and make a sake tonic or a split-base martini (page 206). You can go for a more grownup sake bomb by making a shandy (page 221).

Bar owner and cocktail expert **Kenta Goto** uses sake in many of the cocktails at Bar Goto, his refined, Japanese-inspired bar on the Lower East Side. The Far East Side is one of the bar's most popular drinks. It's a spin on a Southside cocktail, featuring sake and tequila rather than gin. At the bar, he garnishes the cocktail with a couple dashes of house-made yuzu bitters, which we're skipping for this home-friendly version.

FAR EAST SIDE

BAR GOTO · NEW YORK CITY
Serves 1

2 ounces (60 ml) Dassai Junmai Daiginjo sake

¾ ounce (22 ml) St-Germain elderflower liqueur

½ ounce (14 ml) Olmeca Altos Plata tequila

¼ ounce (7 ml) lemon juice

4 shiso leaves

* * * * *

Combine the sake, elderflower liqueur, tequila, lemon juice, and 3 of the shiso leaves in a mixing tin, then muddle the shiso leaves. Fine-strain into a mixing glass and stir with ice cubes.

Strain into a martini glass and garnish with the remaining shiso leaf.

Sushi Rice,
Kanpachi Sashimi,
Far East Side Cocktail

SUSHI RICE

Sushi is defined by the relationship between *neta*, the fish, and *shari*, the rice. The fish certainly gets the glory, but the rice—perfectly cooked, perfectly seasoned—is what separates the great from the sublime. At his stylish, high-end omakase spot in Manhattan, chef Nozomu Abe hews close to the Edomae traditions that form the backbone of contemporary high-end sushi. For his rice vinegar, he opts for the traditional ratio of 80 percent white rice vinegar and 20 percent akazu red vinegar. For accuracy when making this blend, he recommends using a scale. You'll also see that this recipe calls for equal parts water and rice for cooking, which makes things easier if you need to scale this up to serve a crowd. Last, although the stovetop will work, don't hesitate to use your rice cooker. You're aiming for as close to perfection as you can get; the machine will help you get there. You could use this to make hand rolls (see page 142) or serve it with sashimi and pickled vegetables.

Makes about **4** cups

6½ tablespoons (95 ml) white rice vinegar

1½ tablespoons red akazu vinegar

3 tablespoons (35 g) sugar

1 tablespoon (17 g) salt

2½ cups (375 g) sushi rice

In a mixing bowl, combine the vinegar mixture, sugar, and salt. Adjust to taste and set aside.

To wash the rice, place it into a mixing bowl and rinse with cold water. Strain water and put the rice back into the mixing bowl. Repeat this process until the water has a light cloudiness (not clear, as a light cloudiness preserves the rice's natural flavor). Depending on the rice, this will usually take three to five rinses. After the last rinse, strain and replace the rice in the mixing bowl again with fresh water. Let sit for 30 minutes, then strain slowly over the sink, letting it rest in the strainer for 10 to 15 minutes. Using a 1:1 water to rice ratio (2½ cups/375 g rice with 2½ cups/600 ml water, here), transfer the rice to a rice cooker. When done cooking, let the rice sit in the rice cooker or pot for about 5 minutes to allow some of the moisture to evaporate. Then transfer the rice to a larger bowl. The rice should be fluffy, moist, and slightly sticky.

Add the vinegar mixture to the rice gradually, fluffing the rice with a rice paddle as you go to ensure even coverage. Continue fluffing the rice as needed until fully mixed. If the rice is still hot, let it cool down to body temperature before using.

KANPACHI SASHIMI
with Shiro Ponzu Sauce and Sesame Brittle

Chef Nick Bognar grew up in his family's restaurants in St. Louis. In 2019, he partnered with his parents to open Indo, a slick night-out spot that pulls from his experiences running the sushi bar at his family's restaurant Nippon Tei, his time working at experimental Texas sushi mainstay Uchiko, and his travels through Thailand and Cambodia. That means sashimi on the Indo menu isn't just sashimi: It's studded with candied garlic, or paired with coconut jam, or, in the case of this kanpachi sashimi, sitting on a bed of supremed orange segments and topped with sesame brittle. If you are serving this to guests and don't want the pressure of slicing sashimi in front of an audience, you can slice the sashimi, wrap it, put it in the fridge, and then plate it right before guests arrive.

Serves **4**

For the shiro ponzu sauce:
½ cup (120 ml) mirin
½ cup (120 ml) sake
½ cup (120 ml) yuzu juice
½ cup (120 ml) white soy sauce

For the sesame brittle:
¾ cup (149 g) sugar
¼ cup (86 g) honey
¼ teaspoon salt
1 cup (142 g) sesame seeds
2 teaspoons butter
¼ teaspoon baking soda

For the sashimi:
1 pound (455 g) kanpachi loin
4 oranges, sliced into supremes
2 jalapeños, thinly sliced
2 scallions, thinly sliced, green parts only
Olive oil
Finishing salt

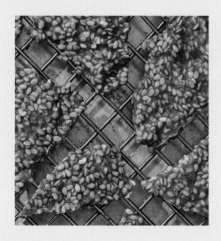

To make the shiro ponzu sauce, combine the mirin and sake in a small saucepan and bring to a boil over high heat. Reduce the heat to medium-high and reduce by half. Transfer to a small bowl and set aside to cool. Add the yuzu and white soy sauce and set aside.

To make the sesame brittle, in a small saucepan, combine the sugar, honey, salt, and 1 tablespoon water and cook over medium-high heat until a thick slurry is formed. Add the sesame seeds and stir constantly until mixture reaches 300°F (150°C) on a candy thermometer. Remove from the heat, then add the butter and baking soda. Pour onto a high-heat silicone mat or parchment paper that has been sprayed with cooking spray. (If using a silicone mat, cool completely.) When cooled, break up the sesame brittle into small pieces with a knife or quickly pulse in a food processor. (If using parchment paper, peel the brittle off while it's still a little warm.)

To prepare the sashimi, if the loin of fish has the skin on, use a very sharp chef's knife or slicer to remove the skin: Pull the very corner of the loin, from the tail end, and place your knife in between the flesh and the skin. Get a firm grip on the skin with your off hand. Use a towel to grip the skin better. In one smooth motion, pull the skin toward yourself with your off hand and push your knife forward, keeping the blade as flat as possible. Try not to force the knife or change the angle. If the skin breaks, flip over the loin and slice off the remaining skin.

Pat the fish dry with paper towels and slice into sashimi-size pieces. You want to use the whole knife: Start at the very heel of your knife and pull it back across to get all the way to the tip. When you feel you're about to finish, push hard with your pointer finger and finish slicing with more pressure to get a clean cut. Do not saw. You want a nice full pull. The sashimi should be relatively thin, about ⅛ inch (3 mm) thick and about 1 inch × 1 inch (2.5 cm × 2.5 cm).

Place the orange supremes in small serving bowls. Line the slices of kanpachi onto the oranges. Then fill the base of the bowl with the shiro ponzu sauce.

Season the kanpachi with salt. Put the jalapeño slices onto the kanpachi. Top the fish with a sprinkle of sesame brittle, then garnish with the scallions. Finish with a light drizzle of olive oil and a little finishing salt.

HOW CHICKEN ACHIEVED MUST-ORDER STATUS

In the early 1980s, the late chef Judy Rodgers's Zuni Café in San Francisco started offering hearth-roasted chicken for two. The restaurant had just installed its now-famous wood-burning oven, and, as Rodgers told Eater back in 2013, "the circumstances and the inspiration collided." She had been thinking about her time living in France, when a spit-roasted chicken could easily and reliably feed her for days—and she wanted to ensure the restaurant didn't become a pizzeria. The Zuni Café chicken for two established roast chicken as a restaurant-worthy meal. In the years that followed, a slew of roasted birds became icons in their own right: the salsa verde–topped roast chicken at Jams and then Barbuto; Balthazar's poulet for two; the A.O.C. Ode to Zuni roast chicken in Los Angeles; the foie-gras-stuffed-and-basted beauty at the NoMad.

Fried chicken also landed front and center on menus. At Momofuku Noodle Bar in New York's East Village, chef David Chang made a special event out of fried chicken in 2009. Diners raced to nab a limited number of reservations for a feast of Southern-inspired and Korean-style fried chicken. Fried chicken became a hip restaurant calling card. At Red Rooster in Harlem, chef Marcus Samuelsson pays thoroughly modern homage to classic Southern fried yardbird, while at Toki in Portland, Oregon, chef Peter Cho goes gonzo, topping twice-fried wings with ramen seasoning. Of course, specialists still, um, rule the roost, so don't sleep on digging into a plate of Nong's Khao Man Gai, where chicken is part of nearly every component on the plate.

Let the work these chefs have put into orchestrating thrilling chicken dishes make your own chicken dinners that much better.

ZUNI'S "CHICKEN FOR TWO" on Your Grill

ZUNI CAFÉ
San Francisco, California

◇◇

The Zuni Café roast chicken for two is perhaps the single most famous chicken entree in the entire country. On the menu at the legendary San Francisco restaurant since the eighties, it boasts wonderfully salty, crispy skin and impossibly juicy meat alongside a bread salad with greens tossed in simple vinaigrette *and* all the pan drippings from the chicken's time in the open hearth. The bird is also one of the most iconic cookbook recipes; Zuni's late chef Judith Rodgers detailed the process over several pages in *The Zuni Café Cookbook*. The multiday salting process is absolutely essential to achieving the proper result. Zuni's former executive chef Nate Norris and chef Ben Cohen developed this grilled version to help achieve that flame-touched feeling without a wood-burning oven. Grilling causes the chicken's juices to fall directly onto the fire, so you'll want to rest the chicken on a tray so you can add them to your salad for that signature Zuni flavor.

Serves **2** to **4**

◇◇◇◇◇◇◇◇◇◇◇◇◇◇◇◇◇◇◇◇◇◇◇◇◇◇◇◇◇◇   ◇◇

1 small chicken, 2¾ to 3¼ pounds (1.25 to 1.5 kg)

Fine sea salt

8 ounces (225 g) slightly stale, chewy, open-crumb bread (not sourdough)

Freshly ground black pepper

10 tablespoons (150 ml) mild olive oil, plus more for brushing the bread and cooking the scallions

2 tablespoons Champagne vinegar or white wine vinegar

1 tablespoon dried currants

1 teaspoon red wine vinegar

1 tablespoon warm water

¼ cup (26 g) thinly slivered scallions, white and green parts

2 to 3 cloves garlic, peeled

2 tablespoons pine nuts

¼ cup (60 g) lightly seasoned salted chicken stock

2½ to 3 cups (43 g) bitter salad greens, such as arugula, frisée, or mustard greens

At least 24 hours and up to 72 hours in advance, trim the chicken and season with salt. While the chicken is resting, think about purchasing bread to dry out for your salad.

When ready to cook, spatchcock the chicken to make it easier to grill. Trim the larger sections of fat around the cavity at the top of the breast near the wings. Using poultry shears, cut closely along both sides of the backbone to remove it. Lay the chicken with its breast facing upward and fold the legs so that the drumsticks run parallel and closely to one another in the center of the bird and the thighs point outward. Use the heel of your hand to apply firm pressure to crack the sternum by pressing on the upper middle area between the breasts and push to further crack the breastbone where it meets the wings. The goal is to create as flat a chicken as possible.

Pat the chicken dry with paper towels. Use 3½ grams salt per 1 pound (455 g) chicken. The thicker sections of muscle, such as the breast, will need more salt than the wings or drumsticks. Distribute the salt accordingly and season with black pepper. Tuck the wing tips underneath the back so the "elbow" points toward the legs and the "wrist" points toward the top of the chicken.

About 1 hour before you plan to eat, heat up your grill. Propane gas will do, but hardwood charcoal is best. Trim the thicker bottom crust off the bread, taking care not to lose any of the bread's interior. Trim most of the top and edge crust (save all these crusts for breadcrumbs or bread pudding) and lightly brush the trimmed surfaces with olive oil. Set this aside while the grill continues to heat up.

Continued

In a small bowl, whisk the olive oil and Champagne vinegar to make a vinaigrette. Season with salt and pepper.

Place the currants in a small bowl and pour the red wine vinegar and warm water over them. Set aside.

In a small skillet, heat a small amount of olive oil over medium-low heat. Add the scallions and garlic and cook until softened and lightly aromatic, about 5 minutes. Set aside.

Once the grill is heated, toast the bread on all sides, so it's lightly crisp and beginning to color. Allow it to cool, then tear it into irregular bite-size pieces 2 to 3 inches (5 to 7 cm) in size. Toss the torn bread with ¼ cup (60 ml) of the prepared vinaigrette and set aside.

Arrange the coals so that you have space to cook the chicken approximately halfway over them. Clean and lightly oil the grill surface, then place the chicken onto it, skin side down, with the breast over the coals. Arrange the grill cover so it is slightly ajar and the vents are open. Cook for about 10 minutes, until the skin releases from the grill and is browning. Rotate the chicken so the legs and thighs are over the coals and cook for about 10 minutes more, until the leg skin is browning. Turn the chicken skin with the breast over the coals and cook for about 10 minutes more. Last, turn the chicken skin side down to re-crisp the skin for another 2 to 3 minutes. The breast temperature should be about 154°F (67°C). Remove from the grill and rest on a rimmed sheet pan for 5 minutes before cutting.

While the chicken is cooking, begin to build the bread salad. In the center of a sheet of heavy-duty aluminum foil, place the toasted bread, scallion-garlic mixture, soaked currants, pine nuts, and chicken stock. Wrap tightly to ensure it does not leak. Once the chicken has cooked for about 15 minutes, place the package in a low heat area of the grill. Cook for 10 minutes, then turn the package over and cook for another 10 minutes. At this point your chicken should be cooked, rested, and ready to cut.

Place the chicken skin side up on a cutting surface. Find the seam between the breast and the thigh and cut along it to remove each thigh and leg. Cut through the joint of each leg to separate the drumstick and the thigh. Slice through the breast on one side of the sternum until the blade reaches the breastbone. Ensure the knife is perpendicular to the cutting board and apply firm pressure to cut the rest of the way through. Repeat on the other breast. Using the same technique of slicing through the meat and firmly chopping through the bone, cut each breast in half crosswise.

Scrape any accumulated juice into a medium mixing bowl, open the aluminum foil package, and empty the contents into the bowl. Add the greens and the remaining vinaigrette. Toss everything together and taste for balanced acidity and full seasoning. Arrange the bread salad in the center of a large plate, reserving about half of the greens. Add the chicken in pieces around the bread salad, and then arrange the remaining greens over the chicken, letting pieces peek out. Serve immediately.

Your Party Needs a Porrón

As told to by Pinch Chinese wine director **Miguel de Leon**.

A porrón is a Spanish drinking vessel made from durable glass that originally hails from Catalonia. It's halfway between a pitcher and a straw. It's built for sharing, with drinkers pouring wine from the spout into their mouths without touching their lips to the glass. Your guests can have a sip here or there; it's not a wine bong, nobody has to chug. It's also a life hack: Having a porrón means not having to wash glasses after a party, and it looks cool on the table without taking up a ton of real estate.

No one will be good at drinking from the spout—that's the point. It's fun, it's communal, and it's a way to have a restaurant-y wine experience that is *not* boring. And who doesn't love a photo of someone successfully drinking from a porrón?

You can serve anything in there. Traditionally, it would be used for cider, piquette, txakoli, or cava—something light and refreshing. You could do Riesling, Grüner Veltliner, or even a chilled red. For a more raucous element at the restaurant, we'll do cocktails. At home, I'll put water in our porrón. It's way more fun than a Yeti, and for a party, it is a great reminder to hydrate.

How to Roast a Chicken

As told to by chef **Kate Williams**, who charmed Detroit with her Lady of the House roast chicken at her restaurant of the same name and at Karl's.

People are afraid of roasting chicken, but they shouldn't be. The easiest place to start is to make sure the bird is *very* dry. Season it with salt, pepper, and maybe some dried herbs and let it dry out in the fridge for a few hours or overnight. This will get you crispy skin and more flavor. Put the chicken in a heavy pan (I often use my stainless steel All-Clad, but a cast-iron works, too). Trussing doesn't need to be fancy: Just tie the legs together above the breast and tuck the wings under. To cook, you really can set it and forget it in a 450°F (230°C) oven. An instant-read digital thermometer is your friend: Take the chicken out once it reaches an internal temperature of 145°F (62°C) and let it rest for 15 minutes, during which it will continue to come up. That's the basic technique, and you can build from there.

To start upgrading, you can add lemon and thyme into the cavity. You could add onions and potatoes to the pan under the bird, so that they cook in the chicken's juices. You could make a compound butter—maybe garlic and rosemary—and rub it under the skin of the breast before cooking it, and as it melts it will flavor the bird and anything else in the pan. You could use the pan drippings to sauté greens or zucchini. You could also make a quick pan sauce: After removing the chicken, pour a little white wine into the pan and scrape up any stuck-on bits with your wooden spoon. Add chopped shallots, tarragon, a squeeze of lemon, and some butter for a delicious sauce to drizzle over your chicken. Add flour and chicken stock, too, and you've made a gravy in a matter of minutes while your chicken is resting. These upgrades can make it feel more special for company, but even a simple roast chicken is a very welcoming, easy-to-love main course.

GRILLED CHICKEN AND COCONUT SAMBAL with Herb and Cabbage Slaw

After a round of pandan-laced rum slushies and shoestring curry fries, the main event arrives at the table: a beautifully charred game hen half, nestled against a small mountain of cabbage slaw and a dish of yellow coconut sambal. This is Oma's Hideaway, the hit restaurant from husband-wife team Mariah Pisha-Duffly and chef Thomas Pisha-Duffly. The menu meanders through inspirations plucked from Thomas Pisha-Duffly's childhood—the Malaysian-Chinese cooking of his grandmother (the restaurant's namesake oma), the nostalgic comforts of a cheeseburger—as well as looking to the hawker fare of Singapore and Malaysia. This dish is an ode to the latter, in particular the coconut sambal, a jammy dip you'll want to use with grilled meats, on top of rice, in a salad, basically everywhere. We've gone ahead and subbed in chicken for game hen, because it's a bit easier and feeds more people. The restaurant is known for its house-party vibe: Consider making this for your next party and serve it with guava–pineapple juice Jell-O shots to bring the Oma's attitude home.

→ NOTES: There are a few interventions in this recipe to make it more home-friendly. Oma's has a charcoal oven; using a grill will get you some of those smoky flavors.

Oma's recipe specifically uses game hens (aka tiny chickens) and serves a half; we've scaled the recipe to a whole spatchcocked chicken for ease at home. If you do want to go with game hen, keep an eye on your cooking time, since a game hen is smaller and therefore will cook faster than a standard chicken.

For the chicken and brine:
1 stalk lemongrass

¼ cup (76 g) salt

1½ tablespoons sugar

3 tablespoons ground turmeric

1 makrut lime leaf

1 (3-pound/1.3 kg) chicken, spatchcocked (see page 151 for instructions or ask your butcher)

For the hen dust:
2 teaspoons ground turmeric

1¼ tablespoons garlic powder

1 tablespoon onion powder

2 teaspoons paprika

1 teaspoon ground fenugreek

2 teaspoons ground cumin

1 tablespoon ground coriander

1 tablespoon ground black pepper

1 teaspoon red chile flakes

1 teaspoon celery seed

For the coconut sambal:
3 stalks (63 g) lemongrass

6 cloves garlic

2 tablespoons chopped shallots

1½ teaspoons sliced Thai bird's eye chile

2 tablespoons candlenuts or cashews

2 tablespoons chopped peeled fresh ginger

2 tablespoons chopped peeled fresh galangal

¼ cup (5 g) makrut lime leaves

1¾ tablespoons yellow curry paste

1 tablespoon ground turmeric

2 tablespoons chopped peeled fresh turmeric

¼ cup (60 ml) coconut oil

¼ cup (60 ml) sweet soy sauce

½ cup (120 ml) coconut milk, plus more for making the sauce

½ cup (120 ml) coconut cream

2¼ teaspoons sugar

½ teaspoon tamarind concentrate

For the salad:
¾ cup (180 ml) fish sauce

¾ cup (180 ml) lime juice

¾ cup (150 g) sugar

2 to 3 Thai bird's eye chiles, or more to taste

2 tablespoons rice wine vinegar

6 cups (420 g) thinly sliced napa cabbage

1 medium red onion, thinly sliced

Chopped fresh mint, basil, and cilantro leaves

Salt and freshly ground black pepper

For the sambal sauce:
1 cup (240 ml) coconut milk

1 tablespoon sugar

2 tablespoons lime juice

Salt

Continued

To make the brine, cut off the bottom inch of the lemongrass stalk and discard (or save for stock). Peel the first layer and discard. Smash the lemongrass with the side of a knife, then chop it. Combine 2 quarts (2 L) water, the salt, sugar, and turmeric in a medium pot and bring to a boil over high heat. Add the lemongrass and lime leaf, remove from the heat, and let cool to room temperature, then transfer to an airtight container (large enough to fit the spatchcocked chicken in the refrigerator to chill). The brine can be made and refrigerated up to 1 day in advance.

To brine the chicken, place the spatchcocked chicken into the container of brine and make sure the brine covers the chicken completely. (You can also use a large zip-top bag.) Place the brined chicken in the refrigerator overnight, or for up to 12 hours.

To make the hen dust, whisk together the turmeric, garlic powder, onion powder, paprika, fenugreek, cumin, coriander, black pepper, red chile flakes, and celery seed in a small bowl. Store in an airtight container for up to 1 week.

To make the coconut sambal, cut off the bottom inch of the lemongrass stalk and discard (or save for stock). Peel the first layer and discard. Smash the lemongrass with the side of a knife, then chop it. Combine the lemongrass, garlic, shallots, bird's eye chiles, candlenuts, ginger, galangal, lime leaf, curry paste, ground turmeric, and fresh turmeric in a blender or food processor. Blend until it turns into a smooth paste; if the mixture looks too dry, add a little water as needed.

In a medium saucepan, heat the coconut oil over medium heat, add the curry paste mixture, and cook until fragrant. Add the sweet soy sauce, coconut milk, coconut cream, and sugar and cook the sambal over low heat for about 20 minutes to allow the flavors to develop. Turn off the heat, add the tamarind concentrate, and cool.

Remove the chicken from the brine (discard the brine) and allow it to air-dry on a roasting rack set on a sheet tray for about 30 minutes.

Meanwhile, preheat the oven to 375°F (190°C) or prepare a charcoal grill.

Season both sides of the chicken with the hen dust. Cook the chicken for about 45 minutes, until an instant-read thermometer inserted in the breast registers 165°F (73°C), basting the chicken with the coconut sambal several times while it cooks. You should have enough leftover to create the coconut sambal sauce.

Meanwhile, make the salad dressing by whisking the fish sauce, lime juice, sugar, chiles, and rice vinegar in a small bowl until the ingredients are incorporated. In another large bowl, combine the sliced napa cabbage, red onions, and chopped mint, basil, and cilantro. Pour the dressing over and toss the salad, taste, and season with salt and pepper before serving.

To make the coconut sambal sauce, thin out the remaining sambal with coconut milk (you might not need the whole cup—you are trying to loosen it and make a saucy consistency). Add the sugar, lime juice, and a pinch of salt. Taste for seasoning and adjust. Set aside until ready to serve.

Serve the chicken with the cabbage salad and sambal sauce on the side.

Glassware 101

Restaurants put a lot of thought and effort into their glassware. Many of our experts recommend building out your personal collection via thrifting, whether at estate sales, vintage shops, or online. You can explore and experiment without committing to a major investment, and then focus your spending on the glassware you find yourself using the most.

WINEGLASSES

If you're just getting started, focus on starting with a really good "all-purpose" or "universal" wineglass—you can also use these for spritzes, egg-white cocktails, and sake. Opt for stemmed glasses, which make it easier to nose the wine in the glass and protect the wine from your hands' heat. Pick according to your budget and, if you like entertaining, get a set of six or eight. The somms we spoke to like Schott Zwiesel, Jancis Robinson, Gabriel-Glas, and Zalto, if you're wanting to upgrade from your starter set of glasses. If you're already pretty into wine, round out your collection with Burgundy and Bordeaux glasses to let your reds properly breathe. Champagne and other sparkling wines are great in a simple white wine glass, so don't feel obligated to get flutes.

ROCKS GLASSES

Also called old-fashioned glasses, these heavy-bottomed glasses can hold a large ice cube, making them a versatile cocktail vessel. Typically used for spirit-forward drinks like old-fashioneds, negronis, and sazeracs, they can also be used for margaritas, sours, and punches. They're also a good option for sipping spirits like whiskey and Scotch neat or on the rocks. If you're ready to invest, seek out Riedel and Rona, and scan thrift stores for estate crystal. Technically anything you can drink in a highball can go in a rocks glass, but do also consider adding highballs to your cabinet for serving gin and tonics, whiskey highballs, and other tall drinks (cocktails made with mixers like juice or soda, like fizzes), and for juice and water.

COUPES

Stemmed glasses like these are meant for cocktails that are served "up" (stirred or shaken with ice but strained to serve without ice), since the stem ensures your hands won't heat things up as you hold it. They're great for martinis, and unlike martini glasses, coupes have curved sides, which makes them less likely to spill. Coupes are an easy way to bring some drama to your collection—they're so eye catching, you won't even need to garnish your drink. You could opt for traditional coupes (these are especially fun to source secondhand) or try out a Nick and Nora glass, which is a bit smaller. Most of the go-to brands mentioned above make lovely coupes, too; Rona is a particular favorite for Nick and Nora glasses. If you do want to go for the traditional V-shaped martini glass, look for Minners Classic Cocktails martini glasses.

Recommended by: John deBary, Natasha Bermudez, Miguel de Leon, Caroline Styne, Helen Johannesen, Seung Hee Lee, Molly Austad, Alyssa Mikiko DiPasquale, Michael Roper

---

EXTRAS

- If you love mezcal or tequila, start collecting clay copitas.

- If you love sake, look for beautiful ceramic ochoko cups.

- If you love beer, stock tall Pilsner glasses, nonic pint glasses for IPAs, porters, and stouts, and goblets for Belgian styles.

KHAO MAN GAI

NONG'S KHAO MAN GAI
Portland, Oregon

Chef Nong Poonsukwattana moved to Portland, Oregon, from her native Bangkok with $70 and a single suitcase. Now her first name is synonymous with her signature dish, khao man gai, the Thai variation of Hainanese chicken rice, which she's served from food carts around town since 2009. The success of the dish, she'll happily tell you, relies on its balance. She layers flavor by infusing each component with parts of the other (the liquid she uses to poach her chicken becomes the "super stock" she uses to cook her rice, which itself was first toasted in chicken fat). This pure, restorative comfort food makes Nong's food cart any Eater staffer's first stop in Portland. She now sells bottles of her sauce online, a great shortcut.

For the chicken:

4 chicken leg quarters (legs and thighs)

1 teaspoon salt

2 teaspoons sugar

1 head garlic, cloves smashed and peeled

1 cup (228 g) sliced peeled fresh ginger

3 pandan leaves (optional)

For the rice:

1 cup (240 g) chicken skins

2 tablespoons chopped garlic

⅓ cup (45 g) chopped shallots

⅓ cup (60 g) minced peeled fresh ginger

3 cups (600 g) jasmine rice

3 cups (720 ml) chicken broth

3 pandan leaves

For the sauce:

¼ cup (44 g) fermented soybean

3 tablespoons white vinegar

3 tablespoons Thai light soy sauce

3 tablespoons simple syrup

2½ tablespoons chopped garlic

2½ tablespoons chopped peeled fresh ginger

3 tablespoons pickled garlic and liquid

2½ tablespoons sweet black soy sauce

1½ tablespoons chopped Thai chile

For the soup:

4 cups (960) chicken broth, from cooking the chicken

2 cups (230 g) Chinese winter squash

2 tablespoons soy sauce

1 teaspoon ground white pepper

2 tablespoons chopped fresh cilantro

2 tablespoons chopped scallion, green and white parts

To make the chicken, in a pot large enough to hold the chicken, bring 2 quarts (2 L) water to a boil. Add the chicken, salt, sugar, garlic, and ginger and pandan leaves, if using, and bring back up to a boil, then turn down the heat and simmer for about 30 minutes, until the internal temperature of the chicken reaches 165°F (75°C). Turn off the heat, and once it's cooled enough to handle, strain the broth and set it aside. Set the chicken aside separately.

To make the rice, heat up the chicken skins in a large skillet over medium heat, allowing the fat to render. It's done when all of the fat is rendered, leaving you about 2 tablespoons fat. Remove the skins from the pan, then add the garlic, shallots, and ginger to the hot fat and cook until golden and fragrant, 5 to 7 minutes. Add the rice to the pan and stir to lightly toast the rice, about 2 minutes.

Transfer to a rice cooker and add the chicken broth and pandan leaves. Cook according to the machine's instructions. When it's finished cooking, leave the rice cooker on warm for about 10 minutes to encourage the residual moisture to evaporate.

Alternatively, if you don't have a rice cooker, transfer the toasted rice and the fat to a medium pot with raised sides. Add the chicken broth, cover with the lid, and cook over medium heat for 8 to 10 minutes, until the rice absorbs the liquid. Check to make sure the liquid has been absorbed, then quickly return the lid to the pot, turn off the heat, and let rest, covered, for about 10 minutes, until the rice is fully cooked and tender.

To make the sauce, combine the fermented soybean, white vinegar, light soy sauce, simple syrup, garlic, ginger, pickled garlic, sweet black soy sauce, and Thai chile in a blender. Blend until well incorporated; the sauce should have texture (it does not need to be totally pureed). The sauce can be made up to 1 day in advance; store in an airtight container in the fridge.

To make the soup, pour the broth into a large pot and bring to a boil over high heat. Add the squash, lower the heat, and simmer for about 20 minutes, until tender. When you are almost ready to serve, add the soy sauce, white pepper, cilantro, and scallion.

You can serve everything family style with the rice, soup, and chicken served in bowls and platters and some sauce on the side, or, if you're plating individual portions, place each chicken quarter on a plate with rice and serve with a bowl of hot soup and a single serving of sauce.

CHICKEN AND CHEESE CURD BRATWURST

It doesn't get more Midwest than cheese curds and sausage or, at chef Gavin Kaysen's Spoon and Stable, cheese curd–stuffed sausage. The dish shows what the team at his Minneapolis flagship does best: coax the flavors of Minnesota out with beautifully plated dishes in the main dining room and gussied up favorites at the bar. A staple of the bar menu, these links come with house-made hot dog buns, pickled shallots, and Dijon aioli. At home, you can go ahead and get store-bought buns, quick-pickle some shallot or onion if you'd like (use a mandoline to get those nice, thin slices), and stir some good Dijon into mayo for a quick condiment. Make the setup easy because you're keeping your eyes on the prize: homemade brats.

Makes 8 to 10 sausages

2 pounds (910 g) ground skin-on chicken thigh meat

1½ tablespoons salt, or more to taste

½ teaspoon sugar

1 teaspoon ground black pepper

¼ teaspoon ground coriander

½ teaspoon garlic powder

½ teaspoon smoked paprika

¼ teaspoon cayenne pepper

¾ cup (157 g) small-diced cheese curds (see Notes)

5 feet (1.5 m) hog casings, rinsed and soaked overnight in water (see Notes)

→ NOTES: Depending on where you live, you might be able to find cheese curds at the grocery store, but if not, there are plenty of vendors (in particular from Wisconsin!) selling online.

Sausage casing can be found at some grocery stores, or you can order online. But an even better option is to buy from your butcher, who can also help you grind the skin-on chicken thighs, plus give you pointers if you'll be making sausage for the first time with this recipe (see page 182).

To make the filling, place the ground chicken in the bowl of a stand mixer fitted with the paddle attachment. Add the salt, sugar, black pepper, coriander, garlic powder, smoked paprika, cayenne, and diced cheese curds. Mix the meat on low speed and continue to paddle until the spices are thoroughly mixed and the meat becomes tacky and bound, about 1 minute.

Taste for seasoning by frying a small piece of the sausage meat in a hot frying pan. Add salt to the mixture if needed. The sausage filling can be stored in the fridge for up to 3 days or frozen for up to 2 months.

To stuff the sausage, place the chicken sausage mixture in a sausage stuffer. With the medium-size hog casing tube, thread the casing over the tube. Take care to avoid tearing. When all the casing has been threaded, tie a knot on one end, then turn the crank to stuff the sausage into the casing. If using a KitchenAid sausage stuffer attachment, turn the mixer speed to low. Use your free hand to keep the casing taut while it fills with the meat. Don't fill the sausages too tight or they will burst when you form the links. It's better to stay on the looser side to be safe. You can always make it tighter later. Continue until all of the sausage meat has been forced into the casing.

Starting on the knotted end of the sausage, form 5-inch (13 cm) long links by pinching the sausage and twisting it over until it becomes plump and full. It should still be slightly soft, or it will burst during cooking. Repeat this step, alternating the direction you twist for each link. When you get to the end, make a knot to secure the meat. The sausage may be stored in the refrigerator for 3 to 4 days or frozen for up to 2 months.

To cook the brats, grill the links slowly on a gas or solid-fuel grill until the internal temperature reaches 160°F (71°C).

Caribbean Cheese and Chicken Patties, Fried Yardbird, Wings with "Essence of Ramen" Dust

CARIBBEAN CHEESE AND CHICKEN PATTIES

THE JERK SHACK
San Antonio, Texas

Amid the wonderful Tex-Mex restaurants of San Antonio, the Jerk Shack is a proudly Caribbean island. Chef Nicola Blaque draws from her childhood in Jamaica, offering an enticing menu promising succulent jerk chicken, killer wings, curry, empanadas, coco rolls, rice and peas, and crackling, plus tropical-feeling sauces on the side. Blaque says the savory stuffed pastries known as patties are both "quintessentially Caribbean" and the perfect way to help people who "need to remix what they have on hand." And so, she developed these Jerk Shack–style patties with a home cook's leftover chicken in mind. You can make this even easier if you go for a store-bought jerk spice blend in your marinade, and, for an extra dose of practicality, Blaque notes that these freeze well—you can pop them right in the oven from frozen on particularly harried days and wind up with a taste of the breezy Jerk Shack dining room.

Makes 12 patties

To make the dough, in the bowl of a stand mixer fitted with the hook attachment, combine the flour, salt, white pepper, sugar, nutritional yeast, and turmeric and mix on low to medium speed to combine. Add the shortening and butter and mix until a breadcrumb-like consistency is formed. Add the ice water in increments until a dough is formed. Remove the dough from the bowl and form it into a ball with your hands. The dough will be slightly sticky. Cover with plastic wrap and refrigerate for 35 minutes.

To make the marinade, combine all the ingredients in a blender with ½ cup (120 ml) water and blend until smooth. Store in an airtight container in the fridge until ready to use, for up to 2 days.

To make the patty filling, combine the chopped rotisserie chicken with the cheese, sour cream, scallions, and ½ cup (120 ml) jerk marinade.

Preheat the oven to 400°F (205°C).

Remove your dough from the refrigerator and cut it into 12 equal pieces. Roll out each piece of dough until round and flat, then use the bottom of the mixing bowl to cut out even circles.

Spoon about 3 tablespoons of the filling on each circle. Spread the filling on one half of the circle but not all the way to the edge. Take the other half of the circle and fold it like a half moon. Take a fork and press the edges together to seal the patty. Repeat with the other circles.

Place the patties on an ungreased baking sheet and bake for 25 to 30 minutes, until the crust begins to look golden and flaky.

Meanwhile, to make the dipping sauce, in a medium bowl, mix all of the ingredients until smooth. Serve the patties with the dipping sauce.

→ **NOTE:** To freeze leftover patties, store in a freezer bag (wrapping individually in parchment paper is helpful but optional). To serve from frozen, warm in an oven or toaster oven.

For the patty dough:
2 cups (240 g) all-purpose flour

1 teaspoon salt

½ teaspoon ground white pepper

½ teaspoon granulated sugar

1 tablespoon nutritional yeast

1 tablespoon ground turmeric or Jamaican curry powder

¼ cup (48 g) cold shortening or lard

½ cup (1 stick/113 g) cold cubed butter

1 to 1½ cups (240 to 360 ml) ice-cold water

For the jerk marinade:
½ bunch Italian parsley

½ bunch thyme (about 8 sprigs), stems removed

½ bunch scallions, whites and greens, roughly chopped

3 cloves garlic, peeled

Peels from ½ lemon

1 habanero chile

1 tablespoon each onion powder, brown sugar, and garlic powder

1 tablespoon salt, or more to taste

1½ teaspoons ground black pepper

½ teaspoon each ground allspice and smoked paprika

¼ teaspoon each ground cinnamon, ground nutmeg, and ground cloves

Pinch of ground cumin

2 tablespoons soy sauce

2 tablespoons olive oil

For the patty filling:
2½ cups (344 g) chopped rotisserie chicken

2 cups (224 g) Colby jack cheese

1 tablespoon sour cream

½ cup (30 g) chopped scallions, white and green parts

½ cup jerk marinade (see above)

For the dipping sauce:
1 cup (235 g) ketchup

1 cup (240 ml) white vinegar

½ cup (170 g) honey

½ cup (120 ml) hot sauce

3 tablespoons jerk marinade (see above)

FRIED YARDBIRD

It takes vision to make a New York City restaurant classic, but that's exactly what chef-restaurateur Marcus Samuelsson and co-founder Andrew Chapman did with their landmark Harlem spot, Red Rooster. Paying tribute to the diverse roots of the historically African American neighborhood and its lasting impact on America's cuisine, the Red Rooster ethos is epitomized by its famous yardbird. At the restaurant, you'll find the signature yardbird tops crispy waffles at brunch; appears as an add-on to radish-and-apple-studded salads; and for a large-format option, it arrives in a magnificent tower, with plenty of cornbread on the side. It's a succulent Southern-style fried chicken, complete with "shake"—Samuelsson's formula for the chicken's seasoning, however, veers from tradition with the inclusion of berbere, a spice blend from his native Ethiopia, that brings plenty of heat and an earthy, herbal punch. Here, Samuelsson riffs on the restaurant's recipe (which he put to paper in the *Red Rooster Cookbook*), adding honey, soy sauce, and lemon as a drizzle to boost the flavor. Samuelsson offers this tip to improve your fried chicken game: "If you want to add an extra layer of flavor to your frying, make sure that the oil has its *own* flavor—you want to season the oil. I like to use rosemary sprigs and garlic. Add it to the hot oil, leave for a few minutes, and take it out before frying your chicken for that additional hit of flavor!"

Serves **4**

For the chicken "shake":

¼ cup (24 g) berbere spice

¼ cup (24 g) hot smoked paprika

2 tablespoons ground cumin

2 tablespoons freshly ground white pepper

2 tablespoons celery salt

1½ teaspoons garlic powder

1½ teaspoons salt

For the chicken brine, marinade, and frying:

1 cup (120 g) salt

4 chicken thighs

4 chicken drumsticks

2 cups (480 ml) buttermilk

¾ cup (180 ml) coconut milk

2 cloves garlic, minced

At least 2 quarts (2 L) peanut oil, for frying

For the dredge:

1 cup (125 g) all-purpose flour

1 cup (160 g) rice flour

¼ cup (45 g) semolina flour

2 tablespoons cornstarch

1 tablespoon freshly ground white pepper

For the drizzle:

1 tablespoon honey

Juice of 1 lemon (1 to 2 tablespoons)

1 tablespoon soy sauce

1 tablespoon peanut oil

To make the chicken "shake," in a small bowl, mix all the ingredients together. Store in an airtight jar out of the light for up to 6 months.

To brine the chicken, put 2 cups (480 ml) water and the salt in a large saucepan over high heat and bring to a simmer. Stir to dissolve the salt, then pour into a large container. Add 6 cups (1.4 L) water and cool to room temperature. Place the chicken in the cooled salt mixture, cover, and refrigerate for at least 1½ hours or up to overnight.

To marinate the chicken, right before taking the brined chicken out of the refrigerator, whisk the buttermilk, coconut milk, garlic, and all but 1 tablespoon of the "shake" together and pour into a 9 × 13-inch (22 × 33 cm) baking dish. Submerge the chicken in the marinade, cover, and refrigerate overnight.

When you're ready to cook, assemble the dredge. Thoroughly mix the all-purpose flour, rice flour, semolina flour, cornstarch, and white pepper in a bowl.

Assemble the drizzle by whisking the honey, lemon juice, soy sauce, and peanut oil in a separate bowl. Set aside.

Continued

Fill a chicken fryer or a Dutch oven one-third full of peanut oil. Set over medium-high heat and heat to 325°F (165°C) as measured on a deep-frying thermometer.

Take the chicken out from the marinade and let any excess drip off. Toss the chicken pieces in the dredge, making sure the pieces are fully coated, and place the dredged chicken pieces on a rack set over a baking sheet. If the coating looks damp, roll it in the flour again.

Fry the chicken in small batches in hot oil for about 20 minutes, until it is a rich brown color and has an internal temperature of 165°F (73°C). Keep an eye on the heat using your deep-frying thermometer and maintain a temperature between 300 and 325°F (150 and 165°C). Transfer the fried yardbird onto a rack set over a baking sheet and season with 1 tablespoon of the chicken "shake." Drizzle with the honey mixture and serve.

What to Drink with Fried Chicken

Great fried chicken deserves a great drink pairing, preferably something light and refreshing to balance it out. Bubbles will cut through the savory fats (there's a reason so many people love Champagne with fried chicken), and you can lean into its saltiness by choosing a drink with some minerality.

Think of **PILSNER** as your go-to beer for pairing with any food. Its clean and spritzy profile works particularly well with fried food.

Recommended by: Hopleaf owner Michael Roper
Go-to bottle: Firestone Walker Pivo Pils

When it comes to wine, anything white and salty works. Seek out **TXAKOLI**, Vinho Verde, Aligoté, Picpoul, or any of the Swiss and Alpine-adjacent wines.

Recommended by: Pinch Chinese wine director Miguel de Leon
Go-to bottle: Ameztoi Txakolina

A white with body and slight sweetness, like **CHENIN BLANC**, especially if you can snag a sparkling one, can match the sometimes subtle spice of fried chicken.

Recommended by: Esmé beverage director Tia Barrett
Go-to bottle: Domaine Huet Vouvray Petillant Brut

If you're in the mood for sake, try spritzing it: Take 2 ounces (60 ml) **YUZU SAKE** and cut it with 4 ounces (120 ml) sparkling water.

Recommended by: Koji Club owner Alyssa Mikiko DiPasquale
Go-to bottle: Joto Yuzu Sake

Fizzy cocktails like **MOJITOS** and **FRENCH 75S** complement the fatty, oily components of a fried chicken dinner.

Recommended by: Over Under bar manager Ashley Richardson

WINGS with "Essence of Ramen" Dust

TOKI
Portland, Oregon

There's only one way to improve the crispy, shattery fried chicken skin of double-fried Korean-style chicken: Dust it with umami-laden, spicy seasoning. These wings first made their appearance at chefs Peter Cho and Sun Young Park's essential Portland restaurant, Han Oak, and are now the star of the menu at the couple's follow-up spot, Toki. The restaurant uses a custom flour blend for their dredge, but for home cooks, Cho likes Bob's Red Mill's gluten-free flour, which will give a similarly crispy effect. And while Cho and his team have devised their own "essence of ramen" seasoning dust, he recommends you use the packets from any instant ramen kit to keep things simple. Cho's favorite for the job—and to have in the house, period—is Nongshim Neoguri spicy seafood flavor. Don't be afraid to use it liberally. These wings are great served with Korean pickles, like sweet-pickled daikon, quick-pickled mu radish, or really anything you like from a Korean grocer like H Mart.

→ **NOTE:** If you want to go full no-cooking mode on this, you could use the ramen packet seasoning on top of takeaway fried chicken or frozen chicken tenders. It won't necessarily have that glassy shell that double-fried Korean-style chicken has, but it will still taste amazing.

Serves **4**

3 tablespoons salt

2 tablespoons sugar

12 whole chicken wings

Peanut oil or other neutral oil, for frying

3 cups (375 g) Bob's Red Mill gluten-free flour

1 tablespoon paprika

1½ cups (360 ml) vodka, plus more if needed

1½ cups (360 ml) makgeolli (Korean unfiltered rice wine), plus more if needed

2 ramen seasoning packets

In a small pot, bring 2 cups (480 ml) water to a boil with the salt and sugar. Once the salt and sugar dissolve, remove from the heat, add 2 cups (480 ml) cool water, and allow to cool.

Place the brine into a zip-top bag with the chicken wings. Push out as much air from the bag as possible, seal, and let it sit anywhere from 12 hours to overnight in the refrigerator.

Set up a chicken fryer or a large Dutch oven on the stovetop. Add enough peanut oil to have 3 to 4 inches (7 to 10 cm) oil in the vessel (enough that the chicken will be fully submerged), set over high heat, and heat until the temperature reaches 350°F (175°C) according to a deep-frying thermometer.

Take the chicken wings out of the brine and set in a colander. Assemble the dry dredge by combining the gluten-free flour and paprika in a large bowl. Coat the chicken wings in the flour and place on a wire rack set over a sheet pan.

Whisk the vodka and makgeolli into the remaining dry dredge. The resulting mixture should be thin, like tempura batter. If batter is too thick or lumpy, add more vodka and makgeolli.

Dip the floured chicken pieces into the batter and fry several of the chicken pieces in the hot oil for about 10 minutes, until the oil's bubbling slows down. Place the cooked chicken pieces on a wire rack set over a sheet pan. Work in small batches, so as not to bring down the temperature, pausing to allow the oil to come back to temperature between batches.

When all the chicken wings are fried, bring the oil back up to temperature and fry the wings again for 5 minutes, or until crisp. Transfer the chicken wings to a sheet pan with a wire rack set on it. Dust with the ramen seasoning.

BOILED WHOLE CHICKEN
with Rice and Soup

MAJORDOMO
Los Angeles, California

At Majordomo, David Chang's perpetually packed LA restaurant, Chang and executive chef Jude Para-Sickels put several dishes on the menu that can serve a whole table. One of them, the boiled chicken, is a must-order—even though Para-Sickels says Chang in particular wanted a boiled chicken on the menu precisely because it is a dish that seems aggressively uncool. But the presentation challenges those expectations—one chicken breast is dressed in vibrant ginger-scallion sauce and the other in fiery red house domojang (a nod to the famous red and green snapper at Contramar in Mexico City), both rest on a bed of gently pan-fried rice, and a chicken noodle soup is served alongside. Para-Sickels has simplified the recipe here; a jar of Momofuku chili crunch is swapped in for domojang, and wonton wrappers for the hand-torn soup noodles. At home, this kind of large-scale cooking project is great for both meal prep (freeze the broth or set aside some meat for salads or stir-fries later in the week) and a dinner party. Don't get too hung up on the plating; it's okay if you, like us, want to do just one topping or the other, or something in between.

Serves **4** to **6**

To make the brine, in a large stockpot, heat 4 cups (960 ml) water and add the salt and sugar. When the salt and sugar are dissolved, remove the pot from the heat and add an additional 4 cups (960) water plus the ice to cool it down. Transfer the cooled brine to a container large enough to submerge the chicken and place the chicken in the refrigerator. Alternatively, you can use a large zip-top bag—whatever you do, the chicken needs to sit in the brine for a full 24 hours.

After the chicken is done brining, bring a large pot of water to a boil. Add the chicken to the pot and boil for 30 minutes. Skim the surface of the boiling water for impurities. Remove the chicken and place in another container or pot and cover with a lid or foil. Allow the chicken to rest until ready to plate. Keep boiling the water that the chicken was cooked in to reduce it until it's flavorful. If you have too much water, you can accelerate the process by taking some of the water out before reducing. If it's not flavorful enough, add chicken bouillon to adjust for flavor.

While the broth is reducing, make the ginger-scallion topping: In a medium pot, heat the oil to 350°F (175°C) on a deep-frying thermometer. Place the scallion whites, ginger, and salt in a heatproof bowl and pour the hot oil on top. Stir in the scallion greens and allow it to cool a bit. When cool enough to touch, taste for seasoning and add more salt if necessary.

Continued

For the brine:
½ cup (130 g) salt

⅓ cup (60 g) sugar

8 cups (2 kg) ice

1 (2½- to 3-pound/1,362 g) whole chicken

For the ginger-scallion topping:
½ cup (120 ml) canola oil

1 cup (113 g) chopped scallions, white and green parts separated

1¼ tablespoons finely chopped peeled fresh ginger

¼ teaspoon salt, plus more if needed

For the chicken soup:
1½ teaspoons chicken bouillon, or more to taste (optional)

Salt

1 clove garlic, thinly sliced

1 teaspoon thinly sliced peeled fresh ginger

1 (12-ounce/340 g) package wonton wrappers

2 cups your choice of vegetables (the restaurant recommends mushrooms, scallion, carrot, bok choy, and peas)

Your choice of liquid seasonings, such as shiro dashi, sesame oil, and/or chili oil

For the rice:
2 cups (500 g) day-old cooked rice

1 tablespoon butter

Salt

To serve:
2 tablespoons Momofuku chili crunch or another chili crisp, or more to taste

Cilantro sprigs, for garnish

Fresh Thai basil leaves, for garnish

To make the soup, once you have reduced the chicken broth to your desired taste, remove all of the leg meat from the chicken, as well as any meat left on the carcass, and shred with a fork. Add the sliced garlic and sliced ginger to the broth and bring it to a boil. Tear wonton wrappers and add them to the pot (these will serve as your noodles). Add your chosen vegetables and the chicken meat. Once the noodles and veggies are cooked, taste the soup for seasoning. Add a splash of shiro dashi, sesame oil, and/or chili oil, as desired. Keep warm until ready to serve.

To make the rice, put 2 cups cooked rice in a sauté pan over low heat. Add some of the cooking broth to moisten the rice and gently heat through. Add the butter and some more broth if needed. Season with salt.

To serve, plate the rice on a serving plate. Carve and slice the chicken breasts and place on top of the rice. Sauce one breast with the ginger-scallion sauce and one breast with the chili crunch. Garnish with the cilantro sprigs. Portion the soup into individual bowls, garnish with Thai basil leaves, and serve with your plated chicken and rice.

A rotisserie chicken in your fridge means you've got meals for a whole week. Shred the meat to bulk up salads and grain bowls, add it to noodles and sandwiches, make tacos with it, dip it in any of the sauces in this chapter for a snack. Yangban chef-owner Katianna Hong will season her shredded chicken before storing it in the fridge. "When you season your chicken with sesame oil and soy or fish sauce before you put it away, it helps it not taste refrigerator-y. It's just a good base seasoning—and then you can do whatever you want with it."

When you've picked the frame of the chicken clean, don't throw the bones away. "I think the true value in a grocery store rotisserie comes from saving all the bones and jus and making a delicious broth out of it," says Golden Diner chef-owner Sam Yoo. The basic technique is simple: Throw the entire carcass and any juices into a Dutch oven, add some aromatics (think garlic, onions, carrots), some peppercorns, and herbs (bay leaf and parsley are typical). Cover with water, bring it to a boil, and then reduce the heat and cover it. Simmer for about 2 hours, or do the whole thing in an Instant Pot, skim it, and store it in the fridge or freezer.

Between the shredded meat and the broth, you now have two base components for countless meals. Here are just a few ways chefs use rotisserie (or leftover roasted or boiled) chickens.

Keep a Rotisserie Chicken in the Fridge

Serve up **CURRIED CHICKEN LETTUCE WRAPS** by combining curry powder and mayonnaise and stirring it into your chopped chicken. Use iceberg lettuce to make the wraps, and if you're able to, pair it with some sort of slaw (like a green papaya salad; see page 67).
Recommended by: Toro chef-owner Jamie Bissonnette

Make **CHICKEN EMPANADAS** with premade pizza dough: Season shredded chicken with garlic and any spices you'd like and add some peppers, onions, and spicy relish. Shape the dough into small, flat circles, fold it over the chicken mixture to create half-moons, and close with a fork. Bake or fry and serve with more relish and avocado.
Recommended by: Fritai chef-owner Charly Pierre

Try a cheater **CHICKEN SHAWARMA** by warming the chicken in your pan with a shawarma spice blend (don't overlook premade spice blends, or see page 90!) and eat it with good pita, lavash, or any flatbread, tahini, and a chopped salad of cucumber, tomato, lemon, and olive oil.
Recommended by: My Abuelas Food chef Luis Martinez

Once you've got a basic chicken broth, add veggies, herbs, noodles, and shredded chicken for **CHICKEN NOODLE SOUP**.
Recommended by: ZoeFoodParty chef Zoë Komarin

Make a homey **JAB CHAI SOUP**: In a large pot, stir-fry some garlic, and then add carrots, napa and green cabbage, daikon, shiitake, bok choy, Chinese celery, Chinese broccoli, and any other vegetables you'd like. Season it with soy sauce, a pinch of brown sugar, and some black pepper. Add rotisserie chicken meat and the bones, cover with water, and simmer for at least an hour. (Remove the bones to serve!)
Recommended by: Luv2Eat Thai chef-owners Noree Pla and Fern Kaewtathip

Make **CONGEE** using chicken broth and rice (you can even toast the rice in chicken fat first if you want), then shred the chicken and add it in when it's almost done.
Recommended by: 886 chef-owner Eric Sze

Take your chicken congee, pour it into a baking dish, and top it with Pillsbury biscuits. Pop it into the oven and bake for a Yangban-style **CONGEE POT PIE**.
Recommended by: Yangban chef-owner Katianna Hong

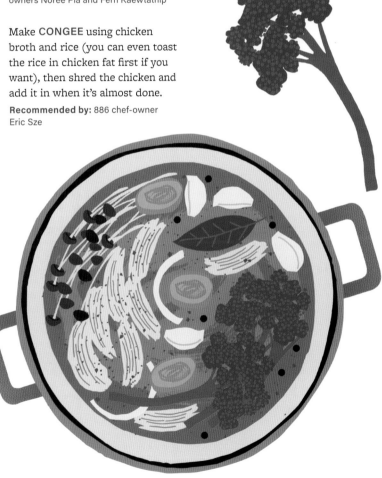

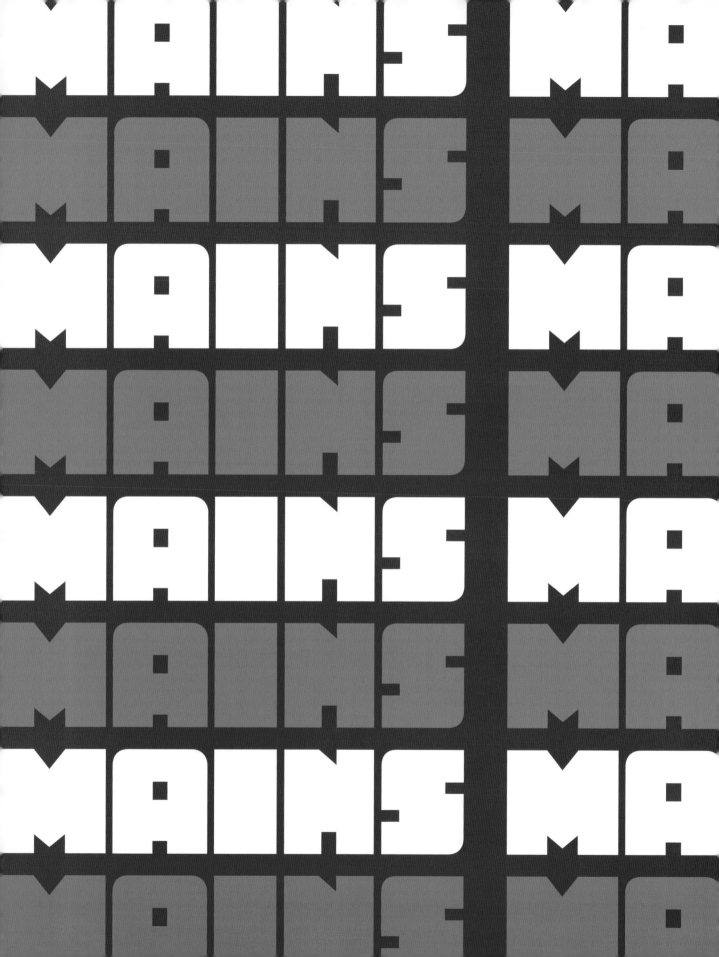

WHAT RESTAURANTS KNOW ABOUT DINNER

Restaurant operators know that every single diner comes in with a unique set of expectations. A regular who comes every Tuesday night for a solo dinner at the bar, a couple coming in on Saturday night for a date, a family celebrating a birthday, bucket-list destination diners—all look to a restaurant meal to provide something they can't find anywhere else, which is not to say they are all looking for the same thing.

Restaurants that succeed at this daunting task often do so when they are clear from the jump about what they do best. That may be hospitality. Whether it's the casual banter of a server taking orders or the expertise of a sommelier helping navigate a wine list, a nimble restaurant staff can meet diners where they are, while conveying the vision and spirit of the restaurant. At home, you can do this, too: It might look like setting a beautiful table for a dinner party or putting effort into your nonalcoholic beverage options. Even if you're just feeding yourself, it's using your good ceramics, playing music, and pouring yourself something properly chilled.

The other major strategy plays out on the menu. A distinct point of view—a clear answer to the question why should someone eat *this specific dish* at *this specific restaurant* for dinner—is a major asset. For home cooks, recipes that come out of that kitchen crucible can be relied upon to offer inspiration, education, and, most of all, the groundwork for forging your own culinary point of view.

SPICED BARBECUE LAMB RIBS
with Labneh

GWEN
Los Angeles, California

◇◇

Gwen is what happened when a star chef, Curtis Stone, and his brother, restaurateur Luke Stone, combined a top-notch butcher shop with a glam restaurant in the heart of Hollywood. Meat is the thing here—in the butcher cases, cooking over live fire in the restaurant's open kitchen, and on the menu, in dishes like bone marrow topped with wagyu chorizo and lamb ribs crusted in fennel, cumin, and coriander seeds and dunked into cooling labneh. At the restaurant, these ribs are typically a starter, with one or two ribs per person. You can absolutely do that when you serve this at home. When you split a rack between two people, you've got yourself dinner.

Serves **4**

For the ribs:
1½ teaspoons coriander seeds

1 teaspoon fennel seeds

¼ teaspoon cumin seeds

1½ teaspoons salt

1½ teaspoons smoked paprika

¼ teaspoon cayenne pepper

2 racks of lamb ribs

1 tablespoon olive oil

For the labneh sauce:
¾ cup (175 g) labneh

3 tablespoons extra-virgin olive oil

1 lemon, zested (½ teaspoon) and juiced (1 tablespoon)

1 fresh long red chile, seeded and finely chopped

1 tablespoon finely chopped fresh Italian parsley

2 teaspoons finely chopped fresh tarragon

1 teaspoon finely chopped fresh rosemary

Salt and freshly ground black pepper

To make the ribs, preheat the oven to 325°F (165°C).

Grind the coriander seeds, fennel seeds, and cumin seeds to a fine powder using a spice grinder. In a small bowl, mix the freshly ground spices with the salt, paprika, and cayenne.

Pat the ribs dry and brush both sides with olive oil, then sprinkle the spice mixture evenly over both sides. Place the ribs on a heavy rimmed baking sheet and cover tightly with aluminum foil. Bake for 1½ to 2 hours, until the meat between the rib bones is tender. Remove the ribs from the oven and set aside to cool.

Meanwhile, make the labneh sauce by whisking all the ingredients together in a small bowl. If the sauce is too thick, thin it out with some water. Sauce can be made one day ahead, stored in an airtight container in the fridge.

When you're ready to serve, prepare a barbecue for medium-high heat. Remove the ribs from the excess fat and pan juices and barbecue the ribs for 2 minutes on each side, or until caramelized.

Cut into individual ribs. Place on a platter and serve with the labneh sauce on the side.

→ **NOTES:** The ribs can be rubbed with spice mixture 1 day ahead, covered, and refrigerated. The ribs can be baked 1 day ahead. Remove the baked ribs from excess fat and drippings, then store in an airtight container in the fridge. When barbecuing the cold baked ribs, cook over medium heat, turning as needed, for about 10 minutes, until caramelized and warmed through.

A butcher can help you source lamb ribs, or you could swap in lamb chops: For a medium-rare lamb chop, pan-sear chops individually, then finish in the oven.

DELICATA SQUASH
with Goat Cheese, Pecans, and Honey

FNB
Scottsdale, Arizona

◇◇◇

In Arizona, this winter squash comes in August. And, in the hands of chef Charleen Badman, it is incredibly light, even when roasted and stuffed with goat cheese and pecans. At once innovative and familiar, dishes like this prove Badman's pioneering when it comes to making vegetables the star of any meal and explains why FnB is considered one of the region's best restaurants. The cavity of a delicata squash isn't that big, but there's enough filling for this to make a great vegetarian entree, especially if you serve it on top of a bed of dressed arugula. Badman suggests roasting and filling the squash ahead of time, pulling them out of the fridge in the morning to bring them to room temperature, and then popping the stuffed squash under the broiler right before serving. It's not dissimilar to how her cooks manage to work through so many orders, she says: "Break it down into stages and you won't get overwhelmed."

Serves **4**

◇◇◇◇◇◇◇◇◇◇◇◇◇◇◇◇◇◇◇◇◇◇◇◇◇◇◇◇◇◇◇   ◇◇

For the squash:
2 delicata squash, halved lengthwise

Salt

Red chile flakes

4 fresh bay leaves, torn in half (2 pieces per squash)

¼ cup (55 g) packed brown sugar

2 tablespoons unsalted butter, cut into chunks

Olive oil, for drizzling

For the stuffing:
3 tablespoons olive oil

1 cup (125 g) diced yellow onions

1 tablespoon minced garlic

1 pound (455 g) goat cheese

1¼ cups (144 g) grated provolone cheese

2 teaspoons minced fresh rosemary

1½ cups (180 g) toasted and chopped pecans

Salt and freshly ground black pepper

To finish:
1 cup (120 g) toasted breadcrumbs

½ cup (170 g) honey

To make the squash, preheat the oven to 350°F (175°C) and line a baking sheet with parchment paper.

Cut the squash in half lengthwise. Scoop and clean out the seeds. Place on the prepared baking sheet, cut sides up, and season each squash with salt, red chile flakes, the torn bay leaves, and brown sugar. Place the butter chunks on each squash and drizzle with olive oil. Roast for 30 to 40 minutes, until the squash is tender but does not take on color. You can test it as you would a cake. Remove the squash from the oven and set aside.

To make the stuffing, heat the olive oil in a small sauté pan over medium heat. Add the onions and garlic and cook until the onions are translucent, 8 to 12 minutes, then transfer to a plate to cool.

In a large bowl, combine the goat cheese, provolone cheese, rosemary, and pecans. Season with salt and pepper. Watch the salt, as the cheeses will be pretty salty. Add the cooled cooked onion mixture and mix well.

To finish the dish, remove the bay leaves from the squash and stuff it with the cheese mixture. Turn the oven to broil and broil the squash until the cheese stuffing is melted, bubbling, and starting to brown. Remove the stuffed squash from the oven and top each half with toasted breadcrumbs and a drizzle of honey.

PAELLA MIXTA

TORO
Boston, Massachusetts

Since 2005, Toro has been where Boston goes for tapas, paella, and a damn good night out, care of chefs and co-owners Ken Oringer and Jamie Bissonnette. You can bring some of Toro's raucous energy to your own table by having friends over for paella. Bissonnette has taught this dish in classes and shared how-tos with friends and family over the years; the recipe below is his attempt to include every tip and trick he's ever passed along. As large-format recipes go, this one has the added bonus of not requiring any sort of serving platters or plating: Let your paella rest, then place your pan in the center of the table and dig in.

→ **NOTE:** If you do not have a paella pan, you could use a large stainless-steel sauté pan or frying pan, or a large shallow Dutch oven. Depending on the size of your pans, you might want to make your paella in two pans to ensure your rice isn't overcrowded and to encourage a crust to form.

Serves **4** to **6**

2 tablespoons (30 ml) Spanish extra-virgin olive oil, plus more for drizzling

½ cup (25 g) diced red bell pepper

¼ cup (35 g) diced Spanish yellow onion

1 bunch scallions, thinly sliced, green and white parts separated

2 cloves garlic, minced

1 cup (140 g) dried Spanish chorizo, sliced into ¼-inch (6 mm) rounds

6 threads saffron

1 (6-ounce/180 g) boneless, skinless chicken breast, or 2 boneless, skinless chicken thighs, diced

Salt and freshly ground black pepper

¼ cup (56 g) tomato paste

1 cup (190 g) Bomba or Calasparra rice (Spanish short-grain rice)

4½ cups (1 L) chicken, seafood, vegetable, or mixed stock

5 littleneck clams

14 mussels

4 to 6 large shrimp, peeled and deveined

1 cup (173 g) fresh or frozen English peas

Place a 14-inch (35 cm) paella pan (see Note) on a large burner over medium heat and add the 2 tablespoons olive oil. Swirl to coat the pan. Add the red pepper, onion, scallion whites, garlic, chorizo, and saffron and cook for 5 to 10 minutes, until the peppers are soft.

Add the chicken to the pan and season with salt and pepper, then increase the heat to high, toss to combine, and cook for 2 more minutes. Add the tomato paste and cook for 1 to 2 minutes, until the paste starts to brown. Add the rice, toss well, and toast until the rice is translucent, about 3 minutes. If the rice isn't coating evenly, add more olive oil.

Add the stock. Once the stock comes to a boil, add the clams, lower the heat to medium-high, and boil for 8 to 10 minutes, until the clams start to open, making sure not to stir the paella. Taste and adjust the seasoning with salt and pepper.

Scatter the mussels and shrimp on top of the paella and turn the heat down to medium. Once the mussels are open and the shrimp is cooked, after 7 to 10 minutes, scatter the peas on top and check the bottom of the paella for a crust of crispy rice. This is called *socarrat*. If the paella does not have a crust, simply turn up the heat and cook until it does. Rotate the pan to cook the base evenly. Once the crust is formed, garnish the paella with the scallion greens and a drizzle of olive oil. Rest for 5 minutes before serving.

TACOS ÁRABES with Sliced Pork Shoulder

NOPALITO
San Francisco, California

◇◇◇

Tacos árabes are where shawarma meets tacos, the delicious commingling of Mexican cooking and the Levantine traditions that immigrants brought with them to Puebla, Mexico, in the first half of the twentieth century. Lamb cooked on a spit became pork al pastor; pita became thinner pan árabe, a wrap that skirts the divide between puffy pita and a flour tortilla. At acclaimed Mexican restaurant Nopalito in San Francisco, chef-owner Gonzalo Guzman—a Veracruz native who also lived in Puebla and Mexico City before landing in San Francisco—goes for marinating rather than spit-roasting, and his pork bursts with the flavors of cumin, thyme, and oregano. You'll want to bookmark this pan árabe recipe: It's perfect for all your dipping, folding, and wrapping needs. Do give yourself time to work on these tacos when you dive in, though. The pork shoulder should marinate for 4 hours, the dough needs to rest for 2, and your salsa needs to simmer for at least 20 minutes. After all that waiting, the cooking and assembly steps will move quickly, making this an ideal meal for a dinner party: There's plenty to do ahead of time, not too much to do in the final hour before folks arrive. And, of course, you could serve this with your favorite store-bought tortillas or flatbread instead of making the wraps.

For the salsa:

1 cup (240 ml) rice bran oil or other neutral oil with a high smoke point (such as avocado or canola oil)

10 morita chiles (40 g)

3 tomatillos, husks removed, rinsed, and halved

½ teaspoon dried oregano

¼ cup (60 ml) distilled white vinegar

2 cloves garlic, peeled

Salt

For the pan árabe:

1 cup (240 ml) warm water

1½ teaspoons honey

¼ teaspoon active dry yeast

1½ teaspoons butter, softened

1½ teaspoons olive oil

¼ cup (70 g) plain Greek yogurt

¾ teaspoon salt

3¾ cups (450 g) all-purpose flour, plus more for dusting

For the meat filling:

¼ medium white onion, peeled

1 tablespoon lime juice

⅓ cup (18 g) chopped fresh Italian parsley

¼ cup (13 g) chopped fresh oregano

1 tablespoon dried thyme

1 tablespoon dried oregano

1 teaspoon cumin seeds

2 cloves garlic, peeled

⅓ cup (80 ml) olive oil

1½ tablespoons salt

2 pounds (908 g) boneless pork shoulder, thinly sliced

3 tablespoons vegetable oil

To serve:

Chopped fresh cilantro

Lime wedges

Diced white onions

To make the salsa, in a medium saucepan, heat the oil to 350°F (175°C) according to a deep-frying thermometer. Fry the chiles for a few seconds, until you start to smell their aroma and they change color.

Bring 2 cups (480 ml) water to a boil in a small saucepan. Put the chiles in the boiling water, lower the heat, and simmer for at least 20 minutes, until the chiles are soft. Strain, reserving the chile water. Transfer the chiles to a blender and add the tomatillos, oregano, vinegar, and garlic. Season with salt. Add a little bit of the chile water and blend until the salsa comes together but still remains somewhat chunky. If making ahead, cool and store in an airtight container in the fridge for up to 4 days.

To make the pan árabe, combine the warm water, honey, and yeast in a small bowl and let the yeast dissolve and get active for about 5 minutes. In a stand mixer fitted with the dough hook, combine the warm water, honey, and yeast mixture with the butter, olive oil, and yogurt. Add the salt, then gradually mix in the flour until a nice soft masa forms—it should not stick to your hands. (You might not need to use all the flour.)

Place the dough on a work area and divide into 8 balls. Sprinkle flour on a tray and lay the dough balls into the flour, then sprinkle more flour on top of the dough balls and wrap them with plastic wrap (the flour should prevent the plastic from sticking). Rest the dough for about 2 hours at room temperature, until nearly double in size and puffy. Heat a griddle or cast-iron skillet over medium-high heat. Roll out eight 8-inch (20 cm) rounds with a rolling pin. Dust the surface and rolling pin with flour to ensure it doesn't stick. Cook the rolled-out rounds on the griddle or skillet for about 30 seconds on each side, until they puff.

To make the meat filling, combine the onion, lime juice, parsley, fresh oregano, dried thyme, dried oregano, cumin seeds, garlic, olive oil, and salt in a blender. Blend until it reaches a paste-like consistency. Place the pork in a large bowl and pour the marinade over. Stir well to combine.

Cover with plastic wrap and refrigerate for at least 4 hours or up to 8 to let the flavors penetrate the meat.

When the pork is done marinating, heat the vegetable oil in a large sauté pan or cast-iron skillet. Cook the meat for about 3 minutes on each side to get a nice char (work in batches to avoid overcrowding). When cooked through, slice the meat into smaller bite-size pieces. To keep warm until ready to serve, keep the meat covered in a very low oven (140ºF/60ºC) so it doesn't dry.

To serve, heat up a pan árabe, spread on some of the salsa, and put as much pork as you want on it. Garnish with cilantro, a squeeze of lime, and onions.

A Good Butcher Will Make You a Better Cook

Better meat means better dinner. To source great meat—as well as charcuterie, tough-to-find or custom cuts, and even bones for stock—you'll want to find a great local butcher.

Honolulu-based butcher Jason Chow offers these starter questions: "Ask about what is important to you in sourcing your meat. Where is the meat from? How is it raised? What is the diet/lifestyle? Is it FRESH OR PREVIOUSLY FROZEN?" And, if your butcher doesn't want to answer questions, "they're probably not asking very many questions of the people they're working with," says Sarah Welch, partner and executive chef of Marrow, the Detroit combination butcher shop–restaurant. "Find someone who wants to answer your questions."

Once you're hooked in with a good butcher, make the most of their expertise. IT ALL COMES DOWN TO TALKING. Tell your butcher your price range, what recipe you're shopping for, and ask for their input on how to get the most out of your purchase. Welch recommends writing down any special instructions or tips they give you about properly cooking whichever cut you choose. Chow likes asking what the butcher would take home for dinner that night and going with that.

"Most butcher shops are retirement homes for line cooks," says Brent Young, the founder of Brooklyn butcher shop the Meat Hook. "Working at the butcher shop is a way to talk with people and get excited about what they're cooking. Trust that YOUR BUTCHER KNOWS SOMETHING ABOUT FOOD."

TEA-SMOKED PORK RIBS

There's perhaps no better place to eat Chinese food in America than in California's San Gabriel Valley. Among the many beloved restaurants in the city of Alhambra, Sichuan Impression's star shines bright for co-owners Lynn Liu's and Kelly Xiao's menu of sophisticated dishes either traditional to or in the style of their native Sichuan province. Nearly every table gets an order of the tea-smoked ribs to start, an example of the restaurant's New Sichuan style of cooking, blending typical Sichuan flavors with innovative, modern technique. The result—fragrant, tender ribs redolent of jasmine tea and delicately complex herbs—is astounding. Sourcing the ingredients to do this at home—even with a shorter spice list than what happens at the restaurant—will take time, as will brining, boiling, smoking, then deep-frying these ribs. But if you do go on this journey, you will learn why so many diners have fallen for Sichuan Impression—and you'll have a well-stocked pantry to boot. Luckily, the herbs you'll need for this recipe will keep for a long time, and, as Xiao will tell you, the spices for the brine can also be adjusted according to availability and your own taste (and the crunchy fried peanuts with garlic, dried chile, and scallions is a game-changing topping to add to your repertoire).

Serves **4** to **6**

For the seasoned brine:
3 pounds (1.5 kg) pork bones

½ chicken (with bones and skin), about 2 pounds (907 g)

½ duck (with bones and skin), about 2 pounds (900 g)

2 pods star anise

2 pods cardamom

1 piece (1 to 2 g) dried shan nai (sand ginger)

1 to 2 pieces angelica (wild celery; optional)

1 cinnamon stick

4 to 5 dried bay leaves

1 to 2 pieces (4 g) licorice root

1 teaspoon ground white cardamom

3 cloves

1 teaspoon dried lemongrass

¼ teaspoon fennel seeds

1 (0.035-ounce/1 g) piece geranium (optional)

1 kernel cape jasmine (optional)

1 tablespoon dried chile (optional)

1 teaspoon Sichuan peppercorns (optional)

For the ribs and baking soda brine:
2 quarts (2 L) cold water

1 tablespoon baking soda

1 leek, cut into 4 segments (trim and discard stringy roots, but keep leafy top)

2 slices fresh ginger (peel and slice off from larger knob)

½ teaspoon ground Sichuan peppercorns

¼ cup (60 ml) Chinese cooking wine

1 whole (2½ to 4 pounds/1.2 to 1.8 kg) rack pork ribs (preferably baby back)

For smoking the ribs:
2½ tablespoons sugar

⅓ cup (100 g) salt

¼ cup (50 g) basmati rice

2 tablespoons fennel seeds

½ cup (30 g) jasmine tea, or any dry tea leaves you like

2 to 3 bay leaves

2 to 3 star anise

1 small pine branch

For deep-frying the ribs:
At least 2 quarts (2 L) vegetable or other neutral oil

To finish:
¼ cup (60 ml) vegetable or other neutral oil

1½ tablespoons dried chile

¼ cup (50 g) dried garlic

¼ cup (50 g) roasted peanuts, chopped

1 tablespoon chicken bouillon powder

Salt

2 scallions, chopped, for garnish

Continued

→ NOTES: Some of these herbs will be available at Asian grocers, but you might also consider shopping at a Chinese medicine shop, where there is a robust herb selection.

As Xiao and Liu explain: "Many Chinese dishes first require cooking a brine, which is an involved and meticulous process. Some recipes cook the meat in the brine, and it is ready to serve. Other recipes use it as a base to add flavor before finishing with an additional cooking method. Brines become generational by reusing the original amount of brine then adding more spices and water (each generation should maintain a total liquid volume of 5¼ quarts/5 liters). Subsequent generations become exponentially more fragrant and flavorful. The ingredients listed above and their amounts are essential for this brine's first to third generations. But when the brine reaches the fourth generation, you should halve the amount of each spice. As a rule, the total amount of spices added for each generation from the fourth on should not exceed 12.5 grams. If you add more than 12.5 grams on these later generations, you will be making traditional Chinese medicine." (Shout out to Xiao and Liu's friend Daniel Ryan, who worked with them on translating this recipe.)

To prepare the seasoned brine, in a large stockpot, combine 5¼ quarts (5 liters) water, the pork bones, chicken half, duck half, star anise, cardamom, shan nai, angelica, cinnamon, bay leaves, licorice, white cardamom, cloves, lemongrass, fennel seeds, cand, if using, the geranium, cape jasmine, dried chile, and Sichuan pepper. Bring to a boil, turn the heat down to medium-low, and simmer continuously for more than 5 hours.

To make the baking soda brine, combine the cold water, baking soda, leek, ginger, Sichuan peppercorns, and cooking wine in a large deep bowl or baking dish that can fit the ribs.

Split the rack of ribs down the middle. Pare away any excess meat (you only want to use the meat that is tight to the bones). Rinse the ribs briefly, then add them to the brine. Make sure the ribs are completely submerged in the brine and cool in the refrigerator for at least 2 hours.

Bring a large stockpot of water to a boil. Take the ribs out of the cold baking soda brine and add them to the pot of boiling water. Parboil for 5 minutes, then remove, rinse, and put them into the boiling seasoned brine. Reduce the heat to medium, simmer for 30 minutes, then turn off the heat. Cover with a lid and let sit in the seasoned brine for 1½ hours.

Take the ribs out of the pot to cool and drain. Allow the seasoned brine to cool, store it in the refrigerator, and take it out to make the next generation (see Notes).

To smoke the ribs, preheat an outdoor grill to 400°F (200°C).

Place all of the smoking ingredients on a thick sheet of aluminum foil with folded-up sides to avoid spilling. Place the foil with the smoking ingredients on the bottom rack of the grill (or, if your grill is only one level, on one side of the grill). Keep the grill on high with the lid closed until it starts to smoke.

Place the cooked ribs on the grill's top grate bone-side down. (If your grill has only one level, place the ribs on the opposite side and shut off the heat to smoke.) Smoke this side for 10 minutes, then turn the ribs over and smoke the meat side for another 10 minutes. When done smoking, use kitchen towels to absorb the surface moisture while the ribs are still hot.

To deep-fry the ribs, heat enough vegetable oil to submerge the ribs in a heavy wok or a large Dutch oven to 300 to 350°F (150 to 175°C) according to a deep-frying thermometer. Fry the smoked ribs in the oil for 1 to 2 minutes, until the surface of the ribs turns golden and develops a crispy-looking exterior. Transfer the ribs to a wire rack set over a sheet pan.

To finish the ribs, heat the ¼ cup (50 g) vegetable oil in a wok over medium heat and add the dry chile, dried garlic, and peanuts. Add the chicken bouillon powder and season with salt. Cook until fragrant, then add the fried, smoked ribs and stir-fry together until the ribs are coated and hot. Remove from the pan to a serving plate and garnish with chopped scallions.

PUN MIENG PAA
(Fried Catfish with Collard Green Wraps and Rice Noodles)

THIP KHAO
Washington, D.C.

Seng Luangrath and her son Boby Pradachith are the chef-restaurateurs behind Thip Khao, an essential D.C. spot and one of the best-known Laotian restaurants in the entire country. At the restaurant, you can order pun mieng with fried tofu or fried catfish. We've gone with catfish here, but at home, feel free to sub in fried tofu, if you prefer, or another flaky fish like cod, black bass, skate wing, trout, halibut, or even shrimp. This is a large-format option, where you'll put the final assembly into the hands of your guests. Here's Pradachith's strategy: Make your leaf your base, then add your noodles, then a piece of the fried fish, and spoon on a little bit of everything *you* want. "Nobody should feel obligated to put anything into their wrap that they don't like." You can either add sauce directly onto your fish or put it on as your last component. Then tuck the ends in and "just go for it."

→ **NOTE:** "Thinking about the materials and visual details of the culture the dish comes from is a way to make your dinner table more restaurant-like, since restaurateurs do this, too," says Pradachith. He recommends setting your table with banana leaves and woven bamboo. You can buy frozen banana leaves at most Asian markets: Just thaw them, and then lay them out like placemats.

186

For the sauce:

2 tablespoons sugar

1½ tablespoons rice vinegar

1 teaspoon salt, plus more as needed

2 tablespoons fermented soybean paste, such as Healthy Boy brand

1 tablespoon fish sauce, such as Three Crab brand

1 tablespoon padaek (fermented fish paste), such as Pantai brand

1 cup (170 g) large-diced pineapple

¼ cup (25 g) peeled and diced fresh ginger

¼ cup (36 g) diced yellow onion

1½ tablespoons lime juice

For the accoutrements and sides:

3 stalks lemongrass

8 ounces (225 g) dried rice vermicelli noodles

1 bunch collard greens

⅓ cup (32 g) peeled and fine-julienned fresh ginger

12 cherry tomatoes, halved

1 cup (125 g) Chinese long beans or green beans, ends removed and cut into 1-inch (2.5 cm) pieces

½ cup (142 g) roasted peanuts

For the fried catfish:

2 quarts (2 L) grapeseed oil, for frying

½ cup (71 g) rice flour

½ cup (76 g) potato starch

½ cup (56 g) cornstarch

1½ tablespoons salt

4 to 6 catfish fillets (1 per person)

To make the sauce, combine the sugar, rice vinegar, and salt in a small saucepan and place over medium heat. Stir occasionally until it's boiling and the sugar is fully dissolved. Remove from the heat and allow to cool completely.

Once it's cooled, pour it into a blender or food processer and add the fermented soybean paste, fish sauce, padaek, pineapple, ginger, onion, and lime juice. Blend until smooth but still pulpy. Taste and add more salt if needed. Reserve in an airtight container in the refrigerator until ready to plate.

To prepare the accoutrements, cut off the bottom inch of the lemongrass stalk and discard (or save for stock). Peel the first layer and discard. Angling the knife on a bias, slice the lemongrass as thinly as possible. Transfer to a container with a damp towel and reserve in the refrigerator until ready to serve.

Place the dried noodles in a medium pot and fill with enough room-temperature water to cover the noodles and place over high heat. Once the water begins to boil, remove from the heat and drain in a colander. Rinse the noodles with cold water to keep from further cooking. Take a bundle of noodles and hold them from one end. Begin to wrap the noodles around your index and middle fingers until the noodles form a doughnut shape. Place the wrapped noodles in a container lined with plastic wrap or parchment paper and top with another layer to keep them from drying. Reserve in the refrigerator until ready for plating.

To make the collard green wraps, remove the stems and cut the leaves into quarters. Reserve in the refrigerator until ready for plating.

To fry the fish, heat the grapeseed oil in a heavy-bottomed pot or Dutch oven over medium-high heat to 350°F (175°C).

To make the dredge, in a medium bowl, combine the rice flour, potato starch, cornstarch, and salt until well incorporated and set aside.

Lightly season the catfish fillets with salt and add to the dredge. Press the dredge onto the fillets to form a crust when frying. Shake off the excess flour and add the fillets to the hot oil. Cook for 2 to 4 minutes, flipping halfway through to achieve an even, golden brown crust. Remove from the heat and drain on paper towels to remove excess oil.

Place a bowl of the sauce in the center of a large platter. Arrange the fried catfish and accoutrements in individual piles around the bowl.

UGALI AND SAMAKI YA KARANGA
(Fish Peanut Stew)

BAOBAB FARE
Detroit, Michigan

◇◇

Wife-and-husband duo Nadia Nijimbere and Hamissi Mamba have made a rich life for themselves in Detroit serving the cuisine of their native Burundi to diners who have welcomed them as cooks, restaurateurs, and neighbors since the couple was granted asylum back in 2017. The menu at their pop-up-turned-restaurant, Baobab Fare, is a parade of beloved East African staples, like slow-simmered beef nyumbani and ugali, a ball of dense cornmeal porridge that the couple serves as a special on Tuesdays. At the restaurant, they typically serve their Tuesday ugali with an okra stew, but for this large-format take, Mamba uses swai, a catfish-like species from Asia. (You might find it's easier to find tilapia or sea bass, both of which would work well here—any neutral, not-too-oily fish will.) You'll make the stew first: The fish will continue to take on flavor while you work on the ugali, which, by contrast, should be served immediately.

Serves **4** to **6**

◇◇◇◇◇◇◇◇◇◇◇◇◇◇◇◇◇◇◇◇◇◇◇◇◇◇   ◇◇

For the fish:

6 white fish fillets

1 teaspoon salt

1 teaspoon ground black pepper

2 tablespoons lemon juice

¼ cup (60 ml) peanut oil or vegetable oil

For the stew:

2 cups (250 g) chopped yellow onion

¼ cup (60 ml) tomato paste

1 teaspoon salt

1 teaspoon garlic powder

¼ teaspoon ground white pepper

1 teaspoon curry powder

½ cup (135 g) peanut butter or roasted peanut paste

3 tablespoons Thai fish sauce

1 cup (145 g) green peas

1 red habanero chile

For the ugali:

2 cups (360 g) fine-ground cornmeal

½ teaspoon salt

2 tablespoons corn oil

Edible flowers (optional)

To cook the fish, season the fish fillets with the salt, black pepper, and lemon juice. Heat the oil in a large skillet, add the fish, and fry for 3 to 5 minutes per side, until flaky. Remove the fish from the pan to a plate and set aside.

To make the stew, in the same frying pan, add the onions and stir until limp and lightly browned, about 5 to 7 minutes Add the tomato paste, salt, garlic, white pepper, and curry powder and stir well. Add the peanut butter and fish sauce and stir to dissolve. Continue to cook the sauce until thick.

Add the fried fish back to the pan with the sauce, then add the green peas and habanero for aroma and keep warm over very low heat while you make the ugali.

To make the ugali, bring 4 cups (960 ml) water to a boil in a large saucepan over high heat. Slowly pour the cornmeal into the boiling water. Avoid forming lumps. Stir continuously and mash any lumps that do form. Add more cornmeal until it is thicker than mashed potatoes, then add the salt and oil. Cook for 3 to 4 minutes, continuing to stir (continued stirring will help thicken the ugali and is the secret to success), until thickened and solid like a dough. Cover and keep warm on the stove for 5 minutes.

Serve the ugali with the fish peanut stew and garnish with the edible flowers, if using.

SHRIMP MIDDLINS
with Carolina Gold Rice Grits

THE GREY
Savannah, Georgia

The Grey's shrimp middlins are just the kind of dish chef Mashama Bailey does best at her acclaimed Savannah restaurant, rich in history and ripe for interpretation. Rice was a high-profit crop; the product of the tremendous amount of knowledge and the work enslaved Africans and their descendants were forced to do in cultivating Carolina Gold rice by hand. While the whole grains were reserved for sale, the broken, discarded bits—the middlins, also known as rice grits or broken rice—would be left for the workers, who would coax out their starches to create a creamy base to absorb all manner of broths and stews. Bailey and chef de cuisine Trevor Elliot have had some version of middlins on the menu for years, and this version is one that reappears often, celebrating Georgia's coastal bounty with a robust shrimp stock and plenty of shrimp in the bowl. While making your own shrimp stock is a project, middlins are wonderfully adaptable: Try cooking them with your favorite chicken broth or beef broth and play with adding additional hearty vegetables (Bailey has done mushrooms, butternut squash, and sunchokes at the restaurant).

For the shrimp stock:

1 pound (455 g) fish heads and bones (see Notes)

1 pound (455 g) royal red shrimp shells

4 cups (500 g) sliced white onion

4 cups (400 g) sliced celery

1 head garlic, cut in half

2 tablespoons vegetable or other neutral oil

¾ cup (196 g) tomato paste

1 cup (240 ml) white wine

1 (28-ounce/794 g) can whole peeled tomatoes

6 tablespoons (100 g) fish bouillon (see Notes)

For the shrimp middlins:

1 cup (125 g) small-diced white onion

½ cup (50 g) small-diced celery

½ cup (70 g) small-diced shallots

¼ cup (60 ml) extra-virgin olive oil

2 cups (360 g) Carolina Gold rice grits (see Notes)

1 cup (240 ml) white wine

¼ cup (½ stick/57 g) butter

1 pound (455 g) royal red shrimp, cut into ½-inch (1.25 cm) pieces

Juice of 1 lemon

2 tablespoons chiffonade fresh tarragon

2 tablespoons chiffonade fresh parsley

2 tablespoons thinly sliced fresh chives

To make the stock, preheat the oven to 350°F (175°C). On a metal baking sheet or pan, roast the fish heads and bones and shrimp shells for 30 minutes, or until browned. In a wide pan over medium-high heat, sweat the onions, celery, and garlic in the neutral oil until the vegetables are soft and the onions are translucent, about 10 minutes. Add the tomato paste and cook until it turns a rich, rust-colored red, about 3 minutes. Add the white wine and scrape up all the bits from the bottom of the pan.

Add the roasted fish bones and shrimp shells. Add the whole tomatoes, fish bouillon, and 4 quarts (4 L) water. Bring to a boil, then lower the heat and simmer for 3 hours. Strain out the bones and shells. If making ahead, cool and refrigerate in an airtight container for up to 3 days. You'll have about 2 quarts (2 L) stock.

To make the middlins, in a large saucepan, bring the shrimp stock with a healthy pinch of salt to a simmer. In a separate wide pot, sweat the onion, celery, and shallots in the olive oil over medium heat until the vegetables are soft and translucent, about 10 minutes. Add the rice grits and stir to coat and toast in the oil, about 5 minutes. Add the white wine and reduce until the pan dries out again, about 5 minutes.

Ladle 2 cups (480 ml) shrimp stock into the pan with the rice grits and stir over a low simmer. Let this reduce and get absorbed by the rice. Keep repeating this process until the rice grits are just cooked, the stock is absorbed, and the rice grits are tender, about 10 minutes. You can let the rice grits cool down at this point if you aren't ready to serve.

To serve, heat the rice grits and loosen them with warm shrimp stock. Mix in half of the butter and keep stirring as the stock reduces. You want a creamy consistency that slowly settles when spooned into a bowl. When the consistency is close, add the remaining butter and the diced shrimp and keep stirring until the shrimp are just cooked. Take the pan off the heat and add the lemon juice and herbs. Portion the shrimp middlins among 4 to 6 bowls.

→ NOTES: Fishmongers often sell fish bones, and some also sell fish stocks.

We've substituted fish bouillon for fish fumet (a concentrated fish stock) in the shrimp stock recipe. You can absolutely make your own fish fumet, which would bring the recipe closer to how Bailey and Elliot do it at the Grey.

The Grey uses Anson Mills rice grits, which you can buy online. Other notable brands from the South include Marsh Hen Mill and Carolina Plantation Rice.

COBIA AL PASTOR
with Pineapple Puree

COSME
New York City

→ **NOTES:** Extra pastor marinade can be stored in the fridge for up to 4 days and in the freezer for 4 months. Olvera recommends using it for marinating any kind of meat, vegetables, and, of course, fish.

If you can't find cobia, look for another fresh, mild fish that can safely be served rare, like mahi-mahi or sea bass.

When acclaimed Mexico City chef Enrique Olvera opened Cosme, his debut New York City restaurant, he electrified the city with his stylish, modern cooking. This dish quickly became one of the restaurant's signatures: a cobia fillet, imbued with the spiced, smoky flavors of trompo- (spit) roasted pork found in tacos al pastor, plated with a bright pineapple puree, and topped with delicate rings of spring onion and slices of serrano chile. It's a triumph of a dish, rewarding the effort you put into creating a potent marinade and thinly slicing all those garnishes. You can make the marinade ahead and store it in the fridge, if you'd like, and you can also swap in another firm, fresh fish for the cobia.

Serves **4**

For the pastor adobo marinade:
12 guajillo chiles (100 g), stems and seeds removed

½ pasilla chile (10 g), stem and seeds removed

¼ small white onion, peeled

2 cloves garlic, peeled

1 teaspoon dried Mexican oregano

2 teaspoons chipotle in adobo, chopped

1½ teaspoons distilled white vinegar

2 teaspoons salt

For the pineapple puree:
1 medium pineapple

½ cup (20 g) butter, cut into cubes, at room temperature

Salt

For the fish:
4 cobia fillets

Salt

1 tablespoon grapeseed oil

To serve:
12 thin pineapple rings (left from making the puree above)

4 key limes, halved

Maldon salt, for garnish

1 spring onion, sliced into thin rings

2 serrano chiles, sliced into thin rings

12 fresh cilantro leaves

Warm tortillas, for serving

To make the marinade, preheat the oven to 375°F (190°C).

Place the chiles, onion, and garlic on a baking sheet and roast for 20 minutes, making sure you rotate the ingredients to get even toasting. It's done when everything looks crisped.

Transfer the toasted mixture into a blender, add the oregano, chipotle in adobo, vinegar, and salt, and blend until smooth. Pass through a fine-mesh strainer and cool. The marinade will keep in the fridge for up to 4 days.

To make the pineapple puree, peel, core, and thinly slice half of the pineapple into rings (you'll need 12 rings). Set aside for garnishing the finished dish. Cut the remaining half pineapple into medium dice. Place in a medium pot over low heat and cook down until all the juice is gone, 7 to 9 minutes, stirring to avoid browning. It should still have a bright yellow color.

Transfer the cooked pineapple to a high-speed blender and blend until smooth, adding the butter in increments. Pass through a fine-mesh strainer and season with salt. Set aside.

To cook the fish, rub each portion of cobia with 1 to 2 tablespoons of the pastor marinade and season with salt. Heat the grapeseed oil over medium heat in a large sauté pan. When hot, sear the cobia for about 10 seconds on all sides. You want the flesh to remain rare, like tuna tataki.

Transfer the fish to a cutting board and thinly slice with a sharp knife, fanning out the slices and keeping the shape of the portion. Squeeze some lime on top and season with Maldon salt.

Transfer a portion of fish onto each of 4 serving plates. Garnish each portion of cobia with 3 pineapple slices, and then add 3 or 4 spring onion rings, 3 or 4 serrano rings, and 3 cilantro leaves. Place a dollop of pineapple puree next to the fish. Serve with warm tortillas.

"MY MOTHER'S" SEAFOOD GUMBO

ROOTS SOUTHERN TABLE
Farmers Branch, Texas

Chef Tiffany Derry named her Dallas-area restaurant Roots Southern Table for a reason: The menu's goal is to delve deep into her own culinary past, to marry the tastes of her childhood in Beaumont, Texas, and Baton Rouge, Louisiana, with her fine-dining work in Dallas. Before she even opened the restaurant, she took her team on a tour through Louisiana, starting at her mother's table. There, they ate the seafood gumbo that inspired the restaurant's signature dish, an homage to that very same welcoming pot, complete with smoky Zummo's sausage, a Cajun-style boudin made in Beaumont. (Availability in grocery stores varies geographically, so if you can't find it, go for your own favorite boudin, Cajun-style andouille, or, in a pinch, pork kielbasa.) Her recipe calls for gumbo filé—dried and ground sassafras leaves, also known as gumbo powder—a traditional ingredient that brings a distinct, almost root beer–like flavor. It's pretty easy to find on grocery store shelves and online (Derry likes Zatarain's); this gumbo isn't the same without it. Derry has helpfully offered up tips for cutting corners, but the fact is your gumbo will need to be cooked with care: Tend to your roux so it doesn't burn, pre-roast your okra so it's not at all slimy, and let this labor of love take a full afternoon.

*Serves **4** to **6***

¾ cup (180 ml) vegetable oil

1 cup plus 2 tablespoons (140 g) all-purpose flour

1 cup (125 g) diced yellow onion

1½ cups (150 g) diced celery

1 cup (145 g) diced green bell pepper

¼ cup (35 g) minced garlic

¼ cup (63 g) canned tomato puree

2 bay leaves

1½ teaspoons cayenne pepper

1½ teaspoons onion powder

1½ teaspoons garlic powder

½ teaspoon dried thyme

1½ teaspoons paprika

1½ teaspoons chile powder

2 quarts (2 L) shrimp stock (page 191) or water

2 quarts (2 L ml) duck stock, chicken stock, or water

2 tablespoons dried shrimp powder (grind in spice grinder or use pre-ground)

1½ tablespoons salt

1½ teaspoons ground black pepper

8 ounces okra, cut into ¼-inch (6 mm) pieces

1½ teaspoons olive oil

1 pound (455 g) chicken breast and/or thighs, cut into large dice, roasted in the oven

8 ounces (225 g) Zummo's sausage, sliced into half moons

Louisiana-style hot sauce, such as Crystal

8 ounces (225 g) blue crab, cleaned and cut into large pieces

2 tablespoons gumbo filé, plus more to finish

8 ounces (225 g) medium shrimp, peeled

4 scallions, sliced, green and white parts

Chopped fresh Italian parsley

Cooked jasmine rice

Continued

Preheat the oven to 375°F (190°C).

To make a roux, heat the vegetable oil in a large cast-iron skillet over medium heat. Add the flour and stir until smooth. Place the pan in the oven and cook for 90 minutes, stirring every 30 minutes. It will turn a dark chocolate brown with no specks. Don't turn the oven off.

Transfer the roux to a large pot. Add the onion, celery, bell pepper, and garlic and cook over medium heat for 8 to 10 minutes, until the vegetables are soft soft. Add the tomato puree, bay leaves, cayenne, onion powder, garlic powder, thyme, paprika, chile powder, shrimp stock, duck stock, and dried shrimp powder and bring to a boil. Lower the heat and simmer for 30 minutes to allow the flavor from the spices to develop. While simmering, skim the surface for oil and impurities. Add the salt and black pepper.

Meanwhile, put the okra in a baking pan and toss with the olive oil. Roast the okra in the oven for 20 minutes. This step is necessary to reduce its slime. Remove from the oven and add the roasted okra to the gumbo.

Add the cooked chicken and sausage to the pot and simmer for another 25 minutes. Taste the seasoning and adjust with a few dashes of hot sauce if necessary. Add the crab and cook for another 5 minutes. Remove 2 cups (480 ml) broth from the pot and mix in the gumbo filé, stirring quickly so it doesn't lump up. Pour the mixture back into the pot.

Add the shrimp, scallion, and parsley, saving some scallion and parsley to use as garnish. Take the pot off the heat and wait for 5 minutes for the shrimp to cook in the hot gumbo.

To serve, ladle the gumbo with chicken, sausage, shrimp, and crab into a bowl. Put a scoop of rice in the center of the bowl and garnish with parsley, green onion, a dash of filé, and hot sauce.

You Don't Need Alcohol to Make a Great Drink

For all the thought we pour into wine pairings or making cocktails at home when we're entertaining, nonalcoholic options sometimes get overlooked. But with a little bit of effort, your zero-proof options can be just as celebratory and fun as your booze. "If it's anything that you've taken the time and effort to curate, to think about, it automatically elevates your drinks beyond just offering Pellegrino," says Helen's Wines owner and sommelier Helen Johannesen. Here's how the pros make alcohol-free drinks feel special.

FANCY UP YOUR WATER
Add slices of cucumber and/or fresh herbs into ice-cold water. Mint, cilantro, and basil all work here, and you can go ahead and include the stems. It will look beautiful in a pitcher, and you can even add straws into the pitcher and make your water into a punch-bowl moment, as Carla Perez-Gallardo did at Lil Deb's Oasis before the Hudson,

New York, restaurant secured its liquor license. This can work with sparkling water, too: Try adding fresh, in-season passion fruit to Topo Chico and serving it over ice for an eye-catching and refreshing summer drink, which Johannesen does with passion fruit she grows herself. You could also go full-tilt agua fresca by blitzing your cucumber and mint with a bit of sugar, lime juice, and water in a blender and straining it into a pitcher.

SHRUBS, VINEGARS, SYRUPS
Serve up nonalcoholic spritzes by combining any shrubs or fruit vinegars you like with citrus juice and soda water. Making your own syrups—from bruised herbs or scraps of fruit or citrus that aren't nice enough to use for garnish—will mean flavorful mocktails and reduce your waste, says Ashley Richardson, the bar director at Miami hotspot Over Under.

STOCK UP ON ZERO-PROOF BASES
The market for zero-proof spirits has never been better. Pinch Chinese wine director Miguel de Leon's favorites include Acid League, Leitz Eins Zwei Zero, Amass, Lyre, Gnista, Ghia, and Figlia. For nonalcoholic beer, Hopleaf owner Michael Roper recommends Athletic Brewing. Consider kombucha for spritzes à la Miller Union chef Steven

Satterfield, or use tea as a base with citrus and herbs.

DON'T FORGET LEMONADE
Making lemonade or limeade isn't hard—fresh-squeezed juice, sugar, and water are all you really need, per Johannesen—and making it from scratch will feel special. Simple syrup isn't necessary, but if you are going to make simple syrup, consider infusing it with something like lavender to further elevate your drink. Add orange blossom water and mint to make your own version of Reem's chef Reem Assil's Damascus lemonade; combine that with black Ceylon tea to make her Sayyid Palmer.

TURN YOUR HOME INTO A STEAK HOUSE

"A steak house vibe is all about celebration and abundance," says executive chef Chris Pandel of Chicago's destination steak house Swift & Sons. That means it's an excellent starting place for a special-occasion dinner party. Here's how the pros do it.

CHOOSE YOUR STEAK CAREFULLY

"Don't look at the individual plates of the guests—filter everything through a family-style format," says Pandel. He finds it best to choose a few large cuts of meat that can be roasted and sliced for the group: think porterhouse (see page 205), tomahawk rib eye, or chateaubriand. He cautions, however, that if you're still getting comfortable cooking steak, you shouldn't dive into the more expensive cuts. "Don't start your cooking adventure with a 64-ounce rib chop."

STARTERS AND SIDES

Chilled shellfish—whether a dozen oysters or shrimp cocktail or a full-blown seafood tower (page 100)—is a luxurious and classic way to kick off a steak house meal. Follow it up with salad: a wedge salad (page 204) is classic, but you could also do a simple green salad with seasonal vegetables. Offer the sides family-style and encourage guests to serve themselves: That's how the steak houses usually do it. Creamed spinach (page 202) will set the mood, but don't be afraid to stick to simpler sides. David Berson, VP of Brooklyn's famed steak house Peter Luger, skips his restaurant's famous steak sauce–drizzled tomato and onion slices at home (though it would be easy to whip up) and instead sticks to grilled vegetables and potatoes. If you want to go all out with your sides, Pandel recommends "looking to the seasons and committing fully." In the summer, try blanched snap peas with fresh horseradish and shaved radishes as well as corn on the cob, and in the winter, go for potato au gratin and glazed root vegetables.

CONDIMENTS WELCOME

Make an easy chimichurri by blitzing olive oil, parsley, cilantro, garlic, and salt in a food processor. Yangban chef Katianna Hong's chopped kimchi vinaigrette (page 44) is perfect for grilled steaks, and she also recommends serving a little kimchi on the side. Plenty of famous steak houses sell their own steak sauce, and while a well-cooked steak doesn't need it, it can be fun to offer it up as an option.

Steak House Dinner

- **Beef Wellington with Mushroom Duxelles and Creamed Spinach**
  SWIFT & SONS · CHICAGO, IL

- **Iceberg Wedge Salad**
  KEENS STEAKHOUSE · NEW YORK CITY

- **Yorkshire Pudding**
  THE TAM O'SHANTER · LOS ANGELES, CA

DON'T FORGET ABOUT THE DRINKS

Part of the fun of a steak house is drinking old-school martinis and ordering a nice bottle of something red. Make some freezer martinis to have when guests arrive (page 206), and Berson likes a classic wine, like a big-bodied Cabernet. For something a bit more unexpected, Graft Wine Shop owners Miles White and Femi Oyediran recommend seeking out a red with a bit more acid, like a Nebbiolo, and chilling it: 2 hours in the fridge, 20 minutes in the freezer (set a timer!), or 5 minutes in an ice bath ought to do it. For an Argentinean steak house vibe, try a chilled Mission grape wine or a Malbec. Once you're putting in the effort to make a whole steak house dinner, it's worth asking your local wine shop pros to help you figure out a game plan that works with your taste and budget. Ultimately, says Pandel, "for pairings, choose wines that you truly will enjoy."

But First, Martinis

In New York City, tourists and locals looking for a night out on the town slink into Bemelmans Bar at the Carlyle, a Rosewood Hotel, which has buzzed with live jazz and chic socialites since it opened in the late 1940s. It's known as much for its famous murals by the artist Ludwig Bemelmans as for its stiff martini. Here's their recipe, ultra-dry and stirred (not shaken!) in the traditional way. Think of this as a starting point; once you've got the basics covered, there are infinite ways to riff on the martini (see page 206).

THE CLASSIC BEMELMANS BAR MARTINI
Serves 1

5 ounces (147 ml) gin (or vodka if preferred)

1 drop vermouth

Lemon twist or olives

Fill a shaker with ice. Add the gin and vermouth and stir gently (so as not to release the botanical oils) until ice cold. Strain half into a martini glass and the other half into a sidecar placed in shaved ice. Garnish with a lemon twist or olives.

Beef Wellington,
Iceberg Wedge Salad,
Yorkshire Pudding,
Porterhouse Steak

BEEF WELLINGTON
with Mushroom Duxelles and Creamed Spinach

Swift & Sons is what happens when a hospitality-obsessed restaurant group decides to take the traditional steak house presets and dial them up to the most luxurious level possible. The Boka Restaurant Group's hit steak house is a glittering, thoroughly modern affair in the heart of Chicago's former meatpacking district. Order the Beef Wellington and a cart will arrive at your table bearing blushing tenderloin wrapped in an impossibly flaky crust—a thrilling throwback. Beef Wellington is a project, so executive chef Chris Pandel encourages you to work with store-bought puff pastry. The mushroom duxelles and creamed spinach pull double-duty: You'll use them in the Wellington, but they should yield enough that you can also serve them on the side to round out the meal.

Serves **4**

For the creamed spinach:

2 pounds (908 g) baby spinach

½ cup (1 stick/113 g) butter

4¼ cups (227 g) diced yellow onion

2 cloves garlic, minced

¼ cup (30 g) all-purpose flour

¾ cup (180 ml) white wine

¼ cup (60 ml) chicken stock

2½ cups (600 ml) whole milk

2½ cups (600 ml) heavy cream

¼ teaspoon ground nutmeg

1 teaspoon each salt and freshly ground pepper

1 teaspooon Tabasco sauce

For the mushroom duxelles:

¼ cup (60 ml) vegetable oil

1 pound (455 g) finely minced button mushrooms

¾ cup (85 g) finely minced yellow onion

4 cloves garlic, finely minced

2 sprigs fresh thyme

¾ cup (180 ml) white wine

½ cup (120 ml) heavy cream

1½ tablespoons salt

1 teaspoon ground black pepper

1½ teaspoons sherry vinegar

For the Beef Wellington:

3 tablespoons canola oil

2 center-cut (10-ounce/284 g) filet mignons

2 tablespoons Dijon mustard

3 tablespoons (57 g) mushroom duxelles (see above)

3 tablespoons (57 g) creamed spinach (see above)

2 sheets store-bought puff pastry, cut into two 7-inch (17 cm) circles (poke a small hole in the center of the larger circles to allow for venting) and two 4-inch (10 cm) circles

2 eggs, beaten with 2 tablespoons heavy cream, for the egg wash

→ **NOTE:** The restaurant's Wellingtons include foie gras, which you could do at home by seasoning some with salt and pepper and quickly searing it on one side for about 90 seconds. Remove the foie gras from the pan, cool completely in the refrigerator, then add it on top of the mushroom duxelles as the final layer before wrapping the fillets.

To make the creamed spinach, bring a large pot of water to a boil and prepare a bowl of ice and water. Add the spinach to the boiling water, leave it for 10 seconds to wilt, then transfer to the ice water. Place the spinach in a colander with a weighted bowl atop to press out any water and reserve.

Melt the butter in a straight-sided pot over medium-low heat. Add the onions and garlic and cook until softened without any color, about 10 minutes. Add the flour and whisk thoroughly. Reduce the heat to low and cook, stirring, for 5 minutes, until no dry flour or lumps remain. Add the white wine and chicken stock and cook, stirring occasionally, until reduced by half, 30 to 45 minutes. Add the milk and cream, then cook, stirring constantly to prevent scorching at the bottom, until the liquid has reduced by a third, 15 to 20 minutes. Add the nutmeg, salt, pepper, and Tabasco.

Using either a stand blender or an immersion hand blender, blend the sauce for about 1 minute, until smooth. Add a pinch of salt, if needed.

Chill the sauce completely in a wide pan or bowl in the fridge (before mixing with the spinach to prevent any browning of the greens). Wring out any additional moisture from the reserved spinach.

Mix the spinach with half of the sauce to start, adding more, if needed, to taste. Refrigerate until ready to serve. You can make the spinach up to a day ahead. You'll use 3 tablespoons (57 g) for the Wellington assembly and serve the rest as a side.

To make the mushroom duxelles, heat a large sauté pan over medium-high heat and add the vegetable oil. Add the mushrooms and sear for 3 to 5 minutes (do not touch during this time). Stir in the onion, garlic, and thyme and cook until the onions are soft and translucent, about 5 minutes. Add the white wine and cook, stirring occasionally, until reduced by half, 5 to 7 minutes. Add the cream, salt, and pepper, and still over medium-high heat and stirring occasionally, bring to a simmer. Remove and discard the thyme sprigs. Remove the pan from the heat and add the vinegar.

Spread the duxelles on a sheet pan and chill completely in the fridge until ready to serve. You can make the duxelles up to a day ahead. You'll use 3 tablespoons (57 g) for the Wellington assembly and serve the rest as a side.

To make the Wellingtons, place a large sauté pan over high heat. Add the oil and heat until it is just beginning to smoke, then add the fillets and sear for 3 minutes on each side, or until both sides are deeply browned. Remove the fillets from the pan, rub them with the mustard, and cool completely.

Place the fillets on a cutting board and top them with the creamed spinach and then the mushroom duxelles. You should now have a fillet on the bottom, creamed spinach in the middle, and mushroom duxelles on top.

For each Wellington, place the topped fillets in the center of the 4-inch (10 cm) puff pastry circle. Gently drape the 7-inch (17 cm) puff pastry circle over the fillet, pressing the top layer of pastry into the smaller base to seal along the edges of the fillet. Trim any excess puff pastry and discard.

Using a pastry brush, gently brush the egg wash all over the outside of the puff pastry. Do not wash the bottom.

Transfer the assembled beef Wellingtons onto a parchment paper–lined sheet pan and store in the fridge until ready to serve, up to 3 hours ahead, or proceed to cooking.

To cook, preheat the oven to 425°F (220°C).

Bake the beef Wellington for 25 minutes, or until the puff pastry is golden brown and the beef is warmed all the way through. Insert an instant-read thermometer and check for desired doneness (135 to 145°F/55 to 60°C for medium-rare to medium, respectively), accounting for 5°F (3°C) temperature variance, because the Wellington needs to rest and will continue to cook outside the oven. Allow the Wellingtons to rest for 10 minutes before serving. While the Wellingtons rest, warm the remaining creamed spinach and mushrooms, taste, and season with salt if needed.

Serve the Wellingtons with the creamed spinach and mushrooms on the side.

ICEBERG WEDGE SALAD

One of the oldest steak houses in the country, Keens Steakhouse is where locals and tourists alike head for a taste of old New York. All the steak house must-haves are here: the room is dark, the martinis are dry, the steaks are USDA prime, and a wedge salad is on the menu. This one does not call for bacon or tomatoes. In fact, neither was allowed on the salad for years, but now they'll let you add either one. Whichever way you like it, make it that way! The restaurant also uses this dressing as a dip for crudités, so keep that in mind the next time you're setting out a veggie tray.

Serves **2** to **4**

For the blue cheese dressing:
1 cup (226 g) mayonnaise

½ cup (114 g) sour cream

¼ cup (35 g) diced white onion

¼ cup (9 g) chopped fresh Italian parsley

¼ teaspoon minced garlic

1 tablespoon lemon juice

1 cup (135 g) crumbled blue cheese

1 teaspoon salt

4 teaspoons ground white pepper

1 teaspoon cayenne pepper

2 teaspoons red wine vinegar

For the salad assembly:
1 head iceberg lettuce

Salt

¼ cup (35 g) blue cheese crumbles, for garnish

Sliced scallions, green parts only, for garnish

Chopped fresh chives, for garnish

To make the dressing, combine all the ingredients in a medium bowl and set aside. Keep refrigerated until ready to use.

To assemble the salad, cut the head of lettuce into 4 equal pieces. Pool a small amount of dressing on each plate. Put 1 or 2 wedges on each plate and dress with the blue cheese dressing. Season with a touch of salt. Garnish with the blue cheese crumbles, sliced scallions, and chopped chives.

How to Perfect a Porterhouse at Home

As told to by **David Berson**, VP of Peter Luger Steakhouse, the legendary Brooklyn steak house known for its porterhouse, served sliced on a plate sizzling with butter.

First, purchase a great porterhouse. At Peter Luger, we focus on quality and only buy USDA prime. Ask your butcher for USDA prime, about 2 inches (5 cm) thick.

Before you cook it, bring it up to room temperature. Leave it out for at least 30 minutes, but plan ahead for 1 hour if you can. Next, heavily salt it—we use kosher salt at the restaurant. Home cooks tend to undersalt steaks, in my opinion, but a steak can really take a lot of salt. Fresh cracked pepper is fine, too, if you like it.

Now, you'll want to preheat your broiler and get a cast-iron pan heated. Use some butter or oil (I like butter), put the steak in the cast-iron, and let it cook for 4 minutes or so. Beware, you *will* set off your fire alarm. You're looking to get a nice char on one side.

Then take the cast-iron off the heat. Remove the fillet and sirloin and cut it into strips, and then, to make it the Peter Luger experience, you'll put the bone back into the skillet—and then put the slices back in the pan, making sure the side that was down is now facing up. Put a little more butter on top and put it under the broiler for about 4 minutes. Don't overcook it. The meat is already sliced at this point, so it will cook

quickly; you can always cook it a little more if needed.

As soon as it's done in the cast-iron, that's the money shot. It should be a beautiful porterhouse, with sizzling, buttery juices. That moment is as close as we can get at home to the Peter Luger steak experience.

If you really want to go all out, you could have some preheated plates. You'll want to give each person a piece of fillet and sirloin and top it with a spoonful of the drippings from the pan.

Martinis Are Surprisingly Adaptable

GO 50/50

A basic 50/50 is a martini with equal parts dry vermouth and gin or vodka. Cocktail expert John deBary appreciates that this version of the cocktail is lower proof. "I like toning it down because you typically have a martini before dinner and then you're sloshed and done at 7 p.m."

Takibi bartender Alex Anderson also prefers a 50/50—"I happen to love love love fortified wines," she says—and she makes hers with Dolin Dry vermouth and a dash of orange bitters and serves it up with a lemon twist. "There is an unfortunate negative connotation with vermouth because most people don't realize that it needs to be refrigerated after it's opened, and you really shouldn't keep it in your fridge after a month."

SPLIT THE BASE

"Cutting your gin with a little sake, soju, or baijiu gives you a totally different flavor profile," says Water Witch bar manager Sam Miller. He recommends experimenting by keeping the basic ratio intact. So, where his standard gin martini is 2½ ounces (74 ml) gin to ½ ounce (14 ml) dry vermouth, Miller will reduce the gin by an ounce and swap in an ounce of a different spirit.

TWIST IT

Sure, lemon twists are classic for a reason, but Caroline Styne, the wine director and co-owner of beloved LA restaurants A.O.C. and Tavern, recommends trying an orange twist in a very dry vodka martini. "This subtle switch makes a big difference," she says, resulting in what she calls "a very elegant variation."

If you're sticking with lemon, Bludorn wine director Molly Austad recommends using a citrus peeler to make lemon swaths. "Actually, twisting a lemon for a drink is very time-consuming and quite difficult to do," she says, "while a swath allows you to get a good amount of lemon oil on the martini itself without having to peel a lemon directly over the glass."

GO FROZEN

Nearly every bartender we talked to about martinis mentioned the key to serving them to a large group is making a large batch in a pitcher and sticking it in the freezer. This also means pre-diluting with water, rather than stirring over ice to order, which is way easier when you are serving a lot of people. Just don't overdo the water. "I like doing a quarter of the volume of the recipe as water," says deBary. "So, if I were making a big batch—a 750 of gin or vodka, with a standard 375 milliliter bottle of vermouth (a 2:1 ratio), I'd just use the 375 bottle as a measuring cup for the water."

For a celebration, step up your garnish game, too. "The showstopper for martinis at a party is offering the special garnishes that restaurants frequently have but are often not found in people's homes. You can pre-stuff olives with blue cheese using a pastry bag. These make a great snack later, if your guests don't use them all for their drinks," says Austad. She also likes to pickle her own onions for Gibsons. "Pickles can keep for a long period of time, so I make a large batch and every time I have a party my guests seem so surprised that I went out of my way to have house-made onions when, really, they've been sitting in my fridge since the day I made them."

YORKSHIRE PUDDING

In an old Tudor building in quiet Atwater Village, the Tam O'Shanter is a neighborhood steak house with history—Walt Disney was a regular back in the day, and it's credited as the oldest operating restaurant in the city. It's the casual cousin to the glitzier Lawry's in Beverly Hills, with which it shares ownership and a great prime rib. These days, the Tam O'Shanter is the kind of place that hosts birthday celebrations and visiting parents; tartans decorate the walls, and it's not uncommon to be served by a bartender who speaks with a Scottish brogue (up to you to decide if it's real). In keeping with the UK theme, every plate of prime rib is served with Yorkshire pudding, an airy, delicate alternative to the boring dinner rolls you'll find at some other steak houses. To bring the full Tam experience home, serve your Yorkshire pudding with steak, mashed potatoes, and gravy, as well as creamed spinach or corn. Or just serve with butter and enjoy with literally anything.

Makes **12**

4 or 5 large eggs (228 g)

½ teaspoon salt

2 cups (250 g) all-purpose flour

1 cup (240 ml) whole milk

Butter, oil, or cooking spray, for greasing

Using a handheld electric mixer or stand mixer, whisk the eggs with the salt on medium speed for 5 minutes until soft and fluffy. Turn the speed down to low and gradually add the flour. Raise the speed back to medium and continue mixing for 10 more minutes. Lower the speed again, add the milk, and mix on low to medium speed for another 10 minutes. Place the batter in an airtight container and refrigerate for 24 hours.

Preheat the oven to 450°F (230°C) and preheat a 12-hole muffin pan in the oven for 10 minutes.

Heavily grease the pan with butter, oil, or cooking spray. Divide the batter into the holes and bake for 20 minutes, or until golden and puffy.

SIDES SIDES SIDES
SIDES SIDES SIDES
SIDES SIDES SIDES
SIDES SIDES SIDES
SIDES SIDES SIDES
SIDES SIDES SIDES

7

EXTRAS REVEAL ALL

The section of a restaurant's menu dedicated to side dishes is like a map legend: It will tell you so much about how to read the rest of the document. A restaurant going for French bistro vibes will have great fries; a restaurant that fancies itself a trattoria will have some lovely verdura. Sides set the scene.

A selection of compelling sides suggests a kitchen that is aiming to do their absolute best work; you're in good hands if even the extras are thoughtful. Something critical also happens to the way we approach ordering when a restaurant has a shareable, must-order dish: Knowing you'll have a serving spoon's worth of pelmeni dumplings on your plate or that you'll have a samosa to claim as your own provides the foundation upon which you build the rest of the order. When that utterly essential taste of the restaurant is on the side, it's a filter through which to experience every other bite on the table.

A composed side dish can take your meals at home from simple to spectacular. Instead of steaming your veggies, you might char them on the grill, then build a salad. Try bathing artichokes in olive oil and roasting them slowly or seasoning them with more than just salt and pepper. A creative approach to a staple side like mofongo can bring a chef's touch to your most comforting meals. A glorious side salad that offers texture upon texture and flavor layered on flavor will make even the easiest main course sing. It might not be the biggest or the loudest dish on the table, but a side can absolutely be the highlight of your meal.

CARCIOFI ALLA ROMANA
(Roman Braised Artichokes)

VIA CAROTA
New York City

Via Carota is equal parts see-and-be-seen spot and West Village institution, a testament to the amazing knack married chef-restaurateurs Jodi Williams and Rita Sodi have for absolutely nailing that effortlessly cool, all-day dining vibe. Their Italian cooking is unpretentious yet uncommonly good. There are no tricks in their seasonal Roman-style braised artichokes, just the knowledge that comes from their combined decades cooking professionally: knowing how to trim these spiky veggies, knowing how to coax big flavors from humble ingredients, knowing that, as the chefs themselves put it, "slow-cooking artichokes in mint, garlic, anchovies, wine, and olive oil for over an hour is transformational." And since these artichokes are meant to be served at room temperature, you can make this elegant spring side dish ahead of time.

Serves **4**

6 large artichokes

1 lemon, halved

4 cloves garlic, peeled

8 anchovy fillets

Handful of fresh mint leaves

Extra-virgin olive oil

Pinch of red chile flakes

½ teaspoon salt

1½ cups (360 ml) dry white wine

Working one artichoke at a time, snap off the tough outer leaves until you reach the softer yellow-green leaves inside. Slice off the top third of each artichoke with a serrated knife or sharp chef's knife (discard the tops and the outer leaves). Trim the stem, keeping about 1 inch (2 to 3 cm). As you work, rub the cut surfaces with the cut side of the lemon halves. (You can also place the trimmed artichokes in a bowl of cold water mixed with the juice of 1 lemon.)

Peel the outer layer of the trimmed artichoke bottom and the stems using a paring knife or vegetable peeler. To remove the choke, hold the artichoke firmly in the palm of your hand and use both thumbs to push open the leaves, turning and nudging the leaves apart until you can reach the center with a spoon. Scoop out any small, sharp leaves from the heart, using a teaspoon to scrape out the fuzzy choke until the artichoke heart is completely clean.

Finely chop the garlic, anchovies, and mint, adding enough olive oil to help the mixture come together into a coarse pesto, roughly 3 tablespoons. Stir in the chile flakes. Rub the pesto all over the artichokes, inside and out.

Arrange the artichokes upright in a pot large enough to hold them snugly and add any extra stems. Season with the salt and add a good pour of olive oil (about ⅓ cup/80 ml) and the wine. Make sure liquid covers the artichokes by two-thirds; add water if needed. Bring to a simmer over medium-high heat, then reduce the heat to low and cook for 10 minutes. Cover the pot and continue cooking until a fork can slide easily into the thickest part of the hearts, 30 to 45 minutes depending on the freshness and size of the artichokes. Uncover the pot occasionally to turn the artichokes in the liquid as they cook. The artichokes can also be cooked this way in the oven—simply place the covered pot in a preheated 375°F (190°C) oven.

Remove from the heat and leave the artichokes to cool in their liquid for at least 20 minutes. The artichokes can be stored in their cooking liquid, refrigerated, for up to 3 days.

VEGAN MOFONGO
with Green Plantains

MY ABUELAS FOOD
Atlanta, Georgia

My Abuelas Food is a shining star in Atlanta's pop-up scene, slinging chef Luis Martinez's Puerto Rican cooking to adoring fans since 2018. Dedicated to his two grandmothers, the abuelas who inspired his approach to Puerto Rican cuisine, his menu of family favorites is deceptively modern. Martinez doesn't hesitate to tinker with tradition, and so: vegan mofongo. Traditionally you would smash fried green plantains with garlic and chicharrones to create this iconic Puerto Rican dish. But for My Abuelas Food, Martinez perfected a vegan version that relies on both raw and toasted garlic to bring depth that he says stays true to "traditional Boricua sazón." Pair it with your favorite vegetables, mojo (see page 72), or protein (shrimp would be especially great with this), and don't skimp on the fresh cilantro.

Serves **4**

3 cups (720 ml) corn oil or other frying oil

2 green plantains, peeled (see Note) and sliced

2 cloves garlic, peeled

1 head garlic, cloves peeled, chopped, and toasted in oil

1 teaspoon salt, or more to taste

½ teaspoon ground black pepper

3 tablespoons chopped fresh cilantro

2 tablespoons extra-virgin olive oil, or more to taste

Avocado slices or your favorite vegetable

→ **NOTE:** Running hot water over the plantain skin will help loosen it, making peeling easier. See page 72 for more details.

Heat the corn oil in a medium skillet over medium heat. Add the plantains and fry for 5 to 8 minutes, until golden brown on all sides and crisp. Transfer the plantains to a plate lined with paper towels to absorb excess grease.

Using a mortar and pestle, mash the fried plantains in batches until the mixture comes together.

Add the raw garlic, toasted garlic, salt, black pepper, cilantro, and olive oil and continue mashing until the mixture looks homogenous. Taste and adjust for seasoning.

Shape the warm mofongo with your hands or use a small bowl or preferred mold and transfer to a serving plate. Serve with your favorite vegetables or with slices of fresh avocado.

JIMMY RED GRITS
with Sorghum-Cured Egg Yolks and Bay Oil

AUDREY
Nashville, Tennessee

◇◇◇

When it opened in Nashville in 2021, Audrey was hailed as a return to the kind of experimental fine dining the celebrated chef Sean Brock first became a household name for at McCrady's in Charleston. As befits Brock's flagship, Audrey's menu still relies on Brock's curiosity and passion for legacy Southern ingredients as its compass. His team makes this menu staple with Jimmy Red grits, a corn varietal spared from extinction, thanks to the work of purveyors like Marsh Hen Mill (who also sells Jimmy Red grits online). The recipe itself is technique-heavy and not shy about calling for specialty ingredients and sub-recipes: We've cut some of those (but if you want to make your own egg white garum or corn aminos to season your grits, we won't stop you). At the restaurant, Brock has served these grits with smoked Ossabaw pork or a skewer of venison. You can take those as inspiration, but trust that this side dish would shine paired with whatever smoked or grilled option you've got planned.

→ **NOTES:** If you want to skip the sorghum egg, try a soft-boiled egg instead (you could give it a splash of soy for the extra umami kick that would come from the curing), or take Brock's suggestion and soak boiled egg yolks in soy sauce overnight and use those instead (he'd also tell you to dehydrate them if you've got time, but we're looking for shortcuts, here!).

Egg whites will keep in the freezer, so consider saving them to make meringues, egg-white omelets, or anything else that calls for egg whites.

For the grits:
1½ cups (250 g) Jimmy Red grits

2 bay leaves

For the grit cream:
10 tablespoons (100 g) Jimmy Red Grits

2 cups (480 ml) heavy cream

For the sorghum-cured egg yolk:
1 cup (200 g) sorghum

3½ teaspoons Redmond Real Salt

6 eggs

For the bay oil:
6½ cups (200 g) fresh bay leaves

2⅓ cups (544 ml) grapeseed oil

For the black truffle puree:
⅔ cup (130 g) whole canned black truffles, plus ¼ cup (60 ml) black truffle juice (from the can)

1½ tablespoons Banyuls vinegar (preferably smoked, or use the highest quality sherry vinegar you can find)

3½ tablespoons grapeseed oil

¾ tablespoon black truffle oil

For the crispy shallots and garlic:
½ cup (50 g) shallots, thinly sliced

⅔ cup (50 g) garlic, thinly sliced

About 1 cup (240 ml) grapeseed oil

To assemble:
Butter, preferably Plugrá

Gluten-free soy sauce

Fresh lemon juice

Redmond's Real Salt

Espelette pepper

To make the grits, combine 4¾ cups (1.1 L) filtered water and the grits in a large bowl, cover, and soak overnight. The next day, skim off any hulls that rose to the top. Be careful to not disturb the mix when handling, which would cause hulls to sink to the bottom. Transfer the grits and soaking water to a large pot, skim any hulls that rise to the top, and bring to a boil over high heat. Boil for 1 to 2 minutes to allow the starches to hydrate. Remove from the heat, cover, and let stand for 10 minutes to allow the grits to relax. Uncover the grits, add the bay leaves, and continue to cook over low heat for 1 hour, or until the grits are very soft.

To make the grit cream, combine the grits and heavy cream in a medium bowl, refrigerate, and allow it to cold steep for at least 24 hours and no more than 36 hours. Strain out and discard the grits, reserving the cream.

To make the cured egg yolks, in a nonreactive container such as a Pyrex, combine 1 cup (240 ml) water with the sorghum and salt to make a brine. Separate the yolks from the whites and place the yolks into the brine. (Discard the whites or save for another use.) Cure the yolks for at least 5 hours, flipping every 30 minutes to ensure that they cure evenly.

To make the bay oil, combine the bay leaves and grapeseed oil in a high-speed blender and blend until the mixture comes up above 140°F (60°C), warm to the touch. Strain through a fine-mesh strainer and reserve.

To make the truffle puree, combine the truffles, truffle juice, and vinegar in a blender and blend until smooth. Slowly drizzle in the oils through the hole in the lid until emulsified.

To make the crispy shallots and garlic, when you are ready to serve, place the shallots and garlic into a shallow pan and add just enough cold oil to cover. Slowly bring the mixture up to 325°F (165°C). Fry over medium-high heat until the shallots are crispy, taking care not to let them burn. Use a slotted spoon to transfer the fried shallots and garlic to a paper towel–lined plate.

To assemble, warm the grits in a pot and season with butter, soy sauce, lemon juice, and salt. Adjust the seasoning to taste—you are going for the absolute best version of buttery movie theater popcorn.

In a separate pot, warm up the grit cream. Season with salt, Espelette pepper, lemon juice, and bay oil (this will be almost like a broken vinaigrette).

In each bowl, place a dollop of the truffle puree and cover with about 1 cup (250 g) seasoned grits. Sprinkle on the crispy shallots and garlic and place a cured yolk right in the center of the bowl. Sprinkle the Espelette pepper on top of the egg and spoon over enough of the seasoned grit cream to cover the rest of the grits.

Broccolini Salad,
Cucumber Salad,
Pipirrana Salad

BROCCOLINI SALAD
with Hearts of Palm and Ginger Vinaigrette

From co-owners chef Jonathan Whitener and front-of-house dynamo Lien Ta, Here's Looking at You is one of those genre-bending, category-defying restaurants that Los Angeles does so well. Occupying a previously nondescript corner on the fringes of K-town, HLAY attracts an equally eclectic mix of guests, the dining room full of date nights, friendly catch-ups, celebratory dinners, and a bar crowd wise to how great the tiki-adjacent cocktails are. The menu is chock-full of small plates that take big swings: This Broccolini salad is a head-scratcher that absolutely slaps. Whitener tops charred Broccolini with every texture you can think of—crunchy fried almonds and peanuts, tender hearts of palm, crispy toasted sesame seeds—and dresses it all in a zingy ginger dressing that will thankfully leave you with enough left over to use for enlivening your salads and veggies all week long.

Serves 4

For the ginger vinaigrette:
1 cup plus 1 tablespoon (254 ml) distilled vinegar

2 tablespoons brown sugar

1¼ cups (230 g) palm sugar

1 makrut lime leaf

1 teaspoon minced garlic

1 Thai chile, minced

1¾ cups (370 g) minced fresh ginger

1 cup (130 g) minced shallots

¾ cup (180 ml) grapeseed oil

2 teaspoons ground white pepper

For the Broccolini salad:
Salt

4 bunches (907 g) Broccolini or Spigarello

1 cup (142 g) almonds, lightly fried and chopped

1 cup (142 g) peanuts, lightly fried and chopped

1 cup (140 g) sunflower seeds, lightly toasted

1 cup (28 g) sorghum, popped

⅓ cup (47 g) black sesame seeds, lightly toasted

⅓ cup (47 g) white sesame seeds, lightly toasted

1 cup (146 g) chopped hearts of palm (preferably fresh, but canned works, too)

1 serrano chile, thinly sliced

To make the ginger vinaigrette, in a medium saucepan, combine ½ cup (120 ml) water, the vinegar, brown sugar, and palm sugar and bring to a simmer, stirring to dissolve the sugars. Turn off the heat and add the lime leaf, garlic, chile, ginger, shallots, grapeseed oil, and white pepper. Let the vinaigrette stand at room temperature for 10 to 15 minutes, then cover and refrigerate (see Notes).

To make the Broccolini, bring a large pot of salted water to a boil and prepare an ice bath. Blanch the Broccolini bunches for about 2 minutes, then transfer them into the ice bath. Drain and dry off the Broccolini with paper towels.

Preheat a grill (see Note) to medium and carefully char the Broccolini, 2 to 3 minutes, making sure to not burn it. Remove the Broccolini from the grill and roughly chop it.

Divide the Broccolini into 4 bowls, placing it in the center. Spoon an equal amount of the nuts, seeds, popped sorghum, hearts of palm, and chile by adding each ingredient side by side in a circular formation over the Broccolini. Drizzle 3 tablespoons of the ginger vinaigrette in the center of each bowl. Serve and encourage everyone to mix their salads.

→ **NOTES:** Leftover ginger vinaigrette can be stored in the refrigerator for up to 1 week.

If you don't have a grill, you can char the Broccolini in a cast-iron pan or a grill pan over medium-high heat.

CUCUMBER SALAD
with Smoked Mussels

DAME
New York City

Smoked fish, cucumbers, and dill are a classic combo, and that's where chef Ed Szymanski started when he was thinking up a salad to offer on Dame's opening menu. It was June 2021, and June in New York can be hot and humid; co-owner Patricia Howard and the servers ended up bringing plate after plate of these cooling salads to outdoor diners. The method here is straightforward but not necessarily simple; you'll be steaming then smoking mussels, creating an emulsion from garlic oil you've created, and garnishing things with dill oil you'll strain through a coffee filter. It's all doable, and worth it for a gorgeous finished dish. And don't hesitate to adapt this one. At Dame, Szymanski will offer up the cucumber salad on its own for vegan diners, and in winter months he'll use the mussel emulsion with cabbage and shaved truffle; you could sub in a different smoked fish entirely.

→ **NOTES:** If you want to save yourself the work of steaming the mussels, you could buy shucked mussels from the grocery store (just make sure they're extremely fresh).

To cold smoke without a gun, place a pan of wood chip embers in the bottom of the oven and a pan of ice in the middle rack. Put the mussels in a perforated pan on the top rack. The ice will ensure that the heat and smoke dissipate before they hit the mussel meat.

Serves **4 to 6**

For the salad assembly:
2 large cucumbers

Salt and lemon zest to taste

¼ cup (60 ml) garlic oil (see above)

1 small piece fresh horseradish (save for serving)

For the dill oil:
1 pound (455 g) fresh dill (with a few sprigs reserved for garnish)

½ to ¾ cup (120 to 180 ml) vegetable or other neutral oil

For the garlic oil:
3 cups (720 ml) vegetable or other neutral oil

2 heads garlic, peeled

For the smoked mussels:
5 pounds (2.25 kg) live mussels, rinsed and scrubbed

Apple, cherry, or oak wood chips, for smoking

¾ cup (180 ml) garlic oil (see above)

¾ cup (180 ml) tamari

For the emulsion:
2½ cups (375 g) cooked mussel meat (see above), plus about 1 cup extra for garnishing

½ cup (120 ml) tamari

Zest of 1 lemon

1 clove garlic, peeled

2 cups (480 ml) garlic oil (see above)

Peel and seed the cucumbers, then cut into bite-size pieces. Place in a bowl, add the salt, lemon zest, and ¼ cup (60 ml) garlic oil, and marinate for about 1 hour, or while you prep everything else.

To make the dill oil, place the dill with the neutral oil in a blender and blend for about 8 minutes on high speed. The blender will get hot on the sides—that's okay! Strain the dill oil through a coffee filter and refrigerate immediately.

To make the garlic oil, combine the vegetable oil and garlic in a medium saucepan and place over the lowest heat. Cook for at least 1 hour, until the garlic has softened. Cool before using.

To make the smoked mussels, steam the mussels in water for 6 to 8 minutes, until they open. Discard any that do not open. Remove from the pot and remove them from their shells. Cold smoke over hardwood for 20 to 30 minutes (see Note) or use a handheld smoking gun with a dome. Place in a bowl, cover the mussels with the ¾ cup (180 ml) garlic oil and the ¾ cup (180 ml) tamari, and let sit for 15 minutes.

Put the 2½ cups (375 g) smoked mussel meat, the tamari, lemon zest, garlic, and ⅓ cup (70 g) water into a blender (the remaining mussel meat is your garnish) and blend until well blended. Drizzle in the 2 cups (480 ml) garlic oil to emulsify.

To assemble the salad, spoon about ¾ cup (175 ml) of mussel emulsion on the bottom of each serving plate. Add the marinated cucumbers and some of the mussel meat on top. Drizzle with dill oil and garnish with dill fronds. Shave some horseradish on the plated dish and serve.

PIPIRRANA SALAD
with Tahini Yogurt

At Brooklyn restaurant La Vara, chefs Alex Raij and Eder Montero explore Spanish cooking, their specialty, through the lens of its Jewish and Moorish influences. There's always been some version of a pipirrana salad on the menu, which traditionally is made from tomatoes, onion, cucumber, and bell peppers. But Raij, in her typical way, let her idea of the dish wander: What if she added greens from the local farmers' market? What if she tipped it toward a tabbouleh with some grains? Her resulting dish—bursting with the fresh flavors of snap peas and cilantro and dressed with a pomegranate vinaigrette *and* a creamy tahini yogurt—is a textbook example of how La Vara explores how a dish moves through a region and takes on different culinary identities. At home, this recipe will have you approaching a salad like a chef does. Having two different sauces is a distinctly restaurant-y approach, and these two are particularly useful to have under your belt: The vinaigrette is a reliable one for salads, and the yogurt makes a great dip. The salad itself is also highly adaptable; some olive-packed tuna would be a great addition for a picnic (maybe skip the yogurt for that one).

Serves **4**

To make the salad, first cook the black-eyed peas or red peas per package instructions. Cool and set aside.

Then blanch the sugar snap peas: Bring a large pot of salted water to a boil and prepare a bowl with ice water. Boil the sugar snaps for 1 to 2 minutes, until bright green. Drain and immediately transfer to the ice bath to cool.

In a large bowl, combine the cooled black-eyed or red peas with the blanched sugar snap peas, cucumber, bell peppers, cherry tomatoes, and about half of the cilantro leaves. Toss to combine.

To make the vinaigrette, combine the lemon juice, garlic, pomegranate molasses, salt, and Aleppo pepper in a blender and process to combine. With the blender still running, slowly add the olive oil through the hole in the lid until emulsified. Set aside and wipe out the blender.

To make the tahini yogurt, combine the yogurt, lukewarm water, tahini, lemon juice, pomegranate molasses, garlic, salt, and cayenne and blend until smooth. With the blender still running, slowly add the olive oil through the hole in the lid until combined. Add the dill and blend briefly, until just combined.

To assemble the salad, toss the black-eyed peas and vegetable mixture with your desired amount of vinaigrette. Taste and add more salt or vinaigrette, if needed. Spread the salad on a large serving platter and generously drizzle with tahini yogurt, garnish with the remaining cilantro, and drizzle with olive oil.

For the salad:

1 cup (260 g) dried black-eyed peas or Anson Mills Sea Island red peas

1 cup (100 g) sugar snap peas

Salt

6 small Persian cucumbers, peeled, seeded, and finely chopped

2 green bell peppers, finely chopped

1 cup (145 g) Sungold or small cherry tomatoes, halved and diced

½ bunch cilantro, leaves picked, stems discarded

For the vinaigrette:

½ cup (120 ml) lemon juice

2 cloves garlic, peeled

1½ tablespoons pomegranate molasses

1½ teaspoons salt

1 tablespoon Aleppo pepper

⅔ cup (140 ml) extra-virgin olive oil

For the tahini yogurt:

½ cup (143 g) plain whole-milk Greek yogurt

⅓ cup (80 ml) lukewarm water

¼ cup (65 g) tahini

2 tablespoons lemon juice

1½ tablespoons pomegranate molasses

1 small clove garlic, roughly chopped

1 teaspoon salt

⅛ teaspoon cayenne pepper

2 tablespoons extra-virgin olive oil, plus more for drizzling

1 tablespoon chopped fresh dill

Shopping List: The Beers Pros Love

- La Fin du Monde
- Tripel Karmeliet
- Golden Monkey
- Leffe Blonde
- Orval Trappist
- Anchor Porter
- Cantillon
- Lindemans Framboise
- Lagunitas IPA
- North Coast Brewing Brother Thelonious
- Sapporo
- Hite
- Guinness
- Miller Lite

Recommended by: Luis Martinez, Tia Barrett, Michael Roper, Miguel de Leon, Reem Assil, Nick Bognar, Ed Szymanski, Ashley Richardson

Get Creative with a Shandy

Easy to make and easy to like, a typical shandy is the delicious combination of beer with lemon soda or ginger ale (or even lemonade). It's wonderfully adaptable, so consider these ideas as jumping-off points to finding your own perfect drink.

AMERICAN LAGER + PINEAPPLE JUICE + TEQUILA
Recommended by: Esmé beverage director Tia Barrett

TENSEI ENDLESS SUMMER TOKUBETSU HONJOZO + OXBOW SURFCASTING FARMHOUSE ALE
Recommended by: Koji Club owner Alyssa Mikiko DiPasquale

RED HORSE BEER + CALAMANSI JUICE + PALM SUGAR
Recommended by: Pinch Chinese wine director Miguel de Leon

FROZEN MARGARITA + BEER + CHILE POWDER + LIME
Recommended by: Miller Union chef Steven Satterfield

Dok Khleh Pork Salad, Brussels Sprouts
Larb, Spiced Potato Vegetable Samosas

DOH KHLEH PORK SALAD
with Onion and Chile

DHAMAKA
New York City

The third restaurant from hitmakers restaurateur Roni Mazumdar and chef Chintan Pandya, Dhamaka took New York City by storm when it opened in 2021 with a capsaicin-laced menu of dishes from India's villages. Their vision of bringing the kind of cooking that happens outside of the country's major cities is a boon for amateur cooks, too; many of these recipes originated in home kitchens. A popular starter since the restaurant's earliest days, doh khleh is a pork salad hailing from the northeast state of Meghalaya. At Dhamaka, Pandya makes the salad with pig head, but for the home cook, he subbed in pork belly. He didn't skimp on heat here, though, layering chile after chile into the dish. The cooking liquid for the pork includes Deggi mirch, a mild red Indian chile powder that, once on your spice rack, makes a compelling substitution for any recipe calling for chile powder and as a topping for fries or even popcorn. The punch comes from red finger chiles and green chiles, with the latter also comprising a major component of the assembled salad.

→ **NOTES:** For the ginger paste, use store-bought or blend peeled, chopped fresh ginger with a bit of neutral oil in a blender or food processor.

For the garlic paste, use store-bought or blend peeled garlic cloves with a bit of neutral oil in a blender or food processor.

Serves **5**

For the pork and cooking liquid:
1 pound (455 g) pork belly, cut into medium pieces

1 quart (960 ml) chicken stock

¾ tablespoon ground turmeric

¾ tablespoon Deggi Mirch chile powder

2 whole dried red finger chiles

2 green chiles

5 peppercorns

2 dried bay leaves

1½ tablespoons ginger paste (see Notes)

1½ tablespoons garlic paste (see Notes)

Salt

For the dressing:
2 tablespoons distilled white vinegar

Juice of 2 lemons

Salt

For the salad:
2 cups (125 g) chopped red onion

2 cups (80 g) chopped fresh cilantro

3 tablespoons chopped green chile

2 tablespoons peeled and chopped fresh ginger

In a pressure cooker, combine all of the ingredients for the cooking liquid, including the pork belly. Cook on high pressure for 45 minutes, then let the pressure naturally release. Remove the lid, set the pork aside, strain the liquid, and reserve it for the dressing.

To make the dressing, in a small bowl, whisk together ½ cup (120 ml) of the reserved cooking liquid, the vinegar, lemon juice, and salt.

Grill the cooked pork belly on a gas or charcoal grill (you can also use a cast-iron skillet or grill pan) just to get a crust, then dice it. Assemble the salad by combining the red onions, cilantro, green chile, and ginger in a bowl. Toss with the dressing, adding more or less depending on your taste. Mix in the diced grilled pork belly and serve.

SPICED POTATO VEGETABLE SAMOSAS

RASA
Washington, D.C.

◇◇◇

When Rahul Vinod and Sahil Rahman—childhood friends whose parents were partners in the restaurant business—went into business together, they had a vision: Rasa would be an approachable quick-service setup that would connect diners with the from-scratch Indian cooking that they love. Now at their locations in D.C., diners can get basmati rice bowls and salads topped with flavorful add-ons like masala beets, sweet potato tikki, and tamarind ginger chutney, and an order of mini samosas on the side. One of Rasa's best-selling sides, the samosas are flaky and crisp and generously stuffed with a classic potato-and-pea filling. They're spicy, savory, and a perfect afternoon pick-me-up. At the restaurant, an order includes two mini samosas; at home, you can stick with minis or go for a medium size and serve them with any chutneys you like as a snack, starter, or side.

Makes about **10** medium
or **20** cocktail-size samosas

For the dough:

1½ cups (180 g) all-purpose flour, plus more for dusting

1 teaspoon ajwain seeds (see Note)

¼ teaspoon salt

¼ cup (60 ml) sunflower oil, vegetable oil, or ghee

For the filling:

4 to 6 tablespoons (60 to 90 ml) sunflower or vegetable oil

½ teaspoon coriander seeds

1 teaspoon cumin seeds

1 teaspoon chopped fresh ginger

2 cups (345 g) fresh or frozen green peas

3 cups (640 g) cooked and mashed potatoes

1½ teaspoons chaat masala spice blend

1½ teaspoons chana masala spice blend

½ teaspoon salt

2 tablespoons chopped fresh cilantro

2 quarts (2 L) vegetable or other frying oil

→ **NOTE:** Ajwain seeds can be purchased online from spice vendors like Spicewalla (which also sells a great chaat masala), at some grocery stores, and at Indian markets. Opt for whole seeds rather than ground ajwain; the whole seeds tend to be higher quality and will keep for longer.

To make the dough, sift the flour into a bowl and mix in the ajwain seeds and the salt. Add the sunflower oil and ½ cup (120 ml) water. Mix the dough by hand until it's firm but not sticky. It's okay to add more water 1 tablespoon at a time if the dough feels stiff; it should be pliable. Cover with a damp towel and set aside for at least 30 minutes and no more than 1 hour. Divide the dough into 5 (or 10 for smaller samosas) equal pieces. Roll each piece into a ball. Using a rolling pin, roll each ball into a very thin circle about 1 mm thick. Cut each in half so you have 2 half moons of dough.

Stack the rolled samosa wrappers on top of each other with a light dusting of flour in between to keep them from sticking. Cover the wrappers with a damp towel or plastic wrap to keep them moist.

To make the filling, heat the sunflower oil in a large skillet over medium-high heat. Add the coriander and cumin seeds—they will crackle and change color almost immediately. Immediately add the ginger and continue to cook until fragrant, about 2 minutes. Add the green peas and cook, stirring, until they are cooked through (if using frozen peas, cook until the water evaporates). Add the mashed potatoes along with the chaat masala, chana masala, salt, and cilantro. Stir thoroughly to combine. Remove from the heat and let the mixture come to room temperature before assembling. (The filling can be prepped the day before and stored in an airtight container in the refrigerator.)

To assemble, take a rolled-out samosa wrapper and place one on your palm. Moisten the edges with a little water and seal to make a cone. Fill the cone with the spiced potato mixture—be careful not to overstuff. Seal the cone well, making sure there are no holes or gaps in between.

In a large heavy-bottomed pot or Dutch oven, heat the frying oil to 350°F (175°C) according to a deep-frying thermometer. Deep-fry the samosas for about 2 minutes on each side, turning to ensure even color, until nicely crisp and browned. Transfer to a paper towel–lined sheet. Serve hot.

BRUSSELS SPROUTS LARB

NIGHT + MARKET SONG
Los Angeles, California

Chef Kris Yenbamroong's story—turning his parents' Thai restaurant into one of the city's hottest destinations—is the stuff of LA legend. Well over a decade in, his restaurant empire remains a party: At Night + Market Song, the raucous Silver Lake mainstay, diners come for irreverent Thai street food and a killer natural wine list curated by the chef and his wife and business partner, Sarah. This brussels sprouts larb first appeared on the Song menu as a one-off, then appeared at his different restaurants as the mood and season saw fit. To make it easier for you at home, we've gone ahead and subbed in vegetarian fish sauce and jarred Thai chile paste for the house vegan chile jam (both of these can be found online and at some Asian grocery stores). You'll still be making your own toasted rice powder, though—store-bought can't compete—and Yenbamroong opts for jasmine rice over the more common glutinous rice. Spicy, salty, and an absolutely dynamite way to serve up a staple fall and winter vegetable, these brussels sprouts will steal the show.

Serves **4**

To make the rice powder, cut off the bottom inch of the lemongrass stalk and discard (or save for stock). Peel the first layer and discard. Angling the knife on a bias, slice the lemongrass as thinly as possible.

Toast the rice in a medium sauté pan over low heat until it is golden brown and the rice grains are easily broken when pressed with your thumb and index finger, 15 to 25 minutes. Be careful not to scorch the rice. Transfer to a small bowl and set aside. Add the lemongrass to the same pan and toast until it is browned and crisp, 5 to 10 minutes, taking care not to let it burn. Remove from the pan and set aside. Add the galangal to the same pan and toast until it is browned, 5 to 10 minutes, then remove and set aside. Finally, toast the lime leaves in the same pan until browned and crisp, 5 minutes, remove, and set aside.

Cool all the toasted ingredients, then blend in a mortar and pestle or spice grinder until it resembles fine sand. Set aside 1 teaspoon of the rice powder to add to the dish and store the rest in an airtight container.

To make the larb, in a heavy pot, heat the oil to 350°F (175°C) according to a deep-frying thermometer. Add the brussels sprouts and fry for 2 minutes, or until crispy and browned.

In a metal mixing bowl, build the sauce by combining the vegan chile paste, vegetarian fish sauce, lime juice, sugar, and chile powder. Whisk well. Add the fried brussels sprouts and toss with the sauce. Add the garlic, lemongrass, Thai basil, cilantro, scallions, culantro, rau ram, mint, and red onion. Toss well. Transfer to a serving plate, sprinkle with the rice powder, and serve.

For the rice powder (see Note):
1 stalk lemongrass

¾ cup (145 g) jasmine rice

⅓ cup (35 g) peeled, small-diced fresh galangal

8 makrut lime leaves

For the brussels sprouts larb:
4 cups (960 ml) vegetable oil, for frying

2½ cups (225 g) trimmed and halved brussels sprouts

2 tablespoons vegetarian Thai chile paste (such as Maepranom brand)

2 tablespoons vegetarian fish sauce or Yondu

2 tablespoons fresh lime juice

½ teaspoon sugar

2 teaspoons chile powder

4 cloves garlic, sliced

2 tablespoons thinly sliced lemongrass

10 leaves fresh Thai basil

1⅓ cups (85 g) chopped fresh cilantro leaves

1 cup (57 g) sliced scallions, green and white parts

1⅓ cups (55 g) whole fresh cilantro leaves

⅔ cup (38 g) whole fresh rau ram leaves

⅔ cup (34 g) whole fresh mint leaves

¼ cup (30 g) sliced red onion

1 teaspoon jasmine rice powder (see above)

→ **NOTE:** The recipe will yield extra rice powder. It can be stored in an airtight container in your pantry for a month and used to thicken soups and dips, season breading for anything you're pan-frying, and, of course, make more larb.

POTATO VARENIKI
with Caviar Beurre Blanc

KACHKA
Portland, Oregon

◇◇

Kachka is a modern landmark in the Portland restaurant scene. Owned by chef Bonnie Frumkin Morales and her husband, Israel, the restaurant's general manager, the menu pays homage to the cuisine and hospitality Bonnie's family knew in Belarus when it was part of the Soviet Union—without being nostalgic or naive about it. The restaurant is pulsingly vital, a place where you can order rounds of infused vodka shots and feast on caviar and dumplings for a raucous night out. More on those dumplings: You'll notice that nearly every table has an order to share, whether it's the cheese-and-chive-filled vareniki or the beef-and-pork pelmeni. At home, vareniki are a fun project that can be done ahead thanks to how well they freeze. If you're already into making dumplings, these will expand your repertoire, and if it's your first foray, these balance the challenge of a new technique with supremely comforting flavors. And nobody will complain about any imperfections in your folding technique when they're enjoying them in luxurious, caviar-studded beurre blanc.

Serves **4** as a side or starter,
2 as a main course

◇◇

For the filling:
3½ cups (500 g) peeled and diced Yukon gold potatoes

4 cups (960 ml) or more whole milk, to cover the potatoes

¼ cup (½ stick/57 g) butter

1 teaspoon salt, plus more if needed

1 large egg, whisked

¼ cup (33 g) "00" semolina flour

¼ cup (15 g) chopped fresh dill

For the dough:
1¾ cups (225 g) all-purpose flour

1½ teaspoons salt

½ large egg

1 cup (240 ml) cold water

For the beurre blanc (see Notes):
½ cup (120 ml) dry white wine

¾ cup (1½ sticks/168 g) butter, cut into 8 pats

Pinch of salt

To serve:
1 ounce (28 g) black caviar (sturgeon or hackleback; see Notes for more)

Smetana or crème fraîche

Chopped fresh chives

To make the filling, place the potatoes in a large pot over medium heat and just barely cover with milk. Bring to a simmer and cook the potatoes until completely cooked through. Drain the milk, saving 2 tablespoons.

Place the cooked potatoes back into the pot and add the 2 tablespoons reserved milk, the butter, and salt. Use a potato masher to gently bring the ingredients together. Transfer the potato mixture into a potato ricer and pass the mixture through. Allow the potato mixture to cool to room temperature. Use a spatula to gently fold in the egg until just combined. Add the semolina and gently fold in until just combined and uniform. Do not overwork. Place in the refrigerator until fully cooled before using, up to 2 days ahead. When ready to make dumplings, add the chopped dill and more salt if needed.

To make the dough, in the bowl of a stand mixer fitted with a dough hook, mix together the flour and salt. Add the egg, then slowly drizzle in the cold water. Mix on medium-low until a dough forms, then knead in the mixer for 10 minutes, or until the dough comes together into a smooth, elastic ball. If you don't have a mixer, you can do this by hand, but you'll need to knead for 20 minutes. (And be prepared to sweat!) Wrap the dough in plastic wrap or place in a covered container and let rest at room temperature for at least 1 hour or up to overnight in the fridge. Let it come back to room temperature before moving on to the next step.

To assemble the dumplings, divide the dough into 4 equal balls and grab a spray bottle of water (or, if you don't have a spray bottle, a dish of water and a pastry brush), a straight-sided rolling pin, and a sheet tray dusted with flour.

Continued

→ NOTES: Kachka sells its dumplings online, shipping them frozen to the continental states, but as of publishing, it doesn't sell these specific potato vareniki.

If you have a dumpling mold or a pelmenitsa, use that instead of shaping by hand. For detailed instructions, check out Frumkin Morales's cookbook, *Kachka: A Return to Russian Cooking*.

Don't break the bank on caviar here, since it's going directly into the sauce. Frumkin Morales recommends using an entry-level sturgeon or hackleback caviar. She recommends the brand Tsar Nicoulai, which can be found at Whole Foods, and going for the classic or estate-grade white sturgeon. If that is out of budget, Frumkin Morales suggests opting for salmon or trout roe (not seaweed caviar or carp eggs). The flavor will be different but still fantastic.

If making ahead, try this restaurant hack: Temper a thermos (make sure it doesn't smell like coffee!) by boiling hot water, adding the hot water to your thermos, and leaving it for a few minutes. Dump the hot water out and pour in your finished sauce. Seal tightly and reserve until ready to finish the sauce with caviar. Otherwise, plan on making the beurre blanc while the dumplings are cooking.

Take one of the dough balls (leaving the rest lightly covered with a dish towel so they don't dry out) and roll it out on a lightly floured countertop until it's the thickness of a fresh pasta sheet—just shy of being transparent.

Take a 2-inch (5 cm) round cutter (or a drinking glass) and cut out rounds of dough. Using two spoons, a small scoop, or a pastry bag, fill each round of dough with a generous blob of filling—about 2 teaspoons. Brush or mist the edges of the dough with water, then fold the round into a half-circle, pressing the edges to seal. Take the edges and pull them to each other, pinching to seal in a tortellini shape. As you shape a few dumplings, you'll get a sense of how much filling you can stuff into each dumpling and still seal it. Transfer the shaped dumplings to your tray and gather the scraps together back into a ball. Repeat with the remaining dough and filling, re-rolling the scraps at the end after they've rested. At this point, the dumplings can be cooked or frozen for future use. (It's best to freeze the dumplings on a tray, then transfer to a freezer bag.)

To cook the dumplings, bring a large pot of salted water to a boil. Add the dumplings, about 20 pelmenitsa-size per batch (fewer if they're larger hand-shaped ones, so the temperature doesn't decrease rapidly). Adjust the heat as needed to maintain a healthy-but-not-too-vigorous boil. While the dumplings cook, give a few good stirs, making sure to get your spoon all the way to the bottom of the pot to free any dumplings that may have stuck there. Cook until the dumplings rise to the surface, and then 1 additional minute (for a total of 5 to 6 minutes). Timing will also depend upon the heat of your burner and whether your dumplings are fresh or frozen. If in doubt, take one cooked dumpling and cut it in half. The filling should be hot in the center.

Meanwhile, to make the beurre blanc, pour the wine into a small sauté pan and let it simmer away over high heat until it's reduced to just 1 tablespoon. Drop the heat to low and begin whisking in the butter, a pat at a time, adding the next pat only when the previous one is incorporated. Make sure that the mixture does not boil, which may cause it to break (or separate). When all of the butter is incorporated into the sauce, whisk in the salt.

When the dumplings are cooked and ready to serve, remove the beurre blanc from the heat and add the caviar, gently folding it into the sauce. Transfer the dumplings into a serving bowl. Add a dollop of smetana or crème fraîche and some chives in the center of the bowl. Spoon the beurre blanc all over the dumplings and serve immediately.

THAI DISCO FRIES

THAI DINER
New York City

◇◇

In their natural habitat of New Jersey, disco fries means a plate of fries topped with brown gravy and melted cheese, served at your local diner. Chefs Ann Redding and Matt Danzer's version speaks to the name of their lively Nolita restaurant. In place of gravy, they smother their fries with spicy Massaman curry. It works like a charm. Like their Jersey predecessor, these curry-topped fries invite everyone at the table to dig in as a shared side with lunch, dinner, or (if you've made the curry ahead of time) a game-changing late-night snack. To make things a bit easier at home, Redding recommends using frozen crinkles. You want most of the fries on the plate to stay as crispy as possible, ensuring they have enough structure to dip or mix into the smoldering curry. To that end, if you've got an air-fryer or convection oven, this is the time to use it, and plan on serving this quickly after plating.

Serves **4**

◇◇◇◇◇◇◇◇◇◇◇◇◇◇◇◇◇◇◇◇◇◇◇◇◇   ◇◇◇◇◇◇◇◇◇◇◇◇◇◇◇◇◇◇◇◇◇◇◇◇◇◇◇◇◇◇◇◇◇◇◇◇

For the curry and fries:

¼ cup (60 ml) coconut cream

4 ounces (113 g) Massaman curry paste

2 (13.5-ounce/400 ml) cans coconut milk

1 cup (240 ml) chicken stock

4 tablespoons (56 g) seedless tamarind paste

¼ cup (60 ml) fish sauce

1 tablespoon and 2 teaspoons (21 g) palm sugar

2 quarts (2 L) vegetable oil (omit if air-frying)

2 quarts (505 g) crinkle-cut frozen fries

For serving:

Fried garlic

Roasted peanuts

Chopped green onion, green parts only

Chopped fresh cilantro

Thai green peppercorns

In a medium pot, heat the coconut cream over medium heat, add the Massaman curry paste, and stir well to incorporate. Cook the mixture until it's fragrant. Add the coconut milk, chicken stock, tamarind paste, fish sauce, and palm sugar and bring to a boil. Once the sugar's dissolved, remove it from the heat and let cool. The Massaman curry sauce can be stored in an airtight container in the fridge for up to 3 days.

Air-fry the frozen fries until golden brown and crispy, or, in a Dutch oven or heavy-bottomed pot, heat the vegetable oil to 375°F (190°C). Fry the frozen fries for 5 to 7 minutes, until golden brown and crispy. Transfer to a baking sheet lined with paper towels to blot out excess oil.

Warm the Massaman curry sauce in a saucepan on the stovetop or in the microwave. Ladle about ¼ to ½ cup of the Massaman curry sauce into your bowl(s), depending on the size. Pile the cooked fries on top of the sauce, and drizzle some more sauce on top of the fries. Top with fried garlic, roasted peanuts, green onions, cilantro, and Thai green peppercorns and serve immediately.

DESSERT
DESSERT
DESSERT
DESSERT
DESSERT
DESSERT
DESSERT
DESSERT
DESSERT
DESSERT
DESSERT
DESSERT
DESSERT
DESSERT
DESSERT
DESSERT
DESSERT
DESSERT
DESSERT
DESSERT
DESSERT
DESSERT
DESSERT
DESSERT
DESSERT
DESSERT

CHAPTER

8

DON'T SKIP IT

When nobody wants the good times to end, a great dessert makes sure they won't, not yet anyway. At a restaurant, the dessert menu compels diners to experience even more of what makes a restaurant worthwhile: delicious, creative food that could only come from the particular team making it. Like a stellar savory dish, a great dessert boasts balance, texture, contrast, a familiar hook, and, often, a surprising turn. But the vocabulary is different: cakes and ice creams, sweet fruits and chocolate, warm spices like cardamom and cinnamon. The end results are as impressive and soul-satisfying as the main event, and often the most pleasing to the eye.

At home, dessert is a wonderful surprise—for you on a Wednesday night or for your loved ones at a languid dinner party. Each of the desserts in this chapter will teach you something about what makes a truly fantastic dessert: Maybe it's the way fresh strawberries in a cobbler announce spring, or the way chopped pistachios elevate a chocolatey truffle. There are projects, too—multilayer cakes, classic soufflé, and composed tarts. All of which are delightfully worth the effort.

Halawa Truffles, Financiers,
Passion Fruit Coconut
Shortbread Tart

HALAWA TRUFFLES

Reem Assil is a chef with a sweet tooth. From the beginning, she's made a name for herself and her eponymous restaurant with phyllo-crusted knafeh and a whole host of sweet bites, as well as her famous za'atar-topped mana'eesh flatbreads. These chocolate-dipped halawa truffles have their own fan base, not surprising to anyone who enjoys the taste of chocolate paired with anything nutty or salty. If you're not practiced at making chocolate shells, they might look a little rustic. That's okay—sprinkle pistachios over the messiest bits and rest assured they'll taste amazing.

Makes **20** to **24** truffles

1½ cups plus 2 tablespoons (375 g) tahini (see Notes)

¾ teaspoon salt

½ cup plus 1 tablespoon (63 g) roughly chopped pistachios, plus 2½ tablespoons finely ground pistachios

1 cup (200 g) sugar

½ cup plus 2 tablespoons (138 g) 70% dark chocolate

3 tablespoons coconut oil

1½ tablespoons ground dried rose petals

Maldon salt, for garnish

→ NOTES: Assil prefers Tarazi brand tahini, which is available online, but any high-quality, light-colored tahini will work well here. You want an easily mixable, light-colored tahini so you have sweeter flavor and no clumps.

You can make the halawa fudge up to a week in advance and store it in an airtight container in the fridge.

To make halawa fudge, in a heatproof bowl, stir the tahini well to loosen, then add the salt and roughly chopped pistachios. Wrap a damp towel into a little "nest" and secure your bowl for easier stirring.

In a small pot with a candy thermometer affixed to it, combine the sugar and 2 tablespoons (30 g) water. Heat over medium heat, and when the syrup reaches 250°F (121°C), carefully drizzle the syrup into the tahini while stirring constantly with a wooden spoon. Alternatively, you can use a stand mixer to make things easier.

To make the chocolate shell, melt the dark chocolate and coconut oil using a double boiler. If you do not have a double boiler, you can make your own: In a small saucepan, bring 1 to 2 inches (2.5 to 5 cm) of water to a simmer. Set a heatproof metal or glass mixing bowl on top of the saucepan (it should fit snugly—try not to let the water touch the bottom of the bowl), add the chocolate, stir with a rubber spatula until melted, and set the bowl onto the counter on top of a dishcloth.

Portion the halawa fudge by rolling it in your hands into 1-ounce (29 g) balls about 1 inch (2.5 cm) in diameter and dip into the chocolate with tongs. Lay out on a cooling rack.

Sprinkle the finely ground pistachios, dried rose petals, and Maldon salt on the truffles and let them set. Finished truffles will keep for 2 to 3 days in the fridge (don't store them on the countertop, as the coconut oil in the chocolate shells will melt).

FINANCIERS

◇◇

At b. Patisserie, the pastry case is flawlessly filled to the brim. A collaboration between pastry chef Belinda Leong and her one-time culinary instructor Michel Suas, the friendly yet sophisticated patisserie attracts long lines for its black sesame kouign-amann and passion fruit bostock. These financiers show why b. Patisserie is such a powerhouse: Something as small and simple as a tiny almond flour cake is a wonder here—moist, nutty, and rich with brown butter. While financiers are traditionally rectangular, Leong uses small silicone mini-dome pans at the bakery; at home you can do that, too, or try a mini muffin pan. Remember to plan ahead; the batter needs to rest for a few hours (or even overnight) before you bake it.

Makes **24 to 48** financiers

◇◇◇◇◇◇◇◇◇◇◇◇◇◇◇◇◇◇◇◇◇◇◇◇◇◇◇◇◇   ◇◇

5 egg whites (130 g) (see Note)

¼ cup plus 1½ teaspoons (63 g) butter

⅓ cup (40 g) almond flour

1⅔ cups (168 g) confectioners' sugar, sifted

⅓ cup (40 g) all-purpose flour

Cooking spray

⅓ cup (24 g) chopped almonds, for garnish

→ NOTE: Egg whites will keep in the freezer, so any time a recipe calls for just the yolks, consider saving them so you can make these financiers, or meringues, or egg white omelets.

Set up a double boiler. If you do not have a double boiler, you can make your own: In a small saucepan, bring 1 to 2 inches (2.5 to 5 cm) water to a simmer. Set a heatproof metal or glass mixing bowl on top of the saucepan (it should fit snugly—try not to let the water touch the bottom of the bowl). Add the egg whites and stir with a rubber spatula until they are warm to the touch, then set the bowl onto the counter on top of a dishcloth.

Brown the butter: Heat the butter in a saucepan over medium-low until it starts to brown at the bottom and smell nutty, 5 to 7 minutes. Stir to incorporate the browned solids. Set aside.

In a stand mixer with a paddle attachment, combine the almond flour and confectioners' sugar. Add the all-purpose flour, then stream in the warm egg whites on low to medium speed. Scrape the sides of the bowl so that everything is evenly mixed.

Stream in the brown butter and mix until the ingredients are homogenous. Transfer the financier batter to a container, cover, and chill in the refrigerator overnight. (The batter will keep covered in the fridge for up to 1½ weeks.)

To bake, preheat the oven to 375°F (190°C). Use a silicone mini-dome mold with a ¾- to 1¼-inch (2 to 3 cm) diameter set against a baking sheet. Alternatively, use a mini muffin pan. Grease the molds or pan with a light coating of cooking spray.

Mix the financier batter thoroughly and transfer to a piping bag. Pipe the financier batter into the molds to fill two-thirds of the way and garnish with the chopped almonds. Bake the financiers for 12 to 17 minutes, until the edges are golden and a toothpick inserted in the middle comes out clean.

Remove the financiers from the molds and transfer to a wire rack to cool completely. You can store them in an airtight container for 3 to 4 days.

PASSION FRUIT COCONUT SHORTBREAD TART

MILLER UNION
Atlanta, Georgia

Claudia Martinez is one of the brightest stars in the Atlanta food scene. She made a name for herself at Tiny Lou's, where she dazzled the city with her playful desserts and technical chops before joining the team at Miller Union. Her desserts often hinge on tropical fruit flavors. For this tart, passion fruit's bright acidity is accentuated with lime juice and mellowed with coconut. Her shortbread cornmeal crust would also be great with a simple lemon curd, chocolate pudding, or berry compote. At the restaurant, she serves the tarts individually; this recipe could yield eight individual tarts, but one larger tart is easier to make at home.

Makes 1 (9-inch/22 cm) tart

For the filling:
3 large egg yolks (54 g)

1 tablespoon Persian lime zest or key lime zest

1 (14-ounce/396 g) can sweetened condensed milk

½ cup (97 g) passion fruit puree

¼ cup (60 g) full-fat sour cream

For the crust:
1½ cups (190 g) all-purpose flour

⅓ cup (56 g) cornmeal

½ cup (50 g) confectioners' sugar

¼ cup (55 g) packed light brown sugar

1 teaspoon baking powder

½ teaspoon salt

½ cup (43 g) sweetened shredded coconut

¾ cup (1½ sticks/170 g) butter, melted

To serve:
Toasted sweetened shredded coconut

Maldon salt

Preheat the oven to 325°F (165°C).

To make the filling, combine the egg yolks, lime zest, condensed milk, passion fruit puree, and sour cream in a blender. Blend until thoroughly mixed, but be careful not to aerate it too much. Strain the passion fruit mixture and set aside.

To make the crust, combine the flour, cornmeal, confectioners' sugar, light brown sugar, baking powder, salt, and sweetened coconut in a large bowl. Drizzle in the melted butter and mix until well combined.

Press the crust mixture into a 9-inch (22 cm) tart pan with a removable bottom (or your desired dish) and bake for 10 minutes. Remove the tart shell from the oven and pour in the passion fruit mixture. Use a toothpick to pop any visible air bubbles and bake for an additional 9 minutes, or until the middle is set. Remove from the oven and cool on a wire rack.

Refrigerate the tart for at least 1 hour before serving. To serve, top with toasted coconut and Maldon salt.

Shopping List: Baking Tools

MUST-HAVES:

MEASURING SPOONS AND CUPS

MIXING BOWLS

DIGITAL SCALE

BENCH SCRAPER

FINE-MESH SIEVE

WHISK

STRAIGHT ROLLING PIN

HALF-SHEET PANS

PARCHMENT PAPER

WIRE RACKS
"These help cool off cakes, cookies, and breads evenly. Racks also help circulate air around your finished product." —MILLER UNION PASTRY CHEF CLAUDIA MARTINEZ

NICE-TO-HAVES:

PASTRY BRUSHES
"Keep one for dry tasks (like brushing excess flour off doughs) and one for wet." —THE PURPLE HOUSE BAKER KRISTA KERN DESJARLAIS

OFFSET SPATULA

STAND MIXER

CAST-IRON PANS

SILPAT MATS

GLASS PIE PLATES
"I just love having glass pie plates— you can rock a small casserole, a pie, a quiche (crustless or not), or a plate of cinnamon rolls." —POOLE'S DINER CHEF ASHLEY CHRISTENSEN

ROUND CUTTERS (for cookies, doughs)

FLEXIBLE RAZOR BLADE (for bread loaves)

DUTCH OVEN

BAKING-NERDS GOTTA-HAVE:

SERRATED UTILITY KNIFE with a 3½-inch (9 cm) blade (for fruit)

DIGITAL INDOOR THERMOMETER OR HYGROMETER
"While not 100 percent necessary (old-school bakers do everything by feel), this can really help a beginner when making sourdough. I glance at the room temperature to determine how warm or cold my mix water should be. Temperature is everything." —APT. 2 BREAD BAKER CARLA FINLEY

BANNETON (a basket to help bread keep its shape while proofing)

PROOFING BOX (to precisely control the humidity and temperature when proofing yeasted doughs)

COUCHE (an untreated, unbleached canvas cloth for making baguettes)

DANSKOS
"These clogs will help you stand for hours." —DOWNTIME BAKERY BAKER DAYNA EVANS

Recommended by: Ashley Christensen, Claudia Martinez, Anita Jaisinghani, Carla Finley, Krista Kern Desjarlais, Steven Satterfield, Dayna Evans

SPICED RICE PUDDING
with Apricots and Nut Dukkah

BAVEL
Los Angeles, California

What do you do after you open one of the hottest restaurants in all of Los Angeles? If you're Ori Menashe and Genevieve Gergis, the married duo behind Bestia, you do it all over again. Where Bestia focused on Italian cuisine, Bavel focuses on the Middle Eastern cooking Menashe grew up eating during his formative years in Israel. Gergis's can't-skip desserts rely on the flavors of the Middle East and the seasonal produce of Southern California, as in a creamy rice pudding topped with apricots and cardamom-laced nut dukkah. The best part about making this recipe at home is how flexible it is: Gergis subs plums in for apricots sometimes at the restaurant, and notes that peaches would also work well here. She also recommends the rice pudding for weekend breakfast or brunch—instead of the caramelized fruit and nut dukkah, top it with fresh fruit and slivered almonds or hazelnuts.

Serves **4**

For the nut dukkah:
¾ cup (80 g) chopped pistachios, almonds, or hazelnuts

1 teaspoon ground cardamom

Pinch of salt

2 teaspoons nut oil, such as almond, or light-flavored olive oil

For the rice pudding:
¾ cup Acquerello rice, or any risotto rice

4 cups (960 ml) whole milk

1 cup (240 ml) heavy cream

⅓ cup (60 g) sugar

¼ teaspoon salt

1 large cinnamon stick

10 pods cardamom, crushed open with the back of a spoon

½ vanilla bean, scraped, or 1½ teaspoons vanilla extract

For the caramelized fruit:
¼ cup (50 g) sugar

1 tablespoon water or ¼ cup (60 ml) amaretto, peach or apricot liqueur, or kirsch

4 apricots, peeled and segmented

To make the nut dukkah, combine all the ingredients in a small bowl. Set aside.

To make the rice pudding, combine the rice, milk, cream, sugar, and salt in a medium pot. Add the cinnamon stick, cardamom, and vanilla. Turn to high heat and cook, stirring occasionally, until it comes to a low boil. Turn the heat down to low and simmer, stirring every 2 to 3 minutes so that the rice cooks evenly and doesn't clump, for 20 to 30 minutes, until the rice grains are soft.

Meanwhile, to make the caramelized fruit, combine the sugar and water or liqueur in a small saucepan. Heat over medium heat until the sugar is mostly melted. Add the apricots and cook until they are just barely soft, 7 to 9 minutes.

To serve, spoon the fruit on top of the rice pudding, either in individual bowls or in one large serving dish. You can sprinkle a spoonful of nut dukkah on top or put in a bowl alongside for self-serving.

STRAWBERRY COBBLER

HIGHLANDS BAR & GRILL
Birmingham, Alabama

Highlands Bar & Grill has been a beacon of fine Southern cooking since the 1980s. Chef Frank Stitt helms the kitchen, while his wife, Pardis, oversees the front of house, and for decades pastry chef Dolester Miles handled desserts. Her sweets are legend: The coconut pecan cake is perhaps her single most famous creation, but her flaky cobblers win plenty of praise from diners and critics alike. Miles has officially retired, but her signature strawberry cobbler still signals the arrival of spring at the restaurant. Diners eagerly dig into individual ramekins, but at home, Miles offers this recipe for making the cobbler in a standard 9 × 13-inch (22 × 33 cm) baking dish. It's easier to work with a single sheet of dough than portioning out individual crusts, and the larger format makes this perfect for a crowd-pleasing dinner party dessert or a winning contribution to a potluck. You could easily trade in blueberries or sliced peaches, if you prefer, and consider serving with fresh whipped cream or vanilla ice cream on the side.

Makes 1 (9 × 13-inch / 22 × 33 cm) cobbler

For the dough:
2½ cups (313 g) all-purpose flour

5 tablespoons (65 g) sugar

2½ teaspoons baking powder

¼ teaspoon salt

½ cup (1 stick/113 g) cold unsalted butter, cut into cubes

1 cup (240 ml) cold heavy cream

For the filling:
8 pints (1,320 g) strawberries

¾ cup (150 g) sugar

Juice of 1 lemon

¼ cup (40 g) cornstarch

For topping:
1 egg, whisked with 1 teaspoon water, for the egg wash

¼ cup (50 g) sugar

Vanilla ice cream or whipped cream (optional)

To make the dough, in a stand mixer fitted with the paddle attachment, combine the flour, sugar, baking powder, and salt. Add the cold butter and mix until the butter is the size of peas. Slowly add the cream and mix until the dough just comes together.

Preheat the oven to 325°F (165°C).

Roll out the dough to about a ¼-inch (6 mm) thickness.

To make the filling, in a very large bowl, combine the strawberries, sugar, lemon juice, and cornstarch. Mix until thoroughly combined.

Transfer the filling to a 9 × 13-inch (22 × 33 cm) baking dish and top with the rolled-out dough. Brush the egg wash over the dough and sprinkle with the sugar. Bake for 35 minutes, or until bubbly and golden brown. Remove from the oven and let rest for at least 30 minutes before serving. Top with vanilla ice cream or freshly whipped cream if you like.

What the Pros Do with Store-Bought Pie Crust

 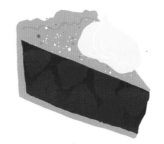 

One of the ultimate convenience foods, premade pie crusts are worth keeping on hand. Take your fillings sweet or savory with these ideas for potlucks, market hauls, and jazzing up leftovers.

BASIC FRUIT PIE: Make a simple fruit filling by combining fresh fruit (berries, stone fruits), a handful of sugar, a pinch of salt, and 2 tablespoons cornstarch or tapioca starch. After tossing it, fill the pie shell generously until the fruit makes a mound. Top that with a lattice or crust, brush it with egg wash, and sprinkle with coarse sugar, then bake until the filling bubbles and the crust is golden.

Recommended by: The Purple House baker Krista Kern Desjarlais

NUTELLA OR COOKIE BUTTER PIE: Mix Nutella with candied hazelnuts, orange segments, and chocolate toffee bits. Or try Biscoff cookie butter: Add it to a baked pie crust and top with whipped cream and fresh fruit.

Recommended by: Miller Union pastry chef Claudia Martinez

SPICED FRUIT PIE: Follow the instructions for Basic Fruit Pie but add a dash of cinnamon and cardamom to sliced stone fruit like peaches and nectarines.

Recommended by: Pondicheri chef-owner Anita Jaisinghani

PUDDING PIE: Blind bake your pie crust, and once it's cooled, fill it with your favorite store-bought or homemade pudding (chocolate, vanilla, or rice pudding all work great). Add any fruit you'd like (try poached fresh figs with rice pudding, for example), then top with lightly sweetened whipped cream and shave some dark chocolate over the whipped cream. Serve chilled.

Recommended by: The Purple House baker Krista Kern Desjarlais

QUICHE: You can go a thousand ways with quiche, and it's a great way to use up leftovers: Just add any cooked meats, veggies, plus cheese into your egg-and-milk-or-cream mixture.

Recommended by: Poole's Diner chef-owner Ashley Christensen

CHICKEN CURRY PIE: Stir-fry diced onion, garlic, small-diced potatoes, curry powder, and cubed or ground chicken, and season with oyster sauce, salt, black pepper, and brown sugar. Fill your pie, top with a crust (leave a hole in the center), and bake until golden.

Recommended by: Luv2Eat Thai chef-owners Noree Pla and Fern Kaewtathip

ALL THE FROZEN PIES: Make a basic semifreddo with sugar, heavy cream, and any flavorful add-ins you want (think matcha, strawberry, chocolate). Soft whip it and then freeze it right in a baked pie crust; when it comes out, you've got an ice cream pie. Or try this one: Blend mangos into heavy cream with some condensed milk and yogurt. If your mangos are soft, save some to put on the bottom of the pie and then add the mango cream on top and freeze for a lassi frozen pie.

Recommended by: Boon Sauce creator and Camphor pastry chef Max Boonthanakit

CHERRY APPLE CRUMBLE PIE

HONEYPIE
Milwaukee, Wisconsin

◇◇◇

Honeypie is part diner, part cafe, part bakeshop, and all-around comfort spot—the kind of place with checkered floors, wood booths, and a big plastic fish on the wall. Founder and "chief pie officer" Valerie Lucks also teaches pie classes, so she knows what it takes to pull them off at home. While some recipes encourage improvisation, it's worth following hers to a T—this pie crust will open up a whole world of baking possibilities. For her cherry apple crumble pie, Lucks uses cherries from scenic Door County, Wisconsin; below, she recommends that you use any tart red cherry (the more local the better). Combined with Granny Smith apples, this pie is one to savor while summer is still high but fall is fast approaching.

◇◇◇◇◇◇◇◇◇◇◇◇◇◇◇◇◇◇◇◇◇◇◇◇◇ ◇◇◇◇◇◇◇◇◇◇◇◇◇◇◇◇◇◇◇◇◇◇◇◇◇◇◇◇◇◇◇◇◇◇◇◇◇◇◇

For the crust:

1¼ cups (155 g) unbleached all-purpose flour

1 tablespoon sugar

½ teaspoon salt

½ cup plus 2 tablespoons (141 g) cold butter, cut into ½-inch (1.25 cm) pieces

5 tablespoons ice water

For the filling:

6 cups (660 g) peeled and sliced Granny Smith apples (6 to 8 apples)

2 cups (76 g) pitted tart red cherries (frozen or fresh)

Zest and juice of ½ lemon (2 tablespoons)

1 teaspoon vanilla extract

1 cup (200 g) sugar

¼ cup (30 g) all-purpose flour

2 tablespoons cornstarch

1 teaspoon salt

½ teaspoon ground cinnamon

For the crumb top:

½ cup (45 g) old-fashioned oats

½ cup (60 g) all-purpose flour

½ cup (110 g) packed light brown sugar

½ teaspoon salt

½ teaspoon ground cinnamon

¼ cup (½ stick/57 g) butter, melted

To make the crust, in a medium bowl, whisk together the flour, sugar, and salt and freeze for 10 minutes. Pull it out of the freezer, scatter the cold butter pieces over the top of the flour, and toss to coat. Use your fingers or a pastry cutter to crumble the butter: The pieces should range from the size of an almond to the size of a pea or smaller. Return the bowl to the freezer for another 10 minutes.

Sprinkle 2 tablespoons of the ice water evenly over your flour mixture. With your hands, toss the flour and water together. Add the remaining 3 tablespoons ice water and toss again. Do not squeeze or pinch the dough, unless it's to break up too large bits of butter. Continue to toss lightly, scooping from the bottom of the bowl upward until you can see a dough forming. If your dough seems dry after tossing for a few minutes, put the bowl in the refrigerator for 15 minutes and let it rest and hydrate. It's ready as soon as it looks like dough (it will be shaggy).

Gently form the mixture into a rough ball by giving the dough a gentle squeeze. Cover the dough in plastic wrap and allow it to rest by refrigerating it for at least 20 minutes or up to 24 hours.

After resting, form the dough into a large disc shape about 1 inch (2.5 cm) thick with very straight edges (if the dough is too cold, let it sit at room temperature for 10 minutes prior to shaping). Transfer the dough to a lightly floured parchment paper and lightly dust the top with flour, then roll it out to a circle that is about ⅛ inch (3 mm) thick and about 12 to 13 inches (25 to 30 cm) in diameter.

Transfer the dough to a 10-inch (25 cm) pie pan and chill for 10 minutes. Trim the dough edges to about 1 inch (2.5 cm) from the edge of the pie pan. Roll the

Continued

pie dough edges up and pinch or crimp to the lip of the pie pan. Place the crust in the freezer.

Preheat the oven to 400°F (200°C).

In a large bowl, mix the apples, cherries, lemon zest and juice, and vanilla. Add the sugar, flour, cornstarch, salt, and cinnamon and toss again until well mixed. Remove the pie crust from the freezer and transfer the filling into the pan. Mound up the filling high, as it will shrink down as it bakes.

Place the pie pan on top of a heavy sheet tray or cookie sheet to catch the juices and crisp the bottom of the crust. Bake the pie for 30 minutes.

While it bakes, make the crumb top: Mix the oats, flour, brown sugar, salt, and cinnamon in a medium bowl. Add the melted butter and toss until the mixture is in small clumps. Remove the pie from the oven and reduce the temperature to 350°F (175°C).

Spread the crumb topping over the filling. If the crust seems too brown, wrap it in aluminum foil or use a pie shield. Return the pie to the oven for another 30 minutes, or until the filling bubbles. There should be no clear or runny liquid in the center of the pie.

Let the pie rest for at least 6 hours before slicing. It will keep at room temperature for 2 to 3 days and can be refrigerated for 4 to 5 days.

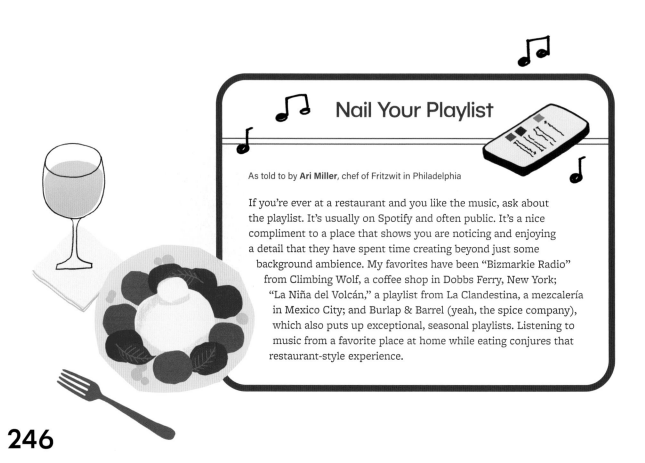

Nail Your Playlist

As told to by **Ari Miller**, chef of Fritzwit in Philadelphia

If you're ever at a restaurant and you like the music, ask about the playlist. It's usually on Spotify and often public. It's a nice compliment to a place that shows you are noticing and enjoying a detail that they have spent time creating beyond just some background ambience. My favorites have been "Bizmarkie Radio" from Climbing Wolf, a coffee shop in Dobbs Ferry, New York; "La Niña del Volcán," a playlist from La Clandestina, a mezcalería in Mexico City; and Burlap & Barrel (yeah, the spice company), which also puts up exceptional, seasonal playlists. Listening to music from a favorite place at home while eating conjures that restaurant-style experience.

POPPY SEED ANGEL FOOD CAKE with Blueberry Yuzu Compote and Thai Basil Mascarpone Cream

STATE BIRD PROVISIONS
San Francisco, California

Husband-and-wife restaurateurs Stuart Brioza and Nicole Krasinski transformed San Francisco's dining scene with their hit restaurants State Bird Provisions, The Progress, and The Anchovy Bar. Brioza handles savory and Krasinski is the pastry chef—this poppy seed angel food cake flaunts her ability to combine unexpected savory components (in this case, Thai basil) with a format that feels familiar but elevated (angel food cake). The cake is fantastic on its own—airy, springy, all the things an angel food cake should be—but the extras take it over the top: The Thai basil–infused mascarpone and blueberry yuzu compote are a surprising but totally fantastic match. This compote recipe is a great technique for so many uses—try it on top of ice cream, stirred into Greek yogurt or oatmeal, topped with whipped cream, strained into lemonade, or in lieu of syrup for waffles or jam for toast.

Makes 1 (9½- or 10-inch/24 or 25 cm) cake

For the angel food cake:
1 cup plus 1 tablespoon (127 g) pastry flour

1½ cups plus 2 teaspoons (306 g) granulated sugar

11 egg whites (365 g)

2 tablespoons lukewarm water

1¼ teaspoons cream of tartar

½ teaspoon fine sea salt

3 tablespoons poppy seeds

For the Thai basil mascarpone:
2 cups (480 ml) heavy cream

¼ cup plus 1 tablespoon (27 g) julienned Thai basil

1 (8-ounce/464 g) package mascarpone cheese, at room temperature

⅓ cup plus 2 tablespoons (90 g) granulated sugar

For the blueberry yuzu compote:
4 cups (580 g) fresh blueberries

1 tablespoon yuzu

2 tablespoons dark muscovado sugar

Pinch of salt

To make the angel food cake, preheat the oven to 325°F (165°C).

Sift the pastry flour and ½ cup plus 1 teaspoon (102 g) of the sugar three times to ensure that there are no lumps and to aerate the mixture.

Make sure the bowl of your stand mixer is very clean. Add the egg whites and lukewarm water and, using the whisk attachment, whisk on medium speed until frothy. Add the cream of tartar and salt, then add the 1 cup plus 1 teaspoon of the sugar in 1-tablespoon increments and whip until stiff peaks form to make a meringue.

Put one-third of the meringue in a bowl. Fold in one-third of the flour mixture. Then fold in another third of the flour mixture and another third of the meringue. Repeat once more, adding the remaining flour and meringue, and add the poppy seeds, making sure to fold gently so the cake batter remains light and airy.

Pour the batter into a 9½- or 10-inch (24 to 25 cm) angel food cake pan and bake for about 45 minutes, until a toothpick comes out clean.

If your pan has "feet," invert the angel food cake on a heatproof surface. Otherwise, invert the pan over a wine bottle to cool completely. This will prevent the cake from deflating.

Continued

To make the Thai basil mascarpone, heat the cream in a small saucepan until just warm. Turn off the heat. Add the Thai basil leaves, cover, and steep for 30 minutes. Strain and cool over an ice bath.

Using a stand mixer with the whisk attachment, mix the mascarpone and sugar. Slowly drizzle in the Thai basil cream and mix until homogeneous. The final texture should be similar to Greek yogurt. Store in an airtight container in the fridge for up to 2 days.

To make the compote, place 2 cups (290 g) of the blueberries in a medium bowl and set aside.

In a medium saucepan, combine 2 tablespoons water with the yuzu and muscovado sugar. Heat over medium heat until the sugar is dissolved. Add the remaining 2 cups (290 g) blueberries to the pan and cook, stirring often, for 8 to 10 minutes, until the mixture is thick and the berries have started to break down.

Pour the warm berry compote over the raw berries in the mixing bowl. Add the salt, stir to combine, and then chill over an ice bath to cool quickly. If making ahead, store in an airtight container in the fridge for up to 2 days.

To serve, spread some Thai basil mascarpone on the bottom of a dessert plate. Put a slice of angel food cake on top of the cream, top with a ladle of the blueberry yuzu compote, and serve.

Serve Dessert Without Making It

CHEESE can be a sophisticated dessert course. Fig jam and goat cheese pair well, and aged Comté offers a tremendous value. Round out a spread of dessert cheeses (any cheese you like can be a dessert, really) with a **LOCAL HONEY** and good fruit preserves.
Recommended by: Dame chef-owner Ed Szymanski, Marrow chef Sarah Welch

You can't go wrong with **FRESH FRUIT**. Berries with homemade whipped cream and a **GOOD CHOCOLATE** bar on the side is an easy, go-to move.
Recommended by: Apt. 2 Bread baker Carla Finley

Make **ICE CREAM** feel fancy by going for luxe toppings like pistachios, cocoa nibs, and **OLIVE OIL**. Try a sweet cream ice cream with chopped nuts, a drizzle of extra-virgin olive oil, a sprinkle of flaky salt, and fresh cracked pepper.
Recommended by: Lil Deb's Oasis chef Carla Perez-Gallardo

"ULTIMATE" COCONUT CAKE

PENINSULA GRILL
Charleston, South Carolina

Coconut cake is a Southern baking staple—its hallmarks are layers of yellow or white cake, creamy filling, and coconut flakes pressed into the frosting giving it its signature look. Among the restaurants that serve coconut cake, perhaps none is more synonymous with this cake than Charleston's Peninsula Grill at Planters Inn. Back in 1997, then-chef Robert Carter introduced an "ultimate" coconut cake, a twelve-layered showstopper crusted in toasted coconut flakes. At home, you'll make twelve layers, too: six layers of cake come from carefully cutting three butter cakes in half and the remaining six from spreading a creamy, coconut-studded filling. It's a long process: You'll want to make the cake the day before, and you can make the filling the night before. The next morning you'll make your frosting and focus on carefully assembling your layers, giving yourself enough time to chill it before serving your lucky, totally stunned guests.

Makes 1 (10-inch/25 cm) cake (Serves 12)

To make the cake, preheat the oven to 325°F (165°C). Spray three 10-inch (25 cm) cake pans with cooking spray and line the bottoms with parchment paper.

In a small bowl combine the cream, vanilla extract, and coconut extract. Beat the butter and sugar together in the bowl of a mixer fitted with the paddle attachment until light and fluffy, about 4 minutes. Add the eggs, one at a time, scraping down the sides of the bowl, and mix until creamy.

Sift the flour, baking powder, and salt together into a separate bowl.

Alternate adding the dry ingredients and the cream-and-extract mixture to the batter in three additions, starting and ending with the dry ingredients.

Divide the batter evenly among the 3 pans and bake until a toothpick inserted into the centers comes out clean, 40 to 45 minutes. Remove to a wire rack and let cool for 10 minutes in the pans. Then remove from the pans, remove the parchment, and let cool completely, preferably overnight (loosely covered).

To make the filling, combine the cream, sugar, and butter in a medium saucepan and bring to a boil over high heat. Mix the cornstarch, vanilla, and ¼ cup (60 ml) water together in a small bowl and slowly add this to the boiling cream mixture, stirring constantly. Bring to a boil and cook, stirring constantly, for 1 minute. Remove from the heat and add the coconut. Cover and refrigerate for at least 6 hours and up to 12 hours.

Continued

For the cake:
Cooking spray

1½ cups (360 ml) heavy cream

1½ tablespoons pure vanilla extract

1 teaspoon coconut extract

2 cups (4 sticks/452 g) unsalted butter, at room temperature

3 cups (594 g) granulated sugar

6 large eggs (360 g)

4½ cups (563 g) all-purpose flour

1½ tablespoons baking powder

½ teaspoon fine sea salt

For the filling:
5 cups (1.2 L) heavy cream

3 cups (594 g) granulated sugar

2 cups (4 sticks) (452 g) unsalted butter

¼ cup (2 g) cornstarch

1 teaspoon pure vanilla extract

9 cups (639 g) shredded sweetened coconut

For the frosting:
8 cups (760 g) flaked sweetened coconut

1 cup (2 sticks/226 g) unsalted butter, at room temperature

1 (8-ounce/227 g) package cream cheese, at room temperature

1 vanilla bean, split lengthwise, seeds scraped out and reserved, or 2 tablespoons pure vanilla extract

5 cups (575 g) confectioners' sugar

For the simple syrup:
1 cup (200 g) granulated sugar

For the coconut anglaise:
1 cup (240 ml) heavy cream

¼ cup (78 g) shredded unsweetened coconut

4 large egg yolks (72 g)

¼ cup (50 g) granulated sugar

To make the frosting, preheat the oven to 325°F (165°C).

Spread the coconut in an even layer on a baking sheet and bake for 15 to 20 minutes, stirring every 5 minutes, until golden brown. Set aside to cool.

Combine the butter and cream cheese in the bowl of a mixer fitted with the paddle attachment and beat on high speed until light and fluffy, scraping the sides and bottom of the bowl occasionally, about 5 minutes. Add the vanilla and beat for 30 seconds. Reduce the speed to low and slowly add the confectioners' sugar. Then raise the speed to high again and beat until smooth and fluffy, about 2 minutes.

To make the simple syrup, in a small bowl, bring 1 cup (240 ml) water and the sugar to a boil. Turn off the heat and let cool. Pour into a squeeze bottle with a small nozzle tip or set aside in a bowl.

To make the coconut anglaise, combine the cream and shredded coconut in a medium saucepan and bring to a boil. Set aside to steep for 20 minutes, then strain and discard the coconut. Return the cream to the saucepan and bring to a simmer.

Whisk together the egg yolks and sugar until the sugar dissolves and the eggs are lighter in color. Pour ½ cup (120 ml) or so of the hot cream into the yolk mixture very slowly, whisking constantly. Pour this mixture back into the hot cream, whisking constantly. Simmer until the mixture coats the back of a spoon. Remove from the heat, strain, and chill.

To assemble, place the chilled filling into a mixer fitted with a paddle attachment. Mix on low speed until the filling has softened, then increase the speed to medium-high and mix until the filling is pale, creamy, and soft enough to spread.

Trim off the domed top of each chilled cake. Carefully cut the cakes horizontally in half, yielding 6 cake layers.

Squeeze the simple syrup in a circular motion on the top of the first layer (or use a pastry brush). Spread 1½ cups (392 g) of the filling evenly on top. Continue with the remaining cake layers, stacking them on top of each other and squeezing each layer with simple syrup before spreading with filling. Refrigerate the cake until firm to the touch, about 4 hours.

Ice the top and sides of the cake with the frosting and pat the toasted coconut around the outside. Chill for at least 2 hours before slicing. To serve, drizzle coconut anglaise on the plate and top with a slice of coconut cake.

→ NOTE: The Peninsula Grill sells its cake online. If you want to purchase the cake but serve it the way they do at the restaurant, whip up the coconut anglaise and add some to each cake plate, then top it off with a slice of your cake.

HALO-HALO
with Leche Flan

KAMAYAN
Atlanta, Georgia

Mia Orino and Carlo Gan have captured Atlanta's heart with their craveable Filipino fare. Their fanciful cups of halo-halo in particular are a hit—they come tricked out with flag snack picks, sprinkles of Fruity Pebbles, and homemade ice cream and toppings like leche flan. The wobbly custard is a classic halo-halo topping; while it is luscious on its own, it brings a deep, creamy caramel flavor to the mix. At family gatherings—and in the recipe below—Orino and Gan's halo-halo is more of a DIY affair. Set up a halo-halo bar at home: You can keep it casual and use bowls or 20-ounce (600 ml) drinking glasses, or you can take a page from how these two do it at home and use empty coconut shells. Stock up on cocktail umbrellas and decorative picks so you can give your halo-halo the Kamayan look.

Serves **4** to **8**

To make the leche flan, in a small heavy-bottomed pan, combine the sugar with 1½ tablespoons water. Cook over low heat until the mixture has some color. Move, swirl, and tilt the pan when the sugar starts to dissolve and becomes a syrup, turning amber. Remove from the heat and pour into an 8-inch (20 cm) square pan. Let the caramel cool and harden.

In a large bowl, whisk together the egg yolks, condensed milk, and vanilla, if using. Add the evaporated milk and mix until well combined. Strain the mixture through a fine-mesh strainer.

Preheat the oven to 325°F (165°C).

Pour the egg mixture into the square pan, covering the caramel. Cover with aluminum foil. Place the pan in a larger baking pan that will accommodate it. Pour hot water into the larger baking pan up to 1 inch (2.5 cm) high or half of the height of the smaller pan.

Bake the flan for about 1 hour, until you can insert a toothpick in the middle and the custard comes out clean. Cool the flan completely and transfer to the refrigerator to chill, preferably overnight.

Slice into 1-inch (2.5 cm) cubes to use as a topping for your halo-halo.

To serve, lay out all your ingredients on the table in serving bowls and encourage guests to make their own halo-halos.

To make a halo-halo, place shaved ice in a 20-ounce (600 ml) glass, dessert bowl, coconut shell, or other serving vessel, then pour in your desired amount of condensed milk or evaporated milk and cow's or nondairy milk. Top with a cube of leche flan, a ball of ube jam, a scoop or two of ice cream, and as much of the optional toppings as you like.

Sprinkle with cereal and garnish with wafer sticks and enjoy immediately.

For the leche flan:

¼ cup (50 g) sugar

5 large egg yolks (250 g)

7 ounces (198 g) condensed milk

2 drops vanilla extract (optional)

6 ounces (177 g) evaporated milk

To serve the halo-halo:

8 cups (1120 g) shaved ice (use a blender or ice shaver)

1 to 2 (12-ounce/354 ml) cans evaporated milk or condensed milk

2 quarts (2 L) cow's, almond, soy, coconut, or oat milk

1 (12-ounce/340 g) bottle ube jam

1 large carton (1.42 L) ube, mango, or coconut ice cream

4 cups (104 g) rice cereal or corn cereal, or other cereal of your choice

2 (2.47-ounce/70 g) packs Pocky Sticks or wafer sticks

Optional toppings:

Jarred tapioca pearls or sago (or if using dried, follow package directions on how to cook)

Jarred banana in syrup

Canned sweet potatoes in syrup

Canned sweetened jackfruit

Canned adzuki or sweet red beans

Jarred coconut jelly (nata de coco)

Jarred kaong (sugar palm fruit jelly)

Jarred sweetened chickpeas

1 (3.17-ounce/90 g) package gulaman (agar-agar), prepared according to package instructions

Canned young coconut strips

Jarred sweetened navy, pinto, or white kidney beans

CHOCOLATE CHIP PANCAKE TRUFFLES

MILK BAR LAB
New York City

◇◇

Christina Tosi built an empire upon her love of nostalgic sweets and her expert, inventive pastry skills: Milk Bar grew from a small bakery at the back of a Momofuku restaurant in New York City's East Village into a thriving multicity chain with a robust online offering and products on grocery store shelves across the country. The Milk Bar Lab is Tosi's R&D team, located in New York and Los Angeles, and it's where the experimental spirit of OG Milk Bar continues to thrive. Here, the lab brings the flavors of a classic diner breakfast to a beloved Milk Bar form: the cake truffle. This recipe is actually a template for how to turn any great cake (even one you buy or make from a box) into a Milk Bar truffle: Start with a delicious cake, soak it through with something that tells what Tosi calls a "flavor story" to form your truffle, lock in the moisture with a chocolate shell, and then add a crumb coating.

Makes **35** to **40** truffles

◇◇

To make the brown butter, melt the butter in a medium saucepan over medium-high heat until it melts. Reduce the heat to medium-low and keep an eye on it until it reaches a deep brown color and gives off a nutty aroma, about 5 minutes. Color equals flavor, so let that butter go until you see it brown. Transfer the butter to a heatproof bowl and stir to distribute the milk solids evenly. Let it cool, then transfer to an airtight container and store at room temperature for up to 5 days or in the fridge for up to 2 weeks.

To make the brown butter cake, preheat the oven to 350°F (175°C).

Combine the granulated sugar, butter, 3 tablespoons (46 g) of the brown butter, and light brown sugar in the bowl of a stand mixer fitted with the paddle attachment and cream together on medium-high speed for 2 to 3 minutes until light and fluffy. Scrape down the sides of the bowl, add the eggs, and mix on medium-high speed again for 2 to 3 minutes until well combined. Scrape down the sides of the bowl once more.

Lower the speed to low and stream in the buttermilk, grapeseed oil, and vanilla. Increase the speed to medium-high and paddle for 4 to 6 minutes, until the mixture is practically white, twice the size of your original fluffy butter-and-sugar mixture, and completely homogenous. Don't rush the process—you're basically forcing too much liquid into an already fatty mixture that doesn't want to make room for the liquid. Stop the mixer and scrape down the sides of the bowl.

On very low speed, add the cake flour, baking powder, and salt. Mix for 45 to 60 seconds, just until your batter comes together and any remnants of dry ingredients have been incorporated. Scrape down the sides of the bowl. If you see any lumps of cake flour in there while you're scraping, mix for another 45 seconds.

For the brown butter:
1 cup (2 sticks/226 g) unsalted butter

For the brown butter cake:
1¼ cups (260 g) granulated sugar

5 tablespoons (72 g) unsalted butter

3 tablespoons (46 g) brown butter (see above)

¼ cup (50 g) packed light brown sugar

3 large eggs (125 g)

½ cup (120 ml) buttermilk

½ cup (120 ml) grapeseed oil

1 teaspoon (4 g) vanilla extract

1½ cups (185 g) cake flour

1 teaspoon (4 g) baking powder

1 teaspoon (4 g) salt

Cooking spray (optional)

For the pancake crumbs:
1½ cups (170 g) all-purpose flour

1 tablespoon (14 g) granulated sugar

½ teaspoon (2 g) salt

7 tablespoons (105 g) brown butter, melted (see above)

For the truffles:
6 tablespoons (125 g) maple syrup

2 tablespoons plus 2 teaspoons (36 g) buttermilk

6 ounces (350 g) white chocolate, melted

1 tablespoon (10 g) neutral oil, such as grapeseed

⅓ cup (80 g) mini chocolate chips

Continued

Spray a quarter sheet pan (13 × 9 inches/33 × 24 cm) and line it with parchment or line the pan with a Silpat. Using a spatula, spread the cake batter in an even layer in the pan. Give the bottom of your pan a tap on the countertop to even out the layer.

Bake the cake for 30 to 35 minutes. The cake will rise and puff, doubling in size, but will remain slightly buttery and dense. At 30 minutes, gently poke the edge of the cake with your finger: The cake should bounce back slightly and the center should no longer be jiggly. Leave the cake in the oven for an extra 3 to 5 minutes if it doesn't pass these tests.

Take the cake out of the oven and lower the oven temperature to 325°F (165°C) to make the pancake crumbs.

Cool the cake on a wire rack or, in a pinch, in the fridge or freezer. The cooled cake can be stored in the fridge, wrapped in plastic wrap, for up to 5 days or in the freezer for up to 1 month.

To make the pancake crumbs, in a medium bowl, combine the flour, sugar, and salt. Toss with your hands to mix. Add 7 tablespoons (105 g) of the melted brown butter and 1 tablespoon (18 g) water and toss gently, just until the mixture comes together to form small clusters.

Spread the clusters on a parchment paper– or Silpat-lined sheet pan and bake for 30 minutes, or until the crumbs look like a sea of golden-brown little rocks and your kitchen smells like brown buttery heaven. Cool the crumbs completely.

Crumble the pancake crumbs into a fine sand texture—you should end up with about 1 cup (300 g). Store in an airtight container in the fridge for up to 1 week or in the freezer for up to 1 month.

To make the truffles, first make the maple buttermilk soak by whisking together the maple syrup and buttermilk.

Then make the white chocolate coating: In a small bowl, whisk together melted white chocolate and neutral oil until homogenous. Keep warm before using.

To assemble your truffles, combine the cake and three-quarters of the maple buttermilk soak in a medium bowl and toss with your hands until moist enough to knead into a ball. If it is not moist enough to do so, slowly add more of the soak. You want the filling to be moist and soft yet structural enough to be rolled into a ball and hold its shape, not dry or crumbly.

Knead in the mini chocolate chips until well distributed.

Using a tablespoon, scoop the mixture, then roll between the palms of your hands to shape and smooth into a round sphere, half the size of a Ping-Pong ball. Repeat until the entire batch is portioned and rounded.

Put the pancake crumbs in a medium bowl and set aside.

With latex gloves on, put 2 tablespoons of the white chocolate coating in the palms of your hand and roll each cake ball around, coating it in a thin layer of melted chocolate; add more chocolate to your palms as needed.

Place the chocolate coated cake ball into the bowl of pancake crumb. Immediately toss it around in the mixture to coat, before the chocolate shell sets and no longer acts as a glue. If this happens, just coat the ball in another thin layer of melted chocolate.

Transfer to a fresh baking sheet or plate. Repeat until the entire batch has been coated in chocolate and rolled in pancake crumbs.

Refrigerate the sheet or plate for at least 10 minutes to fully set the chocolate shell before eating or storing. The truffles will keep in an airtight container for up to 1 week in the fridge or up to 1 month in the freezer.

SOUFFLÉ AU CHOCOLAT
with Chocolate Sauce and Candied Cocoa Nibs

PASJOLI
Santa Monica, California

◇◇

Diners who do their research—the ones who pore over menus and bookmark social media posts—know that when they've finally sat down to dig into must-order fine French classics like pressed duck and gratin dauphinois at chef Dave Beran's smash-hit Santa Monica restaurant Pasjoli, they need to save room for dessert. Specifically, Soufflé au Chocolat. This chocolate soufflé is proper, served individually in a beautiful Mauviel copper soufflé mold with a pitcher of chocolate sauce and a side of the silky house vanilla ice cream nestled on a layer of crunchy chocolate nibs—it's the perfect end to a dinner of French hits. At home, you can use small soufflé molds, too (look for 3- or 4-inch/7.5 to 10 cm diameters and 2-inch/5 cm sides—you want them to be tallish), but a larger, wider ramekin should work, too. The Pasjoli team makes its ice cream using a Pacojet (an expensive machine that basically makes a "micro-puree" out of frozen ice cream base), but we recommend just picking up some great ice cream at the store so you can focus on nailing the soufflé.

Makes 6 soufflés

◇◇◇◇◇◇◇◇◇◇◇◇◇◇◇◇◇◇◇◇◇◇◇◇◇◇◇◇ ◇◇

For the chocolate sauce:
¼ cup (94 g) glucose

⅓ cup (63 g) sugar

½ cup (47 g) cocoa powder (preferably Valrhona)

2 tablespoons (34 g) chopped 70% bitter chocolate

¼ teaspoon (2 g) salt

For the candied nibs:
¼ cup plus 1 tablespoon (63 g) sugar

1 cup plus 3 tablespoons (125 g) cocoa nibs (preferably Valrhona)

For the soufflés:
Room-temperature butter, for greasing the ramekins

½ cup plus 1 tablespoon (120 g) sugar, plus more for the ramekins

⅓ cup (75 g) unsalted butter

½ cup (50 g) all-purpose flour

1⅓ cups (315 ml) whole milk

1 teaspoon (6 g) fine sea salt

1¼ cups (300 g) chopped 70% bitter chocolate

6 large egg yolks (100 g)

7 large egg whites (210 g)

Vanilla ice cream, for serving

To make the chocolate sauce, in a double boiler over very low heat, warm ⅔ cup (150 ml) water, the glucose, sugar, cocoa powder, and chocolate, stirring until all the chocolate is melted. If you do not have a double boiler, you can make your own: In a small saucepan, bring 1 to 2 inches (2.5 to 5 cm) water to a simmer over very low heat. Set a heatproof metal or glass mixing bowl on top of the saucepan (it should fit snugly—try not to let the water touch the bottom of the bowl), add all the ingredients, and stir with a rubber spatula. Strain and add the salt. Set aside, or store in an airtight container in the fridge for up to 2 days.

To make the candied nibs, place the sugar and 1¾ tablespoons (25 g) water in a small pot and bring to a rolling boil. Cook to a syrup-like consistency, about 10 minutes. Add the cocoa nibs and reduce the heat to low. Stir until the moisture cooks out and the sugars crystalize. Remove from the heat and set aside.

To make the soufflés: Preheat the oven to 355°F (175°C). Brush the inside of six 10-ounce (300 ml) ramekins with room-temperature butter in vertical strokes. Then add sugar so it sticks to the butter. Pour off excess sugar.

Melt the butter in a saucepan over low heat. Add the flour and cook to a paste, about 4 minutes, whisking constantly. Add the milk and cook until thick, about 5 minutes, continuing to whisk so that lumps don't form. Add the salt and chocolate and mix until all the chocolate is melted. Remove the mixture from the heat, and then add the egg yolks and whisk until well combined. Set aside.

In a stand mixer, whip the egg whites and ½ cup plus 1 tablespoon (120 g) sugar to medium peaks. Fold the egg whites into the soufflé base.

Continued

Candied Cocoa Nibs

Fill the ramekins about three-quarters full and bake for about 15 minutes, until the soufflés have risen and the tops are smooth.

While the soufflés bake, warm the chocolate sauce over low heat or in a double boiler. Line the bottom of six small bowls with a bed of cocoa nibs, and before taking the soufflés out of the oven, add a single scoop of vanilla ice cream to each bowl.

As soon as the soufflés are out of the oven, serve with warm chocolate sauce on the side in a small ramekin, pitcher, or carafe, and a small bowl of vanilla ice cream. The soufflés will be served hot, so be sure to put a dish or liner under the ramekins.

What to Drink with Dessert

Try splurging on a high-quality **MINT TEA** (RareTea sells to restaurants and retails online). You can turn **COFFEE** into a dessert moment by setting up a creamer bar, with sweetened, flavored milks (see page 37) or by making affogatos (espresso poured over ice cream). **ESPRESSO MARTINIS** are back on restaurant menus; typically they're made with vodka, espresso, coffee liqueur, and simple syrup. To keep things simple, consider serving fruit liqueurs like crème de cassis or Giffard crème de pamplemousse over ice.

Champagne works wonderfully with lighter desserts like strawberries and cream, while **BRACHETTO**, a bubbly, juicy red, pairs well with chocolate, as would a **LAMBRUSCO**. If the drink is the dessert, try something fortified like aged **MADEIRA**, a dessert wine like **SAUTERNES**, or a **BARREL-AGED IMPERIAL STOUT**.

Or let guests serve themselves something warming like **AMARO** or **SCOTCH**. Don't forget to have ice and water at the ready.

Recommended by: Sumi Ali, Nicole Krasinski, Miguel de Leon, Helen Johannesen, Liz Martinez, Ed Szymanski, Michael Roper

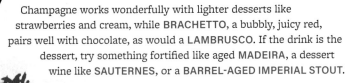

INDEX

Editor: Laura Dozier
Designer: Diane Shaw
Design Manager: Jenice Kim
Managing Editor: Lisa Silverman
Production Manager: Larry Pekarek

Recipe Tester: Louiie Victa
V.P. of Development: Britt Aboutaleb

Library of Congress Control Number: 2023930351

ISBN: 978-1-4197-6576-6
eISBN: 978-1-64700-885-7

Printed and bound in China
10 9 8 7 6 5 4 3 2 1

Abrams books are available at special discounts when purchased
in quantity for premiums and promotions as well as fundraising
or educational use. Special editions can also be created to
specification. For details, contact specialsales@abramsbooks.com
or the address below.

Abrams® is a registered trademark of Harry N. Abrams, Inc.

ABRAMS The Art of Books
195 Broadway, New York, NY 10007
abramsbooks.com

Recipe Credits

"Chilled Zucchini Soup" (page 58) from *The Gramercy Tavern Cookbook* by Michael Anthony, produced by Dorothy Kalins, with a History by Danny Meyer, copyright © 2013 by Gramercy Tavern Corp. Used by permission of Clarkson Potter/ Publishers, an imprint of Random House, a division of Penguin Random House LLC. All rights reserved.

"Baked Goat Cheese with Garden Lettuces" (page 59) is adapted from *Chez Panisse Café Cookbook*, by Alice Waters. Published in 1999 by HarperCollins.

"Grilled Pizza with Asparagus Pesto, Prosciutto, and Burrata" (page 82) is adapted from *Cucina Simpatica* by Johanne Killeen and George Germom. Published in 1991 by HarperCollins.

"Five-Minute Hummus" (page 90) is adapted from *Israeli Soul*, © 2018 by Michael Solomonov and Steven Cook. Photography © 2018 by Michael Persico. Reproduced by permission of Rux Martin Books/Houghton Mifflin Harcourt. All rights reserved.

"Spicy Cumin Lamb with Biang-Biang Noodles" (page 127) is adapted from *Xi'an Famous Foods: The Cuisine of Western China, from New York's Favorite Noodle Shop* by Jason Wang with Jessica Chou. Copyright Jason Wang 2020. Photography by Jenny Huang. Published by Abrams. All rights reserved.

"Diavola Sauce" and "Rigatoni Diavola" (page 135) from *Pasta: The Spirit and Craft of Italy's Greatest Food, with Recipes [A Cookbook]* by Missy Robbins and Talia Baiocchi, copyright © 2021 by Missy Robbins and Talia Baiocchi. Used by permission of Ten Speed Press, an imprint of Random House, a division of Penguin Random House LLC. All rights reserved.

"Fried Yardbird" (page 165) is adapted from *The Red Rooster Cookbook*, copyright © 2016 by Marcus Samuelsson. Published by Harvest.

"Carciofi alla Romana" (page 211) is adapted from *Via Carota*, copyright © 2022 by Jody William and Rita Sodi, published by Alfred A. Knopf. All rights reserved.

"Potato Vareniki" (page 227) is adapted from *Kachka* © 2017 by Bonnie Frumkin Morales with Deena Prichep. Copyright © 2017 by Bonnie Frumkin Morales. Reprinted with permission from Flatiron Books. All rights reserved.

Bemelmans Bar® is a registered trademark, and the Bemelmans Bar is located at The Carlyle, A Rosewood Hotel.

ACKNOWLEDGMENTS

Thank you to the chefs, restaurateurs, bartenders, sommeliers, and experts who so generously shared their recipes, tips, and tricks, and who so graciously answered each and every one of our questions; this book is as much yours as it is ours.

Thank you to our recipe tester, Louiie Victa, who worked tirelessly to make sure these restaurant recipes were home-ready. Thank you to Britt Aboutaleb for dreaming big and being the most ambitious creative partner. Thank you to Stephanie Wu and Erin DeJesus for the unflagging support. Thank you to Ellie Krupnick and Nat Belkov for the enthusiasm, the collaboration, and the feverish Slacking. Thank you to Amanda Kludt, Eater's forever Queen. Thank you to Vox Media's Eric Karp and Hilary Sharp for literally making the deal happen, and to Aude White and Dane McMillan for making sure people know about it.

Thank you to Laura Dozier and Diane Shaw at Abrams for teaching all of us how to make a book! And for wanting that book, this book, to be as magnificent as it could possibly be. Thank you to Natasha Martin, Mamie Sanders, and Danielle Kolodkin at Abrams for their enthusiastic publicity and marketing efforts.

And most importantly, thank you to the sensational writers, editors, reporters, illustrators, and designers who have contributed to Eater over the past fifteen-plus years; this book would not have been possible without your passion and your enduring work.

NONG'S

HERE'S LOOKING *Los Angeles* AT YOU *California*

MY *Abuelas* FOOD

COSME

 THE JERK SHACK

~ MILLER + UNION ~

NIGHT + MARKET **Song**

KAMAYAN ATL

 *Wahpepah's Kitchen*

JIBARITOS *Authentic Puerto Rican food*

VIA CAROTA N.Y.C.

TORO

 *Reem's*

PASJOLI

DHƎMAKA

milk

RASA

nopalito

毛帛城 SICHUAN IMPRES

CHEF & THE FARMER

RED ROOSTER HARLEM

b. patisserie

OTa's

SUSH

BAVEL

Audrey

BAOBAB *fare*

gwen

ROOTS SOUTHERN TABLE

 *dirt candy*

State bird PROVISIONS

the **Tam** O'SHANTER *est. 1922*

PENINSULA GRILL

Nº 3131 FILLMORE ST. BAR CRENN SAN FRANCISCO

Koko Head CAFE

WAX *paper*

 *Saffron* De Twah

Thip Kh 620 cuisi

The **GREY**

LA VARA

SUMMIT DINER

KACHKA

Chez Panisse

— THE — PURPLE HOUSE

Sadelle's

VERACR ▼▼▼▼▼▼ ALL N